MONKee

BUSINESS

THE
REVOLUTIONARY
MADE-FOR-**TV BAND**

ISBN-10 0-943249-00-7
ISBN-13 978-0-943249-00-1
Printed in the USA

Published by Retrofuture Products LLC
PO Box 1611, Port Washington, NY 11050

First Edition, revised

MONKEE BUSINESS

THE REVOLUTIONARY MADE-FOR-TV BAND

ERIC LEFCOWITZ

RETRO FUTURE

I would like to thank all the people who, in one form or another, supported the making of this book: Duane Dimock, Anita Sethi, Henry Diltz, Michael Ventura, Xeth Feinberg, Roger Greenawalt, Joe Poindexter, Bill Inglot, Andrew Sandoval, Harold Bronson, Jason Turner, Mark Pinkus, Kevin Schmid, Randi Waddell, Therra Cathryn Gwyn, Gary Strobl, Jim Marshall, Michael Nesmith, Bobby Hart, Peter Rafelson, Jane Newman, Jennifer Archdekin, Jeff Zeh, Dan Simon, Mitchell and Marjorie Schwarzer, Barbara Lefcowitz, Allan Lefcowitz, Keith Venkiteswaran, David Gaynes, Tony Traguardo, Idan Sims, Frank Raymond, Jeff Rowland, Mark Kleiner, Jennifer Parris, Michael Bennet, Johnny J. Blair, Paul Wargelin, Penn Jillette, Glenn S. Alai, Julie Klausner, Marianne Ways, Ricky Glore, Brad Waddell, Richard Metzger, Wayne Shallabarger, Winifred Boyd, Cindy Justis Simon, and Stephanie Thompson.

Dedicated to my own three Monkees—Nathan, Eli and Avanika.
—Eric Lefcowitz, 2013

Design and layout by Stephanie Thompson
Cover illustration: Wayne Shellabarger (front cover)
and Stephanie Thompson (back cover)

Foreword

THE MONKEES WERE MY ENTRY-LEVEL DRUG to music and art. The Monkees got me started on crazy-ass rock 'n' roll and probably got me started doing my crazy-ass Vegas magic show.

The Monkees were engineered to appeal to the broadest audience possible with no other concerns. The Monkees were sanitized to fit into America's living rooms. My mom and dad would watch the Monkees with me, and other than their stupid haircuts, Mom and Dad weren't bothered much by the Pre-fab Four. The silly Monkees did their thing in the wood veneer TV console under the white doily below the heirloom clock. They didn't shock. They fit comfortably on the same cathode ray tube as Lawrence Welk.

Mom and Dad bought me Monkees records for birthdays and Christmas. I saved money from my paper route and bought my own. I bought teenybopper magazines and had their kissing close pictures up in my room. I think my Dad would have preferred some female pinups, but it didn't seem that unhealthy. Dad worried, but not too much—they were on TV. The Monkees infiltrated our rustic little New England home that my Mom and Dad had designed and built on their own. I read Monkees interviews and through those interviews, learned about a guy named Jimi Hendrix who was the Monkees opening act in cities I couldn't get to. I saw my first live Monkees show after I turned 40 but I saw Frank Zappa of the Mothers of Invention on the Monkees TV show and in their movie, *Head*, at the Garden Theater in Greenfield, Massachusetts. Soon I'd moved from the innocuous to full-blown dangerous rock 'n' roll.

Things that are for everyone sometimes suck us into things that aren't for everyone. The Monkees held my hand and led me out of my parents' home into their world of art. I don't believe the network gave a flying fuck about art but they cast people for the commercial enterprise who did care deeply about art. The Monkees were really good. There was no reason for the Monkees to be good, but that couldn't stop them. There isn't a week that goes by that I don't still listen to them. They are no longer just an entry drug; they are a drug of choice. They each could have been in a "real" rock band but they ended up in a TV rock band and that was just what I needed to knock my head out of Greenfield. They gave me my life and my career.

Many people want to keep rock 'n' roll pure. Hardcore rock fans scoffed at the Monkees. They wanted to ensure electric guitars were for rebels only, but the Monkees got the feeling and beat out there to us provincial children. And some of us, after feeling the beat and digging the feeling, kept going all the way. I got to Dylan, Sun Ra, The Velvet Underground, The Residents, Moondog, David Allen Coe, Modern Lovers, Mothers, Stravinsky, John Hartford, Alban Berg, The Sex Pistols, Miles Davis, Ramones, Clash, Mingus, and Eminem with the Monkees just too busy singing to put anybody down. I'm all their fault and I love them for it.

—*Penn Jillette*

Introduction

I WAS THE PERFECT TARGET AUDIENCE for *The Monkees* TV show when it debuted in 1966—a six-year-old with no access to rock and roll beyond a few brief glimpses at *The Ed Sullivan Show*. The show was a kind of visual LSD for the Kool-Aid set and I drank it down happily whenever I could get my hands on it.

A standout memory for me was the seventh birthday party for my pal Joey Applebaum. He received the Monkees' latest record, *Headquarters*, as a gift. Micky was singing "why don't you cut your hair?" as the sugar buzz from the birthday cake kicked in. It was a great birthday party.

I wanted a copy of *Headquarters* but that wasn't going to happen unless the group changed their names to Peter, Paul and Mary and sang about magic dragons. I had to make do watching the show whenever I could and playing the free record I had gotten from the back of an Alpha-Bits cereal box (music distribution through cereal boxes—this was an idea I could get behind).

They disappeared from my life completely in the 1970s. Occasionally, an intriguing news item would surface in a music magazine. It was reported Peter was waiting tables on roller skates (could that possibly be true?) but otherwise the Monkees stayed out of sight and mind until the early 1980s when a friend played me a recording of the Sex Pistols performing a bizarre cover of "(I'm Not Your) Steppin' Stone." A few days later I found myself in a record store staring at a copy of *The Monkees Greatest Hits* on Arista Records. Four dollars later it was mine.

At the time, I was a fan of the brooding bands like Joy Division and the politically revved-up music of The Clash, Dead Kennedys and Black Flag. At face value, the music of the Monkees had nothing in common with these modern sounds and yet I kept coming back to them for the happy childhood memories they evoked, a dose of musical chicken soup for the soul, you could say.

At some point I caught the bug, an insatiable desire to know more and more about the Monkees. Who were these people who pulled off this unrivalled feat of mercantilism? How had they done it? Why had they gotten so little respect? And, most intriguingly, what did the four Monkees have to say about their experiences?

The establishment rock press had ignored the "Prefab Four" since their break-up. Fortunately a friendly editor at *BAM* magazine named Dave Zimmer let me investigate the subject. It was 1984, and I was living in San Francisco. It wasn't difficult to find out Michael Nesmith was living a few hours drive down in Monterey, California but when I called the offices of Pacific Arts, his video company, I was told he wasn't talking.

On a trip back East to New York City I managed to track Peter Tork down. He was fronting a glorified bar band and eking out an existence giving private guitar lessons. Tork had a story to tell. After years of substance abuse, he had seen the light on the Monkees phenomenon and was now embracing it. This seemed to be an encouraging sign.

Back on the West Coast, I gobbled up all the information I could get my hands on, haunting libraries, tracking down microfilm from the 1960s, catching *Head* at a local revival art house movie theater. I was also working the graveyard shift carrying bags at the Hotel Miyako, a popular stop for visiting musicians and, when I could, I would sneak off into a vacant room at 6 a.m. to watch early morning reruns of *The Monkees* TV show.

An obsession with the Monkees was very difficult to explain to strangers, especially to musical purists of the Bay Area. Even friends and family had no idea what I was going on about for the most part. "I just saw this movie called *Head*," I told anybody who would listen. "It's totally insane!" And then I would try to explain why they should see this cult-classic movie made by the Monkees.

My efforts to tell the story of the "brand that became a band" received a huge boost when the show's co-producer Bert Schneider, who was something of a recluse, agreed to meet me at his Beverly Hills mansion for an interview. He was confident the group's revival was imminent and he was right. Co-producer Bob Rafelson was a quick drive away and provided an extensive interview as well. Both men were clearly proud of the group's legacy.

The pieces were coming together. I followed up with transatlantic calls to Micky and Davy who both provided helpful interviews. And finally I broke through Nesmith's wall of silence. The meeting took place at a video editing suite in Monterey where "Papa Nez" was putting the final touches on his new series, *Television Parts*. Despite a surly reputation, Nesmith seemed not only amiable but quite happy to dispel the misperception that he was still harboring ill feelings about his participation in the Monkees.

I sold the idea of a book called *The Monkees Tale* to comics guru "Baba" Ron Turner whose proudly-disreputable company, Last Gasp of San Francisco, was publishing Bill Griffith's brilliant Zippy the Pinhead comic strips and works by the notorious R. Crumb. Ron gave me three luxurious months to complete the manuscript, and in late 1985 he held a party to celebrate the publication of books by Crumb and me (not since Hendrix opened for the Monkees was there such a mismatch).

MTV made all the difference—to the Monkees and my book. By running every episode of the series back-to-back in a day long marathon, MTV kick-started a full-blown comeback for the group in their 20th anniversary year of 1986.

A few obstinate critics remained, still reluctant to acknowledge the Monkees' influence on the pop landscape. Tom Snyder grilled me on his local TV chat show in Los Angeles, taking well-placed potshots at my horrible '80s fashion sense. An eye-rolling smug interviewer on National Public Radio was another highlight. The general line of questioning was: why write a book on such a fluffy insubstantial band?

There will always be a few nostril-pinching musical purists who never get the Monkees, who don't care that the Beatles, themselves, were fans. They will never acknowledge the craftsmanship of their best pop songs, even if many of the songwriters (Carole King, Harry Nilsson, Neil Diamond) went on to become superstars in their own right. They will conveniently overlook the show's cutting-edge techniques, even though Rafelson and Schneider were instrumental in the New Hollywood movement of the 1970s. And they certainly won't tip their cap to Michael Nesmith, even though, for all intents and purposes, he invented the revolutionary music video format that later became MTV. It's their loss.

The story of the Monkees still remains alluring to me—a fizzy Warhol-like cocktail of instant celebrity, overnight success, and all sorts of delicious behind-the-scenes skullduggery.

Each member of the group brought something to the table. The do-it-yourself spirit that imbues *Headquarters* embodies Peter Tork's heartfelt ambition to capture a real document of the Monkees performing together (and doing it surprisingly well).

Nesmith? Watch an old TV show and check out his comic timing. He's nearly always pitch-perfect whether he's being wry, cynical, wise, or silly, and he always does it with a homespun touch. For a guy with a wool hat who basically walked onto a TV show with no acting experience, it's quite an estimable feat.

Davy Jones was showbiz—an exhibitionist who occupies that rarified strata on planet Earth for those who were born to entertain. They don't make 'em like Davy anymore and they probably won't make 'em like Davy in the future.

Micky, it can be argued, possessed the greatest talent of the four as a pure entertainer. He not only supplied a crystalline pop voice for their greatest hits but typified the antic, and often anarchic, comedic spirit of the enterprise.

Yes I still like the Monkees and they still fascinate me. Like avatars from the future, they seem to embody almost every trend that dominates pop culture today—the branding, the all-pervasive connectivity, the blurring between reality and fantasy, the narrowing of the gap between the audience and the performer and, of course, the Faustian bargain that always accompanies celebrity.

Roll it all together—the high-energy sitcom shenanigans, the classic pop songs, and four wholly-distinct, yet intertwined, biographies—and you get the enduring story of a watershed pop phenomenon that, in my opinion, has never been bettered.

Chapter One

THE ANTICIPATION ON THE NIGHT of February 9, 1964 had reached a fever pitch. Approximately 73 million viewers were tuned in to catch the Beatles' first televised performance in the USA on *The Ed Sullivan Show*. When the cameras cut from the jowly old host to Paul McCartney, John Lennon, George Harrison and Ringo Starr performing "All My Loving," a new era of music began.

College student and aspiring folk musician Michael Nesmith was watching, along with all the future Monkees. "I just went out of my head with it like everybody else," he recalled. Nesmith couldn't have imagined that three years and a day later, he would be a pop star standing in Abbey Road studios watching the Beatles record their masterpiece, "A Day In The Life."

Downtown from the Ed Sullivan Theater, another aspiring folk performer (they were a dime a dozen thanks to Bob Dylan) was plying his trade at pass-the-basket clubs in Greenwich Village. Geographically, the glitzy world of the Sullivan show was only a few subway stops away but philosophically, to a folk purist like Peter Tork, it might as well have been a million miles. Only a few years later, Tork would be strumming a five-string banjo on the soundtrack to George Harrison's film *Wonderwall*.

Micky Dolenz had no purist folk tendencies. In his spare time, he was a greasy-haired lead singer in a five-piece rock and roll cover band named the Missing Links. After seeing the Fab Four perform, like a lot of young American males, Dolenz put away the pomade and got himself a Beatle haircut. A decade later he was partying hard with a gang of rock stars nicknamed the Hollywood Vampires whose inner circle included John Lennon and Ringo Starr.

One future Monkee was on the scene at the Ed Sullivan theatre that night. In between the Beatles' historic performances on the show, an elfin 19-year-old Davy Jones, in the role of the Artful Dodger, performed "I'd Do Anything" with the cast of the hit Broadway musical *Oliver!*

The Beatles on *The Ed Sullivan Show*, February 9, 1964.

After being thoroughly eclipsed by his fellow countrymen, Jones watched backstage with a mix of envy and awe. Later he recalled thinking "I want a bit of this—this is good."

All over America, young male musicians were doing the same calculation—how could they get some of that Beatles action? Seemingly overnight, from basements and garages, bands minted in the image and sound of the world's favorite Liverpudlians began emerging but none shared the group's visionary grasp of musical possibilities.

The Beatles phenomenon traveled at warp speed. A mere six months after *The Ed Sullivan Show*, the group's first full-length motion picture, *A Hard Day's Night*, was released. This surrealistic account of life inside the bubble of a pop phenomenon, directed by Richard Lester, was a box-office sensation as well as a major influence on emerging filmmakers—including the two creators of the Monkees, Bob Rafelson and Bert Schneider.

Thanks to *A Hard Day's Night*, Rafelson's pet project—a weekly TV show chronicling the misadventures of four genial musicians—suddenly had a much greater chance being sold to network television.

Chapter Two

WHILE STRIVING TO MOVE BEYOND the parameters of pop music on the albums *Rubber Soul* and *Revolver*, the Beatles achieved stunning new levels of musical expression and sophistication. They also left something in their wake: a mania gap.

Young fans who had gravitated to the happy-go-lucky Beatles sound of 1964 had a hard time comprehending the alien-sounding "Strawberry Fields Forever." And that was fine with the Beatles. By the summer of 1966, they were sick of the media frenzy. If they were "bigger than Jesus," as John Lennon bluntly put it, what use was a crowd of screaming teenage girls?

On August 28, 1966, the group gave a perfunctory performance at Dodger Stadium in Los Angeles. It was their second-to-last public appearance and lasted only thirty minutes. In attendance that night were producers Bob Rafelson and Bert Schneider and the four young men they had chosen to star in their almost-ready-for-prime-time TV series, *The Monkees*—Davy Jones, Micky Dolenz, Peter Tork and Michael Nesmith.

"I couldn't believe the kids were not listening to them," Tork recalled about the fan reaction at Dodger Stadium. "Here was the greatest single musical operation of all time, and they wouldn't listen. It was all just screaming."

As the Beatles went through the motions, the future superstars could only watch and wonder what was in store for them.

Duplicating the Beatles' success was a seemingly impossible task. The Beach Boys and the Lovin' Spoonful were American groups making inroads against the British Invasion in the fall of 1966 but neither had achieved the proper balance of mystique and musicianship necessary to create a phenomenon. That's what Bob Rafelson and Bert Schneider were actively seeking to do—create a phenomenon.

Their timing was excellent. The lovable lads portrayed in *A Hard Day's Night* had turned into psychedelic shamans singing "Tomorrow Never Knows." A cultural shift was underway where innocence was in short supply. Masters and

Johnson had shattered sexual myths in their book *Human Sexual Response*, *Time* was questioning the role of religion on the cover of their magazine (asking "Is God Dead?"), protests over the war in Vietnam were spilling over into the streets and onto campuses and, in the inner cities and South, racial tensions were peaking.

Meanwhile, efforts to promote an emerging youth-based pop culture were scaling increasingly-bold peaks of capitalistic self-expression. The Scott Paper Company introduced disposable paper dresses for one dollar, strange bands with names like the Thirteenth Floor Elevators, the Chocolate Watchband and the Electric Prunes, were having surprise Top 40 hits and TV shows like *Star Trek* were boldly going where no network executives had gone before.

Rafelson and Schneider had their finger on the pulse of pop culture. Like a West Coast outpost of Andy Warhol's Factory, the ambitious duo were seeking to create superstars out of unknown performers. Rafelson and Schneider realized no organic group could match the collective identity of the four Beatles—it had to be manufactured, scientifically assembled through auditions and use the best songwriting and producing talent available.

Their elaborate game plan was paying off dividends quicker than anyone imagined. On the night of the Beatles' show at Dodger Stadium, before even one episode of *The Monkees* had been broadcast, the first single released by the Monkees, "Last Train to Clarksville," was already a bona fide hit. With a propulsive beat and a guitar riff liberally borrowed from the Beatles' "Paperback Writer," it was top-notch pop.

Only industry insiders knew who or what the Monkees were at this time. To the public, a band name with animal associations was old news—they already had a menagerie of Crickets, Beatles, Turtles, Byrds, and the chirpy animated supergroup Alvin and the Chipmunks.

A sophisticated, immersive promotional campaign ensured the Monkees would not get lost in the already-crowded zoo. Several major entertainment concerns— NBC, Screen Gems, and RCA—had merged in mutual self-interest to make sure the made-for-TV-band would create an immediate impact.

The plan was working. For the latter part of 1966 and the entirety of 1967, to the utter astonishment of almost everybody in the entertainment industry, the records of the Monkees outsold the Beatles. Interestingly, and perhaps crucially in terms of credibility, it turns out the Beatles themselves were not in the least concerned about this development. They liked the Monkees.

The Prefab Four (above), conceived as America's answer to the Beatles.

Chapter Three

WHERE DID IT ALL START? Rafelson, with characteristic bravado, claims his interest in creating a fictional band pre-dated the rise of the Beatles. "I had the idea for the Monkees years before the Beatles arrived," he contended. "I tried to sell it as a folk-rock group, something about which I knew because I had traveled with a group of unruly and somewhat chaotic musicians in Mexico in 1953. We were itinerant musicians and I used many of the incidents that happened to me in Mexico in *The Monkees* episodes. So that's where the idea began."

Unlike Rafelson, Schneider had no reluctance in acknowledging the Beatles' influence on the evolution of the Monkees. "The Beatles made it all happen, that's the reality," Schneider admitted. "Richard Lester is where the credit begins for the Monkees and for Bob and me."

From the start, the maverick duo of Rafelson and Schneider struck a keen equilibrium. The political savvy of Schneider balanced perfectly with Rafelson's insouciance. Schneider built a reputation as a compelling and honest upper-management tactician who knew how to straddle both sides of an issue for the common good. Rafelson had an uncanny knack for spotting unrefined talent. Both possessed a non-conformist bent in business that appealed to young performers.

Rafelson saw kinetic possibilities in an untapped gold mine—a TV series about rock and roll. From the start, he knew it needed to be unique. Neither Rafelson or Schneider had a desire to market a crass, insubstantial product: they knew the kids wouldn't buy it. So they designed a show that snapped, crackled and popped with the latest new wave techniques and talent.

"There was a natural bent for rebellion that was in the air at the time that created a new effort in television. Things didn't have to be so plotted," Rafelson recalled. "People who were eight or nine years old look back on the show and remember there was something different about it—it bombarded their senses."

Youth culture on TV was shackled by a chastity belt—long hair and rock 'n 'roll, if depicted at all, were typically the target for satire and mockery. *The Monkees* aimed to be different. "It wasn't *Father Knows Best*," Schneider contends, "It was the kids know best. The heroes were young people and the heavies were older people."

The series would appeal to the previously undocumented fantasy life of teenagers. By featuring characters that looked and spoke like them, *The Monkees* offered an alternative to the buttoned-up world of TV sitcoms.

A key component was recognizing that rock and roll was about theater as much as it was about reality, purists be damned. The two biggest acts, Elvis Presley and the Beatles, had shown Rafelson and Schneider the way. Elvis' manager, "Colonel" Tom Parker burnished the singer's hillbilly roots by emphasizing his impeccable "nice guy" manners. Similarly, the Beatles' manager Brian Epstein transformed his scruffy Liverpudlians into a smartly-dressed quartet who resurrected the hammy-but-quaint tradition of taking a bow.

Rafelson and Schneider aimed to take the theatrical trappings of "authentic youth culture" one giant leap further by fictionalizing their group's entire backstory. Just how the project was put together—the casting call, the auditions, the screen tests—would wind up being critical parts of the narrative, a metafictional approach that was light years ahead of its time.

Another critical difference was Rafelson and Schneider's embrace of multi-media promotion. Every element available to them—radio, TV, records, advertising, live performances, merchandising and fan magazines—would work together to promote a brand.

Their ambition was vast and it was buoyed by equally important factor: family connections. An advance fund of $225,000 had been provided by former child star Jackie Cooper, an official at Screen Gems. At the time, Screen Gems was the television branch of Columbia Pictures, the entertainment conglomerate headed by Schneider's father, Abe.

An inside job? Perhaps. But no amount of family connections could pull off the kind of made-for-TV band they were plotting. It needed talent, smarts, and crazy energy and Rafelson and Schneider had all three.

The bond between the two producers was uncommonly strong, dating back to a friendship that began in their native New York where Rafelson was working as a story editor for CBS and Schneider was biding time as the treasurer of Screen Gems, the TV division of his father's company.

The strikingly handsome Schneider was clearly marked for greater things.

The masterminds of Monkeemania, Bob Rafelson (left) and Bert Schneider, aka Raybert productions.

"When Bert made an entrance it changed the chemistry of the room," writes Peter Biskind in *Easy Riders, Raging Bulls*, the seminal account of the New Hollywood scene of the early 1970s. "He had the charisma of a movie star, but it was not just looks; he was possessed of extraordinary personal authority."

Despite appearances of nepotism, the one major obstacle standing in Schneider's path, ironically, was his own father. A longtime company man for Columbia Pictures who was conservative by nature, Abe Schneider occupied the top dog's post and showed little interest in promoting his son. Frustrated by the lack of upward mobility after ten years of toil, the not-quite-prodigal son found a rebel soul mate in Bob Rafelson whose confrontational personality was a major part of his modus operandi.

The son of a well-to-do hat manufacturer, Rafelson came from privilege (he was also the nephew of noted playwright and screenwriter Samson Raphaelson) and often acted like it. The suburban existence and private-school upbringing did not satisfy a restless personality. Rafelson, like Schneider, was looking to break out of the old-school conventions of his elders. After a stint in the Army which found him in Japan, he returned to New York full of ideas. Rafelson's ambition of becoming a director of serious movies at times seemed like a pipe dream, especially working on insipid TV fare like *The Wackiest Ship in the Army*. His quicksilver personality earned him a reputation as a hot-head. Reportedly Rafelson had been escorted off the lot of Universal Studios after throwing a chair in an argument with powerful studio boss Lew Wasserman.

Fleeing to the West Coast, Rafelson urged Schneider to join him. He had a grandiose vision: the two of them would remake Hollywood in their own image, building a production company that supported young performers, allowed directors unprecedented control, and encouraged this untested talent to express themselves in bold new ways.

Giving in to Rafelson's enthusiasm, Schneider quit his cushy job in New York and moved to Los Angeles in 1965 to form Raybert Productions. A legendary partnership had begun; in Biskind's words, it was "the tiny company that transformed the industry."

Chapter Four

RAFELSON AND SCHNEIDER'S FIRST PRIORITY was to gather enough capital to bankroll motion picture productions. Then and now, quick money was made on TV. "Our ambitions were to make movies," Schneider explained. "We began with a TV series because that was the foot in the door. It was easier to get a pilot of a TV series made than it was to get a movie made."

The idea of creating a TV series about a fictional band may have originated with Rafelson but it took Schneider's temperament and connections to seal the deal. "Bert was the engineer," insisted Tork. "(Bert) structured the business deals and fought for the terms and got the right pilot deal. Bert was the executive in charge of everything."

Schneider, who later became a significant figure in Hollywood's left-wing counterculture, lent credibility that Rafelson lacked. "To my way of thinking, the thing that sets *The Monkees* apart from all the other TV shows about youth culture of its time was that Bert was a fan," explained Tork. "He was a fan of the Beatles. He liked the spirit of the times."

How and why Rafelson and Schneider picked the name "the Monkees" in retrospect seems pretty obvious—it was a great name that had never been used before. There were other choices. "We kind of fooled around with 'the Creeps,' but we decided it was too negative," Schneider told the *Saturday Evening Post*. Other names, such as The Inevitables, were also briefly bandied about.

Why Monkees? "I don't know why," Schneider quipped. "I'll have to ask my analyst."

After Cooper allocated funds for the pilot, Rafelson and Schneider's first order of business was to cage the proper primates. They adroitly reasoned they needed a mix of professional actors and off-the-street musicians to strike the correct balance for public consumption.

Their quest to find the four Monkees has become the stuff of legend. The duo took out one of the great casting call ads of all-time in *Daily Variety* on September 8, 1965:

Madness!!

Auditions

Folk & Roll Musicians-Singers

for acting roles in new TV series.

Running parts for 4 insane boys, age 17-21.

Want spirited Ben Frank's-types

Have courage to work

Must come down for interview.

Hidden within the ad were several inside jokes designed to weed out the chaff. "Ben Franks" was a reference to a popular Sunset Strip eatery where the mods mused over burgers and fries. "Must come down," according to Rafelson, was "a sly reference to being high."

In all probability, these cryptic allusions mattered little to the over 400 work-starved applicants that swamped Raybert's office. Everybody who was anybody in LA took a crack at the auditions, including the cream of the burgeoning rock scene, among them: Harry Nilsson and Paul Williams (both of whom later penned songs for the Monkees), Danny Hutton (later of Three Dog Night), Bobby "Boris" Pickett (who already had a hit with "The Monster Mash"), Van Dyke Parks (who later collaborated on Beach Boy Brian Wilson's *Smile* album), and legendary disc jockey Rodney Bingenheimer. According to Bingenheimer, Charles Manson also took a stab at the job (an urban legend that was later proven false—Manson was in jail at the time).

Perhaps the most notorious of the Monkees might-have-beens was future rock superstar Stephen Stills. As legend would have it, Stills lost out due to a receding hairline and a recessed tooth. "They could have fixed my teeth," Stills later told writer Dave Zimmer. "What I really wanted to do was write songs for the show. But I found out that I'd have to give up my publishing and that they already had a pair of staff writers in Boyce and Hart."

Schneider had little regret about rejecting Stills, remembering he "had a little less abandon. In order to do this kind of thing, guys really had to have a lot of abandon. I suspect Stephen was a little bit more inhibited." Before leaving Raybert offices, Stills threw one of the great Hail Mary passes in the history of rock and roll by recommending his friend Peter Tork.

One performer not the least bit inhibited was already a shoo-in for the job:

Davy Jones. With a newly-minted contract with Screen Gems under his belt, Jones was, in fact, attached to the project from the very start—an important, though rarely-noted, distinction (one of many Monkees myths is the assumption that all four had answered the ad in *Daily Variety* but, as it turns out, only Nesmith had).

"Screen Gems wanted to find a vehicle for me," Jones later recalled. By 1965, the British-born performer was on the verge of big things—a proto-star with a Tony Award nomination for *Oliver!* and a charismatic personality. One of Jones' charms was that he never denied being a showboat. "Quite honestly, from being a little kid in school I always felt special," he later said. "I was always in the school play. I was always in the limelight, singing and dancing."

Born and raised in class-conscious Manchester, England, Jones came from a resolutely middle-class background. His father Harry worked as an engineer for British Rail. When he was 13, Jones suffered the devastating loss of his mother, Doris, who died of emphysema. His father Harry, harboring hopes his plucky but pint-sized son could become a successful jockey, sent him to live with a horse trainer named Basil Foster.

Whether or not Jones would have succeeded in horse racing will never be known. When Foster was approached with a casting request by a London West End theatrical producer, he recommended the producer take a look at his whippet-sized apprentice. In an instant, Jones' career at the racetrack was over.

With cherubic good looks and a natural stage presence, Jones was a hot prospect on the London scene. In short order he scored a recurring role on the long-running soap opera *Coronation Street* and then won acclaim for *Oliver!*, which opened in London and then moved to New York.

Jones took Broadway by storm. *The New York Times* singled him out for his "impudent charm" in their review of *Oliver!* Judy Garland told him "after tonight, this city is yours." The endorsement of the stage and screen legend, for a young man from Manchester, was truly the stuff of dreams and she wasn't alone—big things were being predicted for the little guy. In July 1965, *Variety* announced he had signed an agreement with Screen Gems to produce television pilots. He also signed to Colpix Records, the company's recording division.

His manager, Ward Sylvester, a former employee at Screen Gems who was friendly with Bert Schneider, provided an inside track to one of the four coveted spots on *The Monkees*. It didn't take a genius to see Jones was a natural fit. For one thing, he possessed something worth its weight in gold at the time: a British accent.

To everyone, except Rafelson, Jones seemed like a perfect fit. "Davy is the one I had the most doubts about. I'll be honest about that," Rafelson admitted. "Davy had the least contact with rock and roll than any of the others, and although he had acting experience, I wasn't sure if he would be able to get into the spirit of the thing." He added, "I was wrong, very wrong."

Jones scored an easy victory when screen tests were used to determine the likability of the Monkees. He had everything it took, including one crucial physical feature: short stature. The reason he became a teen idol, Jones later reasoned, was because he wasn't threatening: "I'm a little guy...I'm not going to jump on you and hurt you and bite you."

In many ways Jones' talents, like his size, were somewhat modest. He was an able dancer but not outstandingly graceful; he could sing adequately but his voice had a distinctively nasal tone that lacked power. "A gimmicky sort of a little thing," was Jones' own description of his singing voice. As a presenter of songs he could get by and occasionally shine (the most notable example being "Daydream Believer") but Jones rarely inhabited the songs with adult emotions. "I make a terrible sound," he told Rafelson during his screen test.

On the other hand, Jones had IT, that ineffable essence that creates celebrities—an enchanting mix of eye-pleasing beauty and affable stage presence. If Rafelson and Schneider didn't want him, there were plenty of other producers who did. That's why he was a shoo-in for the job.

Chapter Five

RAYBERT'S FINELY-TUNED BULLSHIT DETECTOR was on guard for fake rebels. To ensure nobody slipped through the cracks, they employed an intricate and pressure-filled process of elimination. Rafelson had written his college thesis on cultural anthropology and he utilized his knowledge by waging a psychological war among applicants where only the fittest would survive.

The hopefuls, after filling out a questionnaire, were led unwittingly to the producers' offices. Once there, applicants faced a series of intimidation tactics designed to expose their identities. Many, according to the *Saturday Evening Post*, "became flustered when caught in the crossfire as the producers staged mock arguments over their merits, or ignored them while playing catch with a golf ball."

Tork found the atmosphere intimidating. "It was awful, I was so nervous," he said of his audition. To cover up his anxiety he improvised a stage personality he had perfected in Greenwich Village, "a Three Stooges character without the testosterone which I used to protect myself against jokes that didn't work."

Having been recommended by his friend Stills, Tork received a close look. "Stephen was the guy who looked like me on Greenwich Village streets. That's how I recognized him—I walked up to him and said, 'You're the guy that looks like me.' And he said, 'Oh, you're the guy I'm supposed to look like.' So, when they were looking for somebody like him but whose hair and teeth were better, Stephen instantly thought of his friend Peter, threw the bone his way, and took for a consolation prize the Buffalo Springfield and Crosby, Stills, Nash and Young," Tork recalled, adding a sarcastic, "poor guy."

On the face of it, Tork was an unlikely choice. With no record contract and no buzz, Tork had no obvious upside. He wasn't a lead singer or an accomplished songwriter and had no professional experience in recording, theater, or TV. His ability to master musical instruments may have been impressive but some of these instruments, like banjo, were hardly mainstays of rock and roll.

What was Tork's ambition? "To wend my way merrily through life, playing my little banjo and my little guitar and sing my songs" was his answer.

A modest goal, perhaps, but for Tork, any career success in music would be considered a victory. His life before the Monkees had been an itinerant one filled with difficulty. A tumultuous youth found his family moving from Washington, DC, where he was born, to Detroit, then overseas to Berlin then back to Wisconsin before finally settling in Connecticut. By his own admission, Tork was a troubled kid who boasted a "serious inferiority complex."

After a brief marriage failed, Tork flunked out of college. He found himself in New York, staying at his grandmother's apartment on West 57th Street ("a block from the A train, down to the Village in eight minutes") and started singing in coffeehouses. It wasn't much of a living. "You get paid zip," he recalls. "I mean, literally. And you had to make your entire living by passing a basket."

Tork was enamored with the myth of the troubadour roaming from town to town in search of his next musical epiphany. And this did seem to be his destiny before Stills tipped Raybert off about him.

In the attitude and looks department, Tork was just what Rafelson and Schneider needed: a West Coast blonde surfer type a la Dennis Wilson of the Beach Boys. Ironically, Tork's leftist folkie roots were strictly of the East Coast variety and, unlike his role on the show—where he was to play a clueless innocent—he was something of a self-styled intellectual.

To Rafelson and Schneider, the fact that Tork was nobody's idea of a prefab rock star made him even more attractive. He was the authentic street-character they were looking for. "I remember I went to great lengths to contact him," Rafelson later recalled. "I found him working as a dishwasher—not even a musician—so you can imagine it took a while tracing him. But when I heard him, I knew at once he was right. I was knocked out."

Tork remembered Jones walking around "like he owned the place." The diminutive performer with Napoleonic ambitions was keeping score as applicants came and went, keeping a close eye on the appearance of those auditioning. It was important to Jones that he be better looking—beauty, not talent, was his yardstick.

One applicant caught Jones' attention immediately—a lanky Texan going by the name of Michael Blessing. "He had a bag of laundry over his shoulder, his pants tucked into his boots which came up to his knee and he had this wool hat on," Jones recalled with a laugh. "It was like the middle of summer and this guy's just come out of the mountains…and I thought, 'Oh, we got a rare one here!'"

If Rafelson and Schneider were looking for a hard-nosed maverick along the lines of John Lennon, they struck crude oil with this Michael Blessing kid. A mercurial guy with a surly temperament, Blessing, whose real name was Michael Nesmith, drew a diagonal line through the part of the application inquiring about past experience and wrote the word "Life."

In Raybert's universe, this kind of spontaneous confidence was what they were looking for. "Bert wanted strange types," Jones contends. "He wanted raw, new stuff that he alone could bring in."

Strange was a good description for Nesmith. He was a walking contradiction. Never one to suffer fools gladly, he possessed a surprisingly natural gift for comedy. He was driven to succeed to the point of selfishness and yet he could be generous to an extreme.

Growing up in Dallas, the only son of his divorced mom, Nesmith was given to fits of sullenness. His glowering countenance and enigmatic behavior masked a more sensitive, artistic side of his personality. "I'm a street fighter," he later told interviewer Harold Bronson. "Always have been. I grew up with hot rods and fists and all that horseshit."

His mother Bette scraped by as a secretary. When she wasn't on the job she worked tirelessly to promote her new invention—a typewriter correction fluid she called Mistake Out (later renamed Liquid Paper). "Michael came from an extremely poor situation," Tork explained. "I mean, he tells us that his mother would boil up a batch of Liquid Paper on the stove and he would go to Dallas and sell it and they would eat that night on what he made that day."

Surprisingly, the Texas teenager harbored zero ambitions when it came to playing music until the age of 19, when he bought a guitar, taught himself to play, and, with no training, began to write songs. "I had to make up songs in order to have something to play," he recalled matter-of-factly. Nesmith's creative drive and protean nature was firmly rooted in the Lone Star State, where stubborn independence is something of a birthright. His signature song, "Different Drum," perfectly captures his no-nonsense attitude: "I'm not ready for any person, place or thing to try and pull the reins in on me."

True to his word, Nesmith left Texas with wife-to-be Phyllis Barbour and headed off to Los Angeles in search of a lucky break. Like many of his contemporaries,

Folkie upstart Nesmith (below) performing with future wife Phyllis Barbour.

Nesmith's stage persona represented another in a long line of Bob Dylan imitators. Dressed in denim, guitar in hand and a harmonica rig around his neck, he was operating on the fringes of the LA folk scene, a regular at hootenannies hosted at the legendary nightclub, The Troubadour.

After adopting his stage name out of a phone book ("I didn't find anything in the A's that I liked so by the time I got to the B's, Blessing seemed pretty good…I liked the implications of it") he managed to score an agent and released a few unsuccessful singles for Colpix records, coincidentally the same label that had already signed Jones.

By the time he sauntered into Rafelson and Schneider's offices to audition, Nesmith had reached a crucial make-or-break moment in his career. He was already married, had a son and was flat broke. Somewhat sheepishly he admitted he was unemployed during the making of his screen test and then added with a sly smile "I hope I get this series."

Rafelson and Schneider loved everything about him, even the wool hat he incongruously wore on his head in sunny Southern California. But it was clear from the start he could be stubborn and confrontational. When the producers sought to nickname him "Wool Hat," Nesmith drew a line in the sand—he was not going to be caricatured. Rafelson recalled, "He said, 'I will not be called Wool Hat.'" And that was that.

Chapter Six

UNLIKE HIS FUTURE BANDMATES NESMITH AND TORK, Micky Dolenz was an unflappable pro from the get-go. Having been cast in the lead role of TV's *Circus Boy* at the age of 11, he was something of a showbiz vet. Auditioning was part of his weekly routine.

Under the stage name Mickey Braddock, Dolenz won national fame as Corky, the blonde-haired cherub smiling widely as he rode the back of camels. For a young boy growing up in the 1950s, he was living a charmed life. According to the *Los Angeles Times*, Dolenz was "the envy of every youngster in his neighborhood" for taking a balloon ride during the making of the series. The ride was "more fun than baseball," he cheerfully told the reporter.

Theatrical behavior came naturally to Dolenz. Raised in the world of show business, his father George, a well-regarded actor, was best known as the swash-buckling hero on TV's *The Count of Monte Cristo.* Later, he owned a restaurant, the Marquis, a popular hang-out spot for Hollywood bon vivants on Sunset Boulevard.

The apple didn't fall far from the Dolenz tree. From an early age, George Michael Dolenz, Jr. displayed the innate mutability of an actor. Whether it was dyeing his hair blonde to play Corky on *Circus Boy*, growing an afro and wearing paisley as a psychedelized Monkee, or donning a debonair hat and playing country music on a reality TV series, Dolenz was always comfortable slipping on a disguise.

Dolenz immediately seized upon the potential of The Monkees. "It was pilot season and there was like three or four other shows about music that they were trying to get on the air," he recalled. "There was one about a Beach Boys kind of act, there was another like Peter, Paul and Mary—two guys and a girl—and this was by far the most unique."

Coming from old school entertainment circles, Dolenz, Jr. was initially dumbstruck by the ramshackle appearance of Rafelson and Schneider's office. "I walked into this office and pizza cartons and Coke cans were everywhere and

Final cut pros: Dolenz, Jones, Nesmith and Tork emerged as the four survivors from auditions.

two guys were sitting around in jeans and t-shirts. I thought they were gofers," he remembered. "And they were the producers!"

Dolenz had three things going for him: he was familiar with producing a weekly TV series, he possessed an ingratiating singing style of unusual depth and elasticity, and just as importantly, he harbored a friendly-but-snarky comic edge. This was the kind of irreverent spirit Raybert were looking for. According to the *Saturday Evening Post*, "Dolenz found Rafelson and Schneider seated on opposite sides of a desk, absorbed in balancing a pile of soda bottles, glasses and paper cups. Impulsively, he snatched a cup off the desk, balanced it on top of the stack and shouted, 'Checkmate!'"

The use of confrontational tactics, Rafelson later argued, was both necessary and intentional: "As a rule, actors come into an audition prepared. Usually, they've heard very little about the project that's real. For example, their agents, who don't know anything, have told them they're looking for somebody sexy. So the girl comes into your office and tries to be sexy. The thing is to unmask those people as quickly as possible to find out who they are. This is what we did with the Monkees."

Before Rafelson and Schneider settled on the "chosen four," they winnowed the possibilities down to a select group to be given screen tests. Even Jones, who had all but clinched his role, had to pass Hollywood's traditional test of fire.

The screen tests, like everything else associated with the Monkees, were far from traditional. Potential cast members faced a volley of unpredictable questions. Portions of Jones and Nesmith's tests later grafted onto the pilot episode remain fascinating artifacts, revealing as much about the subjects as they do the off-camera inquisitor. At various times Rafelson is heard ridiculing Jones' attempt to show off "song and dance" moves; he cajoles Nesmith into admitting he's been a "failure."

The mix of self-effacing honesty and cheeky artifice was the quixotic brew that Raybert were intent on serving the public. Rafelson set the tone—he was loose, unafraid and in your face.

After taping the screen tests, Rafelson and Schneider began mixing and matching the applicants in an effort to achieve a balance of style, personality and appearance. Once they narrowed their choices down to eight finalists, the producers took the screen tests to Audience Studies Incorporated (ASI), a research subsidiary of Screen Gems that measured random samples of a viewing audience and computerized their findings. The final results were tallied. David Jones, unsurprisingly, was the audience favorite. Micky Dolenz, Peter Tork and Michael Nesmith also scored highly enough to make the cut.

Over the years, much ballyhoo has been made over the laboratory Darwinism employed by Rafelson and Schneider. What was perceived as unnecessary cruelty in the auditioning process later became the stock-in-trade of reality TV shows like *Survivor* and *American Idol*—just one example of how Rafelson and Schneider were pushing the boundaries.

Their boldest stroke—casting two actors, Dolenz and Jones, with two musicians, Nesmith and Tork—proved to be a critical component in elevating the project to greater creative heights as the musicians learned to act and the actors learned to become musicians. Casting idiosyncratic personalities rather than professional actors was another crucial decision. Although advised to the contrary, Raybert stuck to their guns. "I would rather work with amateur actors," Rafelson told the *New York Times*. "If you hired professionals you wouldn't get the primitiveness we were looking for."

As production on the pilot was readied, a large stone lay unturned: how well would headstrong survivors of Raybert's arduous casting techniques get along? Four distinct personalities with four distinct backgrounds, their chemistry was

Two actors meet two musicians. The question was: would they harmonize?

untested. The prevailing mood, described by Tork as "always some tension, always some jealousy" set the tone.

They were about to embark on a remarkable journey but they were barely familiar with each other. Jones, a constant presence at auditions, had already met the others. He quickly struck up a friendship with Dolenz. The two were natural allies. Both were experienced hands in the entertainment industry with impressive resumes. "Davy and I hit it off immediately," Dolenz confirmed, "because of our theatrical, cinematic backgrounds."

Prior to winning their roles on *The Monkees*, Nesmith and Tork had crossed paths at The Troubadour but they were oddly mismatched personalities. Although both shared the mentality of an outsider, their highly individualistic characters were destined to clash. "In every group of four there are six pairs," Tork said diplomatically. "There were six fights, one each."

Nesmith's take was more blunt. He contended, "It wasn't one for all and all for one. There was a very clear, distinct barrier between each one of us—a real individuality in each one of us. And in a way that may be one of the things that made it work."

Chapter Seven

THERE WAS NO TIME TO MAKE LONG-TERM ASSESSMENTS about whether they would get along—the pre-scheduled production of the pilot ensured that. It was time to begin shooting. The director of the pilot was Mike Elliott, better known at the time as a director of TV commercials (he would later film the Monkees shilling for Kellogg's Rice Krispies and Yardley Black Label After-Shave).

Production commenced on November 11, 1965. The risky nature of putting a quartet of willful young men together (Jones was the youngest at 19, followed by Dolenz, 20, Nesmith, 22, and Tork, 23) became instantly apparent. The four brash young Monkees instigated a public food fight during a break between shooting scenes at the Hotel Del Coronado in San Diego, an incident that lead to the group being permanently banned from the hotel. As malfeasances go, it was minor and perhaps inevitable given the pressure of the situation. It was also prescient—future incidents of a similar nature were to follow.

In the meantime, behind the scenes, decisions were being made that would affect (some might say haunt) the project until its dying days. At the behest of Schneider, the talented songwriting team of Tommy Boyce and Bobby Hart had been commissioned to score the pilot.

Fresh from the stables of New York's Brill Building—songwriting central of its day—Boyce and Hart were a thoroughbred writing team who had scored major hits such as "Come a Little Bit Closer" by Jay and the Americans. Their knack for knocking out three-minute melodies sufficiently impressed song publisher Don Kirshner who recommended the duo to Schneider (Kirshner was a music impresario who lorded over a wealth of Screen Gems songwriting copyrights and would later become the savior as well as devil incarnate of the Monkees phenomenon).

In short order, Boyce and Hart composed three songs, "(Theme from) The Monkees," "I Wanna Be Free" and "Let's Dance On."

The four chosen ones were eager to become a self-contained musical unit.

"We had to have those tracks made before the group ever existed," Schneider explained. "I can remember meeting with Boyce and Hart at the same time we were interviewing kids to be in the Monkees. In fact, Boyce and Hart were hoping to be in the group themselves."

Of the three songs written for the pilot none was more important to the project's success than "(Theme from) The Monkees." Featuring an ominous momentum thanks to its slow/fast dynamic, the theme song had a cinematic quality that was altogether winning. Its clever lyrics straddled a fine line between outright manipulation ("we're the young generation and we've got something to say") and chummy felicity ("we're too busy singing to put anybody down"). Most importantly, it was an ear worm—once heard it was never forgotten.

For the songwriting duo of Boyce and Hart it was an impressive start. Moreover, it set a crucial precedent. Having the Monkees lip-sync the vocals of Boyce and Hart (the group's vocals were later dubbed back in when the pilot aired) was a harbinger of things to come. Although Nesmith and Tork had been given vague promises they would eventually get the opportunity to express themselves musically, it was clear from the start the idea was nice but not entirely necessary.

Consumed by the sudden whirlwind pace of events, the quartet had no time

Long before MTV, the Monkees revolutionized the concept of music videos.

to protest. In only a few weeks, they landed prized roles and began filming a pilot. Musical control was far from foremost on their minds—making the show successful was and besides, as Schneider later contended, "it was inconceivable that they would have become a cohesive group that fast."

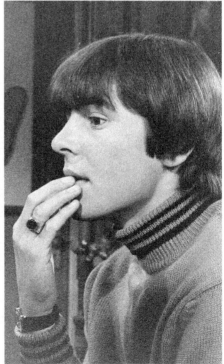

Chapter Eight

THE PILOT—WHICH LATER AIRED WITH SOME CHANGES as episode ten of the series—established the thematic arc of the series. Written by Paul Mazursky (later a successful Hollywood director) with partner Larry Tucker, the storyline was straightforward: the Monkees are hired to perform at a sweet-sixteen party, things go awry when Davy falls in love with the hostess—predictably much to her parents' disapproval—and then all sorts of madcap Monkee business ensues.

It had two outstanding qualities—it was funny and it was new. Amidst all the Hollywood hokum of the simplistic plot lurked a benevolent yet pointedly modern edge to the show, in particular, a forthrightness unseen elsewhere. The Monkees were portrayed as regular bumbling Joes instead of untouchable rock icons—a thematic ploy which softened the show's subtle anti-establishment stance. Except for a long-suffering manager (who appeared in the pilot but never returned in future episodes) the Monkees operated without adult supervision. The distinction was important because it allowed viewers to immerse themselves in a total fantasy. There was never a mention of school or dishes to do.

"We were the only TV show ever from that time," Tork claimed, "and for 15 or 20 years afterwards to have young adult figures without an older authority figure. That made it unique."

Tork, who was never a fan of Rafelson's domineering ways, maintained that Schneider deserves credit for letting the Monkees be independent. "That never could have happened if Bert had been a cigar-chomping older executive. [It] reflects Bert's rare qualities, unique for television at that point, that he saw that there was no need for an authority figure."

The visual presentation of *The Monkees* pilot was also an unexplored entity on network television. With a nod to Richard Lester's *A Hard Day's Night* as well as silent-screen masters Charlie Chaplin, Buster Keaton and Mack Sennett, Rafelson and his staff brought an entirely new language to network programming. Gone was the static visual stylization of sitcoms past. Match cuts and continuity were thrown into the wind. By shooting film, a galaxy of effects were possible. Abrupt cutaways and sped-up action added a Dadaesque element to the proceedings. In one freeze-frame sequence at the end of the pilot, a cartoon-like bubble appears next to a dancing nymphet, asking "A typical teenager?" only to be answered by another bubble reading "No, a friend of the producers."

"We came up with every technique we could think of in order to make it visually interesting," remembered James Frawley, director of half of the show's 58 episodes. "We used mirror shots, trick shots, upside-down angles, weird lenses, anything we wanted."

Flat lighting—the standard TV technique of lighting the entire set—was scrapped altogether. Rafelson explained, "I believed very strongly at the time that background in television counted for naught. All you ever looked at was the foreground because there's no depth to the medium. So I said, 'light the foreground, fuck the background, let's shoot fast and we'll make it in the editing room.' It caused a monumental amount of editing."

Instead of the established twenty-five or so set-ups used for a sitcom, the Monkees used as many as ninety. Rafelson's boast to *TV Guide*—"I do not regard film as a sacred parchment but as a pliable thing"—became an overall operating philosophy, particularly in the two musical sequences per episode, free-form romps that were often the highlight of the show.

It is Nesmith's contention that the power of these mini-musical moments are what contributed to the misperception that *The Monkees* episodes were pure improvisation. "The magic to the show wasn't the scripts," argued Nesmith. "The magic was the musical numbers and they were almost entirely ad-libbed. But they weren't ad-libbed by us necessarily, they were ad-libbed by Jim Frawley and the camera crew."

"I had the freedom that most directors pray for," Frawley corroborated. "It gave me the kind of autonomy that spoiled me for working with other people because I had absolute and total freedom, which is very nurturing to a young director. If I wanted to shoot an entire episode with one lens just to see what it looked like, I could do that. If I wanted to try cutting experiments, I could do that, too, because every show had a couple of musical numbers which were pretty free-form."

Incorporating six or seven minutes of each episode, the Monkees' musical sequences were a revolutionary development for television and proved to be highly influential in years to come. Up until *The Monkees*, a musical performance

on television usually featured a group lip-syncing to a pre-recorded track in an imitation of a real performance. Rafelson and Frawley promoted the concept of music videos becoming a form of narrative interwoven into the show's plot.

Doubts still lingered as to whether the public would buy these new techniques and the frantic antics of long-haired rock musicians. When Rafelson and Schneider screened the pilot for a test audience, it laid an egg, scoring one of the lowest ratings ever. "What we found in the original testing," Schneider explained, "was for those in the audience who didn't know who these guys were, the anti-establishment stance was too much of an affront of their sensibilities and attitudes. Those kind of testing services bring in the whole demographic, a typical TV audience, so you're going to have all the older people in there as well as the younger. Well, the older people just hated the kids—you couldn't get past that. In other words, they weren't prepared to see the humor because they had already turned off their minds."

Instead of throwing in the towel, Rafelson immediately took the pilot back into the editing room, where he strategically re-cut the episode by placing Jones and Nesmith's screen tests at the beginning of the show. "I spent 48 straight hours in the editing room," Rafelson recalled, "and put the interviews at the very beginning so people could get to know the Monkees and therefore buy some of their so-called anti-establishment." He had stumbled upon a winning formula.

Rafelson's gamble hit pay-dirt—only two days after the show bombed, it scored a high-enough rating to have it considered by NBC for their primetime line-up. While NBC executives mulled it over, the four cast members nervously waited. Each kept busy in his own way. Nesmith kept singing his Michael Blessing material, made promotional appearances and hosted open-mike nights at The Troubadour. Dolenz auditioned for more TV roles (at least one of which was another rock-themed show) and Tork traveled back to the East Coast to visit friends and family.

Of the four would-be Monkees, only Jones had the security of a contract with Screen Gems but this guaranteed him nothing. In the ever-changing world of pop culture his success was far from assured. The anemic "twee pop" he was recording for Colpix Records was creating zero buzz. It was complete treacle.

Prior to making *The Monkees* pilot, Jones had filmed an appearance on the medical drama *Ben Casey* which aired on December 27, 1965. Uncharacteristically, he played a wife-beating glue-sniffing reprobate, a far cry from the ingratiating roles he usually landed.

A little more than one month later, on February 9, 1966, the waiting came to an end. It was news they were hoping for—NBC had commissioned a full season of *The Monkees*. The long and strange journey had just begun.

Chapter Nine

FOR RAYBERT, THE EXCITEMENT OF SELLING THE SERIES did not last very long. Only five days after getting approval from NBC to start making episodes, *Variety* announced legal action had been taken against Raybert by producers David Gordon and David Yarnell, whose show *Liverpool USA* had been pitched to Screen Gems in late 1964.

The format of Gordon and Yarnell's show, featuring a group of two American and two British musicians bore a more-than-passing resemblance to *The Monkees*. It, too, was going to star the charming British moppet named Davy Jones. In fact, discussions between Jones' manager Ward Sylvester and Gordon and Yarnell had already taken place. Moreover, the duo had already pitched the idea to Don Kirshner, the same music-publishing magnate who had recommended hiring Boyce and Hart.

A lawsuit loomed but Raybert had other important issues to contend with. The four Monkees, particularly TV newbies Nesmith and Tork, would soon have to face the cameras and the daily grind of creating a weekly sitcom. Preparation was essential. Under the auspices of James Frawley, the group started a six-week improvisational workshop at Screen Gems Stage #3 where a sign warned, "Monkees—Keep Out!"

Frawley, who had up to this time only directed two experimental films, was skilled in the art of improvisation. As a member of an innovative New York comedy troupe named The Premise, he had honed his talents with the able likes of Buck Henry, a co-creator of the madcap spy comedy *Get Smart* (Henry was also a close friend of Schneider and Rafelson).

Tasked with whipping the Monkees into shape, Frawley was suddenly immersed into the world of TV production, a virtual rookie in Hollywood's big league. But Raybert's faith in untested talent was undiminished. If anything it was the central premise of their hell-bent, go-for-broke attitude. "If you're going in a direction that requires that you be innovative," Schneider explained, "it's impossible to reach into the same pool of talent where everybody else reaches because then you're not going to get innovators, you'll get imitators. Our attitude was 'we're jumping off the bridge here, there's no point in going halfway.'"

As it turns out, Frawley's relative inexperience was perfectly suited to the Monkees, who were green themselves, and anxious to boot. To loosen them up, Frawley had the boys run through improvisational exercises that found them imitating animals or impersonating celebrities. "These sessions gave the guys a chance to improvise together and to establish a feel of ensemble," said Frawley. "Also, it gave Bob, Bert and me a chance to determine where the strengths and weaknesses of each of the boys lay."

Nesmith remembered the experience as "very nurturing," lauding Frawley's ability "to create a safe haven and make it okay to be silly." The four Monkees were treated to screenings of classic comedy troupes like the Marx Brothers and the Three Stooges and encouraged to act with abandon.

Although rehearsals helped establish a personal rapport between the four cast members, the spontaneous anarchy generated in these sessions, when unleashed in public, created a new set of problems. At a meeting of NBC affiliates previewing the fall line-up at the venerable Chasen's restaurant in Beverly Hills, the Monkees made a shambles of a highly-opportune moment.

TV Guide later reported the incident in full detail: "Somebody had dragged along a stuffed peacock. They played volleyball with it, stopping traffic on Beverly Boulevard. Micky got into the restaurant's switch box and turned off all the lights. Finally they were introduced to Dick Clark. Since they hadn't any musical instruments...they did 'comedy' material. Micky shaved with the microphone. Davy pretended he was a duck. The jokes began to die."

The network and the show paid dearly for this display. Several affiliates were sufficiently offended by the group's lack of decorum and rejected the show without seeing it. According to *TV Guide*, at least five key stations failed to pick up the series, which, in turn, resulted in lower national ratings throughout the entire run of the series. As a result, *The Monkees* show, despite its popularity and its critical standing, never cracked the Top 25 in the Nielsen ratings.

If past is prologue then the Chasen's debacle was a sign of things to come. Strange and sometimes unpleasant things seemed to happen when the four Monkees were not under the strict control of directors and producers. Any vacuum in authority was quickly filled with spontaneous attention-seeking antics of four young men with expanding egos. When order was replaced by anarchy, disaster was lurking around the corner.

Chapter Ten

AS THE NETWORK DEBUT OF *THE MONKEES* **GREW CLOSER**, Rafelson and Schneider realized they had one major problem—there was no music ready beyond the pilot. Already, a recording session with Snuff Garrett (Gary Lewis and the Playboys) had been deemed a failure. In-demand British music producer Mickie Most (the Animals, Herman's Hermits, Donovan) took a pass. And when songwriter Carole King gave it a shot, she clashed with Nesmith and left the studio in tears.

Adding to the complexity of the task was the musical ambitions of Nesmith and Tork, both of whom were agitating for studio time to prove themselves. To appease their enthusiastic charges, Rafelson and Schneider assured them they shared their goal of becoming a real band but, in the short run, they would have to be patient and wait.

Tork felt his integrity was at stake. "I was raised in the Pete Seeger tradition of authenticity and folk singing and integrity and honor and I thought bands played their own music," he explained.

Hoping to show off his chops, an eager Tork arrived uninvited at a Boyce and Hart recording session with guitar in hand only to be turned away. "I was distraught," Tork recalled about the incident. "(And) the worst thing was that nobody seemed to notice."

While Tork's reaction was emotional, Nesmith was analytical and calculated. He could be appeased in the short term by having his songs appear on Monkees records but clearly he was in the pursuit of a bigger stake in the process. With an entrepreneur's zeal like his mother, Nesmith brandished a knife to make sure he would receive a slice of the cake. After repeated demands and much agitation, he finally got his way. On June 25, 1966, Nesmith was granted access to RCA Studio A with a stipulation: he could produce his own songs but not perform on them.

Pouncing on the opportunity, Nesmith assembled a dream team—the crème de la crème of session players—many of them legendary musicians. Drummer Jim Gordon, bassist Larry Knechtel and two titans of the guitar, James Burton and Glen

Campbell, were among hired hands that gathered together to create instrumental tracks for "All the King's Horses," a Nesmith original and "The Kind of Girl I Could Love," co-written with Roger Atkins.

The results were impressive, two country-inflected songs, a new and interesting hybrid that exhibited solid pop values that were later deemed worthy of running on early episodes of the TV series. It was plain to see Nesmith was not going to be ignored. Now that he had proved his mettle in the recording studio, he could begin turning his attention to a larger, and much more difficult, task. Like Tork, he wanted the Monkees to develop into an actual working band. This ambition was more than mere vanity. The desire to play together had been evident as early as the making of the pilot when the foursome performed an impromptu version of Chuck Berry's "Johnny B. Goode" in front of the production crew.

Positions in the band had already been determined through casting. No one, least of all Jones, wanted to be hidden behind the drums—they were a theatrical liability. In an act of self-sacrifice, Dolenz agreed to do it. "I thought it would be great fun," Dolenz said of the challenge of becoming a drummer. "I started practicing immediately and I'm sure they were all waiting around with bated breath wondering if I could ever be able to cut it. And I managed."

Almost by default Nesmith was the guitarist. He donned a customized 12-string guitar donated by Gretsch, one of the group's sponsors. Tork assumed bass duties, and Jones added percussion on tambourine and maracas. On-set jam sessions became part of the daily work ritual. "A lot of the (instruments) were already hooked up," explained Nesmith, "So we would sit around and play." His verdict? "Didn't sound good," he wryly commented, "but it didn't sound bad."

The Monkees made an interesting sound—earnest, slightly amateurish garage rock that was on par with contemporaries like the Seeds and the Standells. Despite being tossed together they still managed to possess a certain organic charm.

Rafelson and Schneider did not want to discourage the group from bonding but they were far more pessimistic about the prospect of them becoming a functioning band. "Groups as a rule, up until this time, took years of consolidation on the streets," Rafelson contended. "A bass player meets a drummer—they join one group, they pick up another guitarist, they move over to another group, they fire two guys until finally it gets consolidated, just like the Beatles, over a long period of time. A harmonious sense of what the sound should be is born of a lot of trial and error. Well, these guys never had that opportunity and so for them to find out what kind of music they wanted to create and who was going to be the boss was a bit of a jumble."

The band concept was indulged by Raybert but the necessity of getting two or three songs ready for each weekly episode required a different approach; in fact, a whole new level of mass production. Meanwhile, the clock was ticking. Stacks of tracks were needed pronto and there was only one person who could deliver the goods: the Man With The Golden Ear.

Who was this supernatural hit-maker? It was song publisher extraordinaire Don Kirshner, the dictionary definition of a double-edged sword. There was no denying the man's uncanny knack for divining the latest smash hits but he was hardly the reticent type. His boast to *Time*—"I can hear a kid hit a note and I know whether he has it or not"—illustrated the problematic nature of his out-sized personality.

On one hand there was the Golden Ear, the infallible hitmaker; on the other, an incorrigible megalomaniac. "Kirshner had an ego that transcended everything else," argued Schneider. "It's sad because it was that ego of his that caused real conflicts and ended up in a very bad fight with the group."

Kirshner's conceit was not entirely unfounded. At 32, the hottest music publisher in the business could brag about having sold over 150 million recordings. As president of Screen Gems Music Publishing, he lorded over a virtual goldmine of songwriting talent, including Carole King and Gerry Goffin, Barry Mann and Cynthia Weil and a superstar-in-the-making named Neil Diamond.

Donnie—as he was popularly known—had nurtured the Brill Building pop sound with extraordinary aplomb. With a personality marked by an unselfconscious pomposity, not unlike the preening abrasiveness of Simon Cowell on *American Idol*, he had risen to the top of the industry. "Kirshner plays only one instrument," *Time* reported, "the telephone. There are 14 of them in his South Orange, N.J., home, and an eleven-channel radiophone in his chauffeured Fleetwood."

It wasn't like he hadn't tried to play music. As a teenager growing up in the Bronx, Kirshner had taken a crack at writing commercial jingles with Robert Walden Cassoto (later Bobby Darin). His pal, it turned out, was a lot more talented. Kirshner turned to selling songs which, given his persuasive abilities, he seemed destined to do. With partner Al Nevins, he formed the Aldon Music publishing company which capitalized on the songwriting talents of Neil Sedaka and Carole King. After amassing a small fortune, Kirshner sold the company to Columbia Pictures in 1963. At the time Schneider contacted him, he was supervising musical

Don Kirshner (center) lends a golden ear to Monkee tunesmiths Tommy Boyce (left) and Bobby Hart.

content over Screen Gems TV series such as *Bewitched* and *I Dream of Jeannie*.

"I had always felt that the wedding of television and music would be important," Kirshner explained. "The Monkees project was the culmination of what I had started a couple of years before."

Kirshner was seeking a princely sum for his services—15% of music-related sales. Initially Raybert balked but by the summer of 1966 Schneider was on bended knee, pleading, "Donnie, we need a miracle!" Kirshner got his sweetheart deal including a royalty rate that was triple what the Monkees were making *combined*.

Like Raybert, Kirshner realized a window of opportunity existed because of the artistic maturation of the Beatles. "When I did the Monkees, the Beatles were getting married. They weren't touchable to the public anymore; they lost their innocence. I knew that if a group like the Monkees came to TV, it would take all the marbles," he later said.

There were lots of marbles to be made. Now that the Monkees were his four-headed Frankenstein and the Brill Building was his laboratory, Kirshner faced a series of crucial decisions; foremost, choosing a producer. Almost by default, the job fell to Boyce and Hart. "All this time we were tugging at Donnie's sleeves. Finally after all of these fiascoes, time was short, the show was going on the air and they needed to have a record out, so we got the job," Hart remembered.

Overcoming his fear of flying, Kirshner landed in LA with Schneider's "miracle"—dozens of demo recordings ready to roll. Under his guidance, the Monkees only needed to dub their voices over pre-recorded tracks that were cranked out with machine-like efficiency.

"We were all real nervous about it," Kirshner later recalled. "They were pre-stars and were a little frightened about being on TV. I was there to do business because I had records to get out."

Kirshner negotiated a partnership with RCA Victor to create a brand new label called Colgems which would exclusively distribute Monkees singles and LPs. With the debut of the TV series only two months away, Boyce and Hart assembled the Candy Store Prophets, a cheekily-named studio band, which consisted of seasoned session players, including guitar maestro Louis Shelton and drummer Hal Blaine. The latter had already played on hit records by the Mamas and the Papas, the Beach Boys and the Byrds. The Candy Store Prophets were quintessential session players: quick, efficient, and thoroughly professional.

From the get-go, Nesmith and Tork were at odds with the process. Kirshner rejected the idea of having them play on their records. Tapes of the Monkees' maiden musical efforts had been sent to him. "I heard them," Kirshner later told *TV Guide*. "They were loud. It was not the right sound of today."

The garage rock created by the four Monkees had nothing in common with the clean-cut mainstream pop Kirshner preferred. His vision of the group's sound was personality-driven. "I wanted a musical sex image. Something you'd recognize next time you heard it. Davy was OK—for musical comedy. Mike was the weakest singer as far as I was concerned. Micky was a natural mimic and he had the best voice for our purposes."

Kirshner seemed to relish the power he exercised. "I walked in with four ringers—four studio men—because I assumed the Monkees would give me a hard time," he recalled in typical blustery fashion. "And after they clowned around for the first ten minutes, I said, 'All right, fellas—out!' And I brought in the four ringers. I put them on the mics and the boys came back right away and we made some great records."

But the bruised egos could not be easily swept under the rug. To placate Nesmith, Kirshner allowed him to continue producing. Nesmith, in turn, threw a bone to his aggrieved bandmate, inviting Tork to play guitar on the session that produced "Papa Gene's Blues." Tork was barely audible in the mix. Five guitarists played on the session. For the time being, it would have to do.

Chapter Eleven

THE PACE WAS GRUELING. An average week found the Monkees filming an episode of the TV series, providing vocals on recordings and, in their spare time, rehearsing to become a real band. There were also photo shoots, TV commercials, and an endless series of promotional commitments.

The pace created tension, an environment where tempers easily flared. Rafelson's volcanic personality often clashed with Screen Gems officials. During location shooting at a farm, Rafelson, confronted by a locked gate, suggested to a studio official ("a typical bureaucrat") they knock it over and worry later. "So I sent him to look for the farmer," recounted Rafelson, "then I took the first truck and I rammed the gate, broke it open and we marched in. After all, to pay for a gate was going to cost $500, but it cost $10,000 an hour to shoot. Well, we proceeded to shoot the shit out of the day and that set a pattern for leaving us alone."

While the Monkees were busy filming new episodes, Boyce and Hart were in the recording studio finishing tracks. On July 25th, the duo finally struck gold, recording their newly-penned composition "Last Train To Clarksville." It was a slice of pop perfection, highlighted by a jangling guitar break, several stop-on-a-dime pauses, and a wonderfully theatrical Dolenz vocal. In less than three weeks the song would become the Monkees' first single.

The lyrics of "Last Train to Clarksville" were slyly-subversive, the lament of a drafted soldier desperate to see his girlfriend one last time before going off to battle. Even if the hidden message was lost on most listeners it didn't matter—the ringing guitar licks and propulsive beat sold the song.

Given the high quality of the production, it is fair to speculate that "Last Train to Clarksville" would have been a hit without any television exposure. RCA Victor, however, was taking no chances. The record company forked out the then-formidable sum of $100,000 for promotion. A team of 76 advance men were commissioned to saturate the market with hype. Bumper stickers proclaiming "Monkee Business Is Big

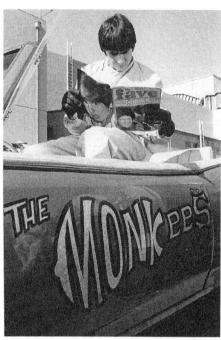

Jones had "impudent charm" according to the *New York Times*. A British accent didn't hurt, either.

Business" were distributed across the country. A commercial on NBC promised the show was "the wildest ride of your life with the world's zaniest string quartet." Flyers were handed out at concerts. Preview records were sent to six thousand disc jockeys. The media took the bait. "Synthetic Quartet Will Hit Tube Hard" promised a headline in the *Washington Post*, reporting a "wholly manufactured singing group" assembled by "white coats with nets" aimed to "woo the younger generation." The article anticipated that "critics will cry foul" and "longhairs will demand, outraged, that they be removed from the air" and concluded with the prediction "kids will adore The Monkees; you can bet on it."

Suddenly everybody wanted a piece of the action, despite the fact that the show had yet to air. Tommy Boyce remembered the anticipatory excitement: "All the corporate people flew in from around the world to Hollywood and said, 'what's the first record going to be? Whatever it is, it will be number one in three weeks.'"

Competition in the pop sweepstakes was fierce. "Last Train To Clarksville/ Take A Giant Step" was released on August 16, 1966. The number one song on the charts was the Lovin' Spoonful's "Summer In The City" and the top-selling album was the Beatles' *Yesterday and Today*. But if any doubts lingered regarding the quality of the Monkees' maiden effort, they were quelled by *Billboard's* review: "All the excitement generated by the promotional campaign…is justified by this debut disk loaded with exciting teen dance beats."

The effectiveness of the publicity campaign became fully evident during the Monkees first public appearance. On September 9, 1966, in front of an audience described by Vince Canby of the *New York Times* as "too old for Barbie dolls and too young for mini-skirts," the Monkees took the stage at the Broadway Theater in New York and the crowd went ape. Rafelson remembered the reaction: "There was so much hoopla about the coming show, with ads on TV, and kids were so quick to attach themselves to fads, that when the Monkees came to New York, minus their instruments, it was pandemonium. All they did was stand there and introduce themselves."

For Rafelson and Schneider it was a moment of vindication. It had been exactly one year and one day since they had advertised for "four insane boys." But there was more to prove. Had they picked the right ones? Would the critics buy it? More importantly, would the kids buy it?

A brash comment made by Rafelson to the *New York Times*—"You can fool some of the kids some of the time"—reflected the state of unease at Raybert Productions. They were attempting to do the impossible: pull off a manufactured pop music phenomenon

and a weekly television sitcom at the same time. It was a supremely ambitious agenda but there were plenty of landmines. If fooling "some of the kids some of the time" was the goal then almost inevitably the issue of credibility was going to be raised.

The idea that music could unite the masses was being treated with quasi-religious significance by the counterculture. 1966 was the year when John Lennon's immortal words "we're more popular than Jesus" couldn't be dismissed as the mad ravings of a drunk lunatic. To fans of the Beatles, the very idea of a band assembled for TV, especially one called the Monkees, was bound to be viewed with skepticism, if not outright hostility. Were they only in it for the money? Could they play their own instruments? Were they even talented?

On September 11, 1966, the day before the show's premiere, the quartet performed in public for the first time. The site of the show was Del Mar, California, a coastal community renamed "Clarksville" for the day. In keeping with the theme of the Monkees' hit single, lucky radio-contestants boarded a train to the seaside town to witness a PR stunt of the highest order. The spectacle was carried off with military precision. Four helicopters, each carrying a payload of one Monkee, approached from the sky and landed in formation. Out came the group dressed in their signature double-breasted Gene Ashman-designed shirts. The mayor of Del Mar presented them the keys to the city. Then, strapping on instruments and taking the stage, they performed two sprightly songs, Nesmith's "Papa Gene's Blues" and a cover of "She's So Far Out, She's In."

In a whirlwind it was over. The Monkees jumped on the helicopters and were whisked away. They were ready for prime time.

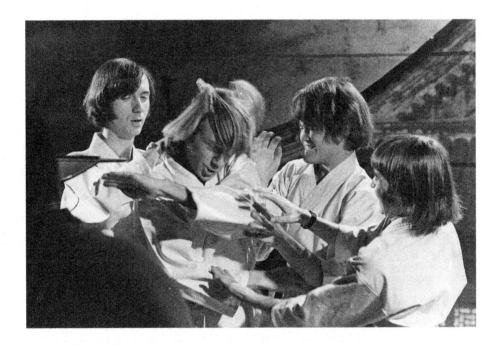

Chapter Twelve

AT 7:30 P.M. EASTERN STANDARD TIME on Monday, September 12, 1966, *The Monkees* debuted in living color on NBC. The trill of a tom-tom and the finger-popping beat of "(Theme from) The Monkees" announced their arrival with an ominous prediction:

> "Hey, hey, we're the Monkees,
> You'll never know where we'll be found.
> So you'd better get ready,
> We may be coming to your town."

Over at producer Bert Schneider's house, all four Monkees gathered to watch the debut of TV's first rock and roll situation comedy. Actress Natalie Wood and assorted guests joined the festivities. In half an hour, it was over.

The next day would bring the most important news—the Nielsen ratings—which were less encouraging than expected, a fact at least partially attributable to the damage done at Chasen's. Of 200 NBC affiliates, only 160 had chosen to run the show.

Another factor in the less-than-stellar ratings was the series' head-to-head competition with ABC's *Gilligan's Island*, a sacred cow among teens. For discerning couch potatoes, the grave decision whether to watch *The Monkees* or *Gilligan's Island* was akin to choosing between Bach and Handel (remember, fair reader, these were prehistoric times when recording shows for playback later was impossible).

In contrast to the ratings, reviews were glowing. The *Los Angeles Times* raved about moments of ingenuity, while the *New York Times* marked the Monkees as "the Marx Brothers in adolescence," noting that "progress can turn up in the strangest places."

Daily Variety singled out the abundance of fresh talent. "Run your eye over the credits and there's not one name that strikes a note of familiarity," the paper reported. "It's that kind of show, too, newly concepted for TV."

A few writers tempered their enthusiasm with back-handed swipes regarding the Monkees' debt to the Beatles. *Time* hailed the show as "bright, unaffected and zany" only to conclude it was a "half-hour steal of the Beatles." *Newsweek* wrote that the show was "fresh stuff for TV," but then countered that the Monkees were "direct videological descendents of the Beatles" and that "television is a medium that thrives on thievery."

It was inevitable, the Monkees were going to be compared to the Beatles, and no amount of Rafelson bluster was going to mitigate that fact. And yet, Jim Frawley, who did much to shape the TV image of the group, always begged to differ. "The Beatles' humor was much more English, really, it was subtle and drier," he argued. "Ours was much more American—it was bombastic and slapstick. We were more inspired by the Marx Brothers whereas Lester's style with the Beatles was inspired by *The Goon Show* in England."

There was another crucial difference, Dolenz notes. "*The Monkees* was a television show about a group that wanted to be like the Beatles (but) we never made it on the show. We were always the underdogs. It was one of the elements people didn't always get but it was one of the things that made it charming."

The debut episode, *Royal Flush*, set an irreverent tone that would be maintained throughout the entire run of the series. The plot—involving the Duchess of Harmonica and her evil Uncle Otto—was nearly incidental to the action. It was the cumulative effect of visual wit, winning performances and music that mattered. One thing stood out right away: Unlike standard sitcom fare, *The Monkees* did not condescend to its audience. The music was rock and roll, the fashions were mod and, for the first time, there were no sage parental figures or dowdy old schoolmasters preaching their gospel.

Underneath the zaniness, *The Monkees* aimed to capture the era's most important catch-phrase: freedom. "Believe it or not, long hair at that time was still synonymous with crimes against nature," claimed Dolenz. "Anything to do with music and long hair and hippies and beads and flowers was anti-American. It was stuff that you got shot for."

On a subliminal level *The Monkees* established a conduit to mainstream America, allowing kids to connect, however ephemerally, to the counterculture that was emerging in the 1960s. By the fall of 1966, all but the youngest knew there was a change in the air. A new form of youth culture had begun to express

itself with throbbing psychedelic intensity. In stepped *The Monkees* which, despite its innocent appearance, was further proof that a cultural and generational shift was well underway.

The homespun corn of *The Beverly Hillbillies, Petticoat Junction* and *Mayberry RFD*, dominating the airwaves for most of the decade, met its match with *The Monkees*, the first show offering an accessible, cleaned-up carbon copy of youth culture. Long hair and rock and roll had entered the living rooms of Wheatfield, Indiana and nothing would ever be the same.

In terms of television programming, *The Monkees* had broken new ground. One year later, almost to the day, adults would get *their* zany show featuring witty gags, quick-cutting visuals and groovy music called *Rowan & Martin's Laugh-In* and it, too, was on NBC. "Most TV is like dope," Dolenz told *Seventeen* magazine in 1967. "It's just there to put people into a state where they'll believe anything anybody says– like the announcer of the six o'clock news. Our show gives you the idea of being an individual. That's what we represent to the kids: an effort to be an individual, an attempt to find your own personality."

A tectonic shift was underway, the dawning of a new era in show business. The

Monkees were the new model. Combining the cross-marketing power of a weekly TV series with a constant flow of music recordings and merchandise, it was a radical, exciting, untapped method of promoting an entertainment franchise.

Rafelson and Schneider had given birth to an influential new force—the cross-promoted brand—and executed it to perfection. The seeming ease in which they pulled it off was cause for alarm. It wasn't just old-school showbiz types who were feeling threatened. To purists of the flower power generation, the Monkees were as phony as a fake hit of acid sold by an undercover narc. Up in San Francisco, the new cultural vanguard saw the made-for-TV-band as symbolic of everything wrong with mainstream culture. The Monkees had co-opted their treasured romantic vision of rock and roll as a revolutionary agent of change—they were peddling it at J.C. Penney.

A battle was erupting. All over America, older siblings and their younger counterparts went to war over the Monkees. If you were the older sibling and a Beatles fan, it was easy to heap ridicule on your little sister's watered-down facsimile of the real thing.

It took true devotion to be a Monkees fan in the face of these obstacles. Toting your Monkees lunch box to school meant risking the Baby Boomer death penalty— you might be identified as uncool. In the inner sanctums of the most sanctimonious the Monkees were about as uncool as uncool could be.

Years later, the dilemma of the long-suffering Monkees fan was captured to comic perfection in an episode of *The Simpsons* when Marge Simpson reveals to her psychologist Dr. Zweig the humiliating teasing she had taken for liking a band that didn't play its own instruments. "The Monkees weren't about music, Marge," Dr. Zweig advises her, "they were about rebellion, about political and social upheaval!"

Chapter Thirteen

THE MONKEES WAS A TRAILBLAZING SHOW. Of all its innovations, perhaps the most significant was the invention of an episode-ending tag, short candid interviews that caught the Monkees with their guard down.

Frawley explained how the unscripted moments became a recurring feature of the series: "The first show was too long so we edited and edited until we got it down a minute and a half under length. And rather than lay in a minute and a half of film after we had toiled to get down to length, we just did an experiment, which was to sit the four boys in director's chairs on the set and ask them questions. It turned out they were very amusing in their responses and it became a very warm, real part of the show."

Rafelson felt the episode tags allowed the group to "talk directly to the audience. They sat there unmasked, if you will, and addressed the common concerns of their audience. As a consequence, people felt they knew the Monkees."

The technique of knocking down the fourth wall—later adopted by nearly every reality TV program—was cutting-edge stuff. It brought the four young personalities face-to-face with their audience. As always, Rafelson and Schneider were intent on pushing the boundaries of audience identification as far they could go. From the very start they insisted the four Monkees retain their real names on the TV show, another move that made the line between fantasy and reality fuzzier.

(Dolenz, who had adopted a separate stage persona, Mickey Braddock, during his *Circus Boy* days, regretted the decision: "I think in retrospect I would have used a character name. I would have named myself Jerry—'Micky Dolenz as Jerry.")

For Dolenz, Jones, Nesmith and Tork there was no longer any easy refuge from the ruckus they had helped create. Suddenly and irrevocably, the anonymity they had enjoyed evaporated. They were now instantly recognizable TV superstars.

This brought a whole new set of problems. A public sighting of a Monkee had the potential to create a mob scene of clutching, screaming teenyboppers, ravenously grabbing for a piece of their heroes. "If there were only two or three kids, they'd come within a certain distance of you and stop cold," Tork explained about the psychology of a mob. "Because there was a distance they couldn't cross. But when behind them was three thousand more kids pushing to get as close to the ones in the front were, then you had a recipe for disaster."

Dolenz found out the hard way. Absentmindedly shopping for holiday presents at a local mall, he experienced a sudden jolt of fear when a crowd of screaming people started running toward him. Believing there must be a calamity of some sort, Dolenz turned and ran in the same direction of the stampede until it dawned on him he was the cause of the commotion. How did Dolenz react? "I just got pissed off," he recalled. "I had to leave. I couldn't do my shopping. But that's the first time I realized how successful the show had been."

Pandemonium created potentially lethal situations. Once, on tour, the group took evasive action from a gathering crowd by spontaneously jumping into the back of a police car, begging the stunned occupants to drive (it didn't help matters that one member was carrying a stash of smoke-able contraband).

Security was one issue. Privacy was another huge concern. Tork, from the start, was conflicted about implications of celebrity. "The privacy aspect was very distressing," he recalled. "You didn't really know for sure who your friends were. Even people who had been friends of mine before suddenly took on a new attitude towards me after the fame hit."

Nesmith was equally wary, if not more so. Surrendering his private self to the media machine went against every fiber of his combative personality. Dolenz and Jones, on the other hand, had no such concerns. If anything, having both been professional entertainers since childhood, they were embracing the moment for all it was worth. While driving to a house they were sharing in Benedict Canyon, Dolenz and Jones heard "Last Train to Clarksville" on the radio for the first time. Knowing they were officially the "next big thing," they pulled the car over and did a happy jig on the side of the road as traffic passed by.

Chapter Fourteen

WITH THE DEBUT SINGLE CLIMBING to the top of the charts, Kirshner's next big move was releasing the group's eponymous debut album. It had been only three weeks since the show had gone on the air and market research was signaling the Monkees were the real deal—a money-making juggernaut rivaling the Beatles.

Parents were the ones that paid the price. They risked rebellion in their homes if they did not comply with the loyal Monkees fans in their ranks. The hush money was handed over en masse. "I told people I would outsell the Beatles and they laughed at me," Kirshner cackled years later. "Then the first album sold four million and outsold the Beatles."

The album was a unique kind of triumph. Kirshner managed to create an appealing musical buffet that magically cohered despite its stylistic disparities. Certain moments of ingratiating charm stood out. Gerry Goffin and Carole King's proto-psychedelic song, "Take a Giant Step," and Nesmith's genial "Papa Gene's Blues," were two such moments.

Taking no chances, Kirshner made sure there was something for everybody—rousing rockers such as "Tomorrow's Gonna Be Another Day," gentle ballads like "I Wanna Be Free," and the soon-to-be-obligatory novelty song "Gonna Buy Me A Dog."

The latter tune was off-beat, friendly and full of personality, featuring the spontaneous studio tomfoolery of Dolenz and Jones. "We knew our fans were young, but this was for prenatal people," Dolenz later cracked. "We must have been in a silly mood, probably ripped out of our brains, and just started goofing on it, just probably to alleviate the boredom."

A "Monkees sound" had emerged primarily thanks to Dolenz's remarkably facile pop vocals. Who knew the former Circus Boy had such amazing pipes? When they were combined with the "studio garage rock" of Boyce and Hart an identifiable musical direction emerged, one, gratefully, with very little connection to the Beatles. The only recognizable influence of the Beatles' work was actually the debut album's cover shot which ripped off the balcony pose of the Beatles' *Please Please Me*.

One notable feature of that photo is the oddly churlish look on Nesmith's face, apparently the result of the impatient wool-hat wearing Texan counting down how many shots the photographer had to get it right.

The success of the LP was a testament to the pop instincts of Kirshner and his teams of songwriters and producers. Everybody, that is, but the Monkees themselves. Only Nesmith, through his sheer force of will, had managed artistic leeway but "Papa Gene's Blues" and "Sweet Young Thing," the fascinating country-rock hybrid collaboration with Goffin and King, were tainted victories; like the others, he had been relegated to vocal-only, non-performing status. Did the fans care? Probably not. The Monkees were white hot, the fastest selling act since the Beatles. They had a momentum that bypassed authenticity. By early November, the album resided at number one on the *Billboard* charts where it would stay for 13 weeks, a record for a debut album that stood for nearly 20 years. Overall, over 3 million units were shifted in less than three months and considering the last-minute haggling in the studio, it was a remarkable sum. All in all, the LP stayed on the charts for 78 weeks.

"Last Train to Clarksville" took a skyward leap up the charts. On November 5, the debut single bumped "96 Tears" by ? and the Mysterians from the top spot on *Billboard*'s Hot 100 on the way to becoming the sixth-most popular song of 1966.

It was a goldmine for the suits at RCA Records. But a follow-up was needed right away, and Kirshner was ready. His trump card was "I'm a Believer." Without a note being heard, the Monkees' next single boasted an astounding 1,051,280 advance orders—the biggest pre-sale order since the Beatles' hit "Can't Buy Me Love." *Billboard's* confident expectations—"blockbuster sides that will have immediate impact"—were easily met. The single vaulted straight to number one.

Like every other aspect of the Monkees project, "I'm a Believer," had been the source of fierce behind-the-scenes squabbling. Its author, Neil Diamond, who had just scored a hit with "Cherry Cherry," was dead set against surrendering all publishing rights to Kirshner.

"When Neil Diamond walked in and played it for me, I knew it was a major, major giant song," Kirshner later recalled. "But Neil gave me a hard time because he wanted half the publishing, although I wound up with the whole thing. I was a nervous wreck for about a month because he held out. I kept visualizing that if

The Golden Ear presents Gold Record awards for their million-selling debut album.

Micky Dolenz would sing it, it would be unbelievable."

The Monkees phenomenon scaled staggering new peaks with the release of the single "I'm a Believer"/"(I'm Not Your) Steppin' Stone" which, to this day, remains one of the great double-sided hits in pop history. Propelled by Dolenz's mock-angst vocals and one of the cheesiest organ riffs this side of the local roller rink, "I'm A Believer" was an optimistic crowd-pleaser with an irresistible sing-along chorus which instantly became the Monkees' signature musical moment.

The flip side, Boyce and Hart's, "(I'm Not Your) Steppin' Stone," was a garage rock classic. Again, Dolenz shined, lending the song an air of theatrical menace. On its own merits, "Steppin' Stone" became a chart hit, peaking at number 20. Years later, it lived on in the repertoire of many fledgling rock bands including the Sex Pistols and Minor Threat. "It's kind of a phenomenon," explained coauthor Bobby Hart regarding the song's evergreen appeal. "It's one of the first songs that every garage rock band in the country learns to play. That's probably because it's an easy four chords." (That's E-G-A-C for all you guitar heroes out there.)

The fortuitous release of "I'm a Believer"/"(I'm Not Your) Steppin' Stone" was the last piece in the puzzle. The Monkees were now two-hit wonders. And with over 10 million copies of the single sold worldwide, one thing was for sure: they wouldn't be stepping stones for very much longer.

Chapter Fifteen

THE THIRST FOR MONKEES PRODUCT was unslakable. One Southern California radio station played a Monkees track every 15 minutes for an entire month. NBC was inundated by 50,000 fan letters a week. Merchandise was moving faster than they could ship it out.

For NBC and the show's sponsors, Kellogg's Cereals and Yardley Cosmetics, the financial dividends were both welcome and a bit of a relief. Reservations over Raybert's unorthodox approach to business had been simmering from the very start. "I don't think anybody was too thrilled about it," Schneider recalled. "I mean, the network was never too thrilled about it, except that it worked. Who's going to argue with that? They were counting the money. At that point, as long as nobody did anything egregiously wrong, they just stayed away."

Remarkably, for such a successful enterprise, nearly every major creative player was a newcomer to network television—Rafelson and Schneider were new to producing, Frawley was new to directing, and the rag-tag staff of writers, with the exception of Dee Caruso and Gerald Gardner (formerly of *Get Smart*), were all new to the medium. Rafelson recounted "a freewheeling madness in the office. We were just whaling and gunning—that's the way the show evolved."

Almost everything had gone right for Rafelson and Schneider—finding four boys who connected with the public, creating an innovative, critically-hailed TV series, and releasing huge hit records that were going to number one.

But equaling the force of teenage consumption was a new opposing force that had an ax to grind: the media. As journalists began digging into the back-story of the Monkees, they began focusing on how the music was being put together by Kirshner's hit factory.

Raybert knew in advance that the "plastic" issue was their Achilles heel. "It was a chink," Schneider explained. "It was something they could attack."

The producers braced themselves for the backlash. Their initial strategy was a

Nice perk department. Each Monkee got a customized Pontiac GTO with four bucket seats.

flawed one with damaging ramifications—stalling all efforts to interview the four Monkees. Forbidding access to the group in the short term made sense, but in the long run it merely served to ratchet up suspicions that somebody was trying to pull the wool over the public's eyes.

Early reports claiming the Monkees did not perform on their records had risen from vague rumor to full-blown controversy. As far as Nesmith and Tork were concerned, the worst thing about the rumors was their validity. The pained expression on Nesmith's face as he "finger-synched" the lick to "I'm A Believer" on the TV show said all you needed to know.

From a modern perspective, the amount of hair-pulling over whether or not the Monkees played their own instruments may seem vaguely ludicrous. Even at the time of the Monkees' first successes, many popular groups like the Byrds, the Beach Boys and the Mamas and the Papas were being aided by studio musicians, not to mention Berry Gordy's roster at Motown Records and the Wall of Sound productions of Phil Spector.

But red herring or not, these issues had incalculable power. With no adequate answers being offered, inquisitive reporters became even more intrigued about how

A media firestorm was already brewing but the Monkees lacked a forum for their own defense.

the Monkees were being put together. Who was the Great Oz pulling the strings behind this money-minting enterprise? The hounds of the press were sniffing around for the answers.

Kirshner was happy to tell one and all about the pivotal role he was playing. He loved branding himself the Golden Ear. It was good for business. This was just one more reason Raybert was seeking to stymie press access to the group's members. If Nesmith and Tork's displeasure with Kirshner's methods leaked out it would shatter the carefully-crafted image they'd worked so hard to polish for public consumption.

The situation was untenable as far as Nesmith was concerned. Having asked for more musical control and been thrown a few measly crumbs, he watched in dismay as Kirshner's assembly line kicked into high gear. Under that wool hat, Nesmith was bristling with righteous anger. Not only did he have to defend a product he couldn't stand, bubblegum music, but he was being shut out of the creative process. "Tommy (Boyce) and Bobby (Hart) were doing some cool stuff and I liked 'Last Train to Clarksville' and I loved the way Micky sang…but the rest of it was just hopeless junk," Nesmith maintained. "And I thought, 'Well, I don't really want to be a part of this if this is going to be this bad.'"

Nesmith was constitutionally incapable of taking the matter sitting down. So he did what he always did: he devised a plan. Convinced the group needed an outside producer to help them advance their musical ambitions, he began searching for one. After attending a show by the Turtles, he approached the group's bass player Chip Douglas and offered him the job on the spot. Years later, Douglas remembered the conversation, "I said, 'I never produced a record in my life.' I had no idea about the highs and lows and volumes and levels. And he said, 'that's alright, I'll teach you everything you need to know.'"

A former member of the Modern Folk Quartet (a group which included Jerry Yester, one of the finalists at the Monkees auditions, as well as Henry "Tad" Diltz, the unofficial photographer of the Monkees), Douglas had only one true distinction when it came to hit records, having arranged the Turtles' "Happy Together," the sunshine pop classic that was bubbling up the charts in late 1966.

Although Nesmith pursued the goal more aggressively, fellow cast member Tork also felt a sympathetic outside producer was essential. He advocated for Stephen Stills, the friend who had gotten him the job in the first place. Stills had joined forces with Neil Young in the much-buzzed Buffalo Springfield, whose chart-topping single "For What It's Worth" was just then being readied for release.

Tork's bid to get his buddy Stills into the mix was rebuffed by Nesmith, a sign (the first of many) that ol' Wool Hat had an upper hand in internal group politics. Tork's interpretation, many years later, was Nesmith "was not into the group as such. Mike, it turns out, in my estimation, was about gaining control."

Above: Club-wielding cops protect the boys. "If the girls got to us," claimed Jones, "they'd tear us apart." Below: Monkeemaniacs greet their heroes at the airport. Dig those frames!

Chapter Sixteen

NESMITH AND TORK KNEW THE KIND of artificial pop music the Monkees represented was out-of-synch with the arbiters of what was hip and cool. Their peers, the "peace, love, and flowers generation," were the kind of people who reflexively sneered at the heresy of programmed pop.

The prevailing attitude was summed up by the Byrds' hit "Do You Want to Be a Rock 'n' Roll Star?" A vicious pop thrill, it offered cynical advice to young musicians to "just get a guitar and learn how to play." Some of the lines—"sell your soul to the company, who are waiting there to sell plastic ware"—seemed to strike directly at the heart of the Monkees' dilemma. Years later, members of the Byrds denied the song was about the Monkees, but that was beside the point. If the public was interpreting the song to be about the Monkees, that was bad news.

Word on the street was spreading among the hippies—*The Monkees* was a con job being perpetuated by calculating hucksters who were manufacturing public interest to increase their profits. The word "fake" summed it up. It was a put down that, in certain circles, fatally doomed the project from ever attaining a shred of credibility.

Authenticity, or at least the appearance of it, was suddenly crucial. It didn't matter that only one member of the Byrds, Roger McGuinn, had played on "Mr. Tambourine Man" or that *Pet Sounds* was practically a Brian Wilson solo album even though it was credited to the Beach Boys. Those bands, and countless others, were viewed as organic musical ventures while the Monkees and their TV show were not.

Everyone in the inner circle—Rafelson, Schneider, Nesmith, Tork, Dolenz and Jones—agreed the solution was to have the Monkees prove their musical prowess in front of a live audience. It was a situation with very little precedent. Four actors playing rock musicians for an unseen TV audience were being asked to become a real band playing in front of a paying audience.

Life had surely imitated art before, but never in such ludicrous circumstances. Consider poor Micky Dolenz, already having taken lessons so he could realistically

fake playing the drums, now having to take a crash course in keeping the beat as he sang Monkees hits. Dolenz would later modestly say "it wasn't exactly brain surgery." It wasn't exactly a piece of cake either (you can count on your hand the famous lead singers who played drums in the history of rock and roll).

As the targets of a nasty whispering campaign, the Monkees were eager to prove themselves before a live audience. The four rehearsed, working furiously into the night and on weekends, knowing they would have to live up to the considerable hype that preceded them. This would be the final and most pressure-packed test of all. "Regardless of how successful the records were, if they couldn't be good onstage, no one was going to see them. Word gets around awfully fast. It's awfully hard to be the number one act in the world and you've never worked in a recording studio," maintained Schneider.

The test of fire was scheduled for December 3, 1966 at the Honolulu International Center Arena in Hawaii. In the great tradition of Broadway, the group would break in out of town or, in this case, off the continent altogether.

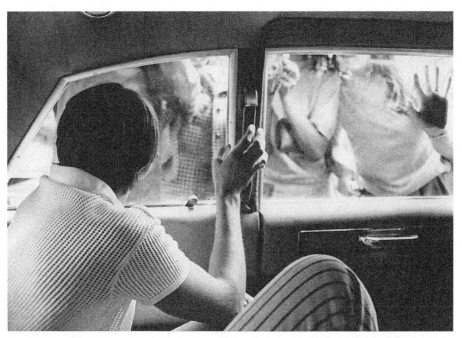

Dreamboat Davy Jones, object of desire, watches the commotion from the safety of his limo.

Although understandably nervous about their first live gig, the Monkees needn't have worried—the pandemonium all but eclipsed the quality of their performance. In fact, the ear-shattering roar of 8,364 fans that met their entrance (the Monkees burst from fake speakers in a neat bit of stagecraft) was so overwhelming that for a split-second the members feared for their safety.

The set list, concentrating on material from the first LP, opened with their first smash hit "Last Train to Clarksville" and closed with their second smash hit, "I'm a Believer." In between, audiences were treated to a real-screen projection system— still a cutting-edge technique at the time—that flashed visuals as the Monkees sang. Providing moral and musical support during the solo performances were Bobby Hart's session musicians, the Candy Store Prophets, and for all their trouble they could have stayed behind since hardly a note was audible. After intermission, the four Monkees all performed solo spots. Each had a telling choice for material. Tork tackled the traditional, "East Virginia," on banjo; Nesmith slyly covered Willie Dixon's "You Can't Judge a Book by the Cover," and Jones went full-blown, over-the-top theatrical on his version of Anthony Newley's "The Joker." But it was Dolenz who stole the show with a somersaulting, high-energy performance of the Ray Charles classic, "I Got a Woman," borrowing some mock histrionics from R&B king James Brown.

The show had been choreographed by David Winters, formerly of the swinging '60s musical variety show *Hullabaloo*. Winters' fast-paced revue and the Monkees' winning performances received positive press. "They are highly compatible with the flair of seasoned pros," a reviewer raved in the *Honolulu Advertiser*. The concert had been a financial hit as well, reportedly grossing $36,000 in box office receipts.

It was a double triumph. Accusations of their complete musical ineptitude were stopped (at least momentarily); at the same time, they had paved the way for more in-concert appearances. On December 26, 1966, the group commenced a short tour of mid-America starting in Denver, Colorado. This dry run of shows would conspicuously avoid the media hotspots of Los Angeles and New York. They'd tackle those later.

The whirlwind 12-stop tour, conducted on weekends between shooting TV episodes, was greeted with enthusiasm and standing room only crowds in every city from Detroit and Cincinnati to Memphis and Nashville. Local media coverage saturated their appearances. How did the Monkees rate their performances? "I don't know if we were good or not," said Jones. "All I know is that we played it. We did it. We're pretty, you know, average. What is average? We were good enough for our fans. They weren't there to criticize us; they were there to enjoy. And we had a great time."

A concert in Phoenix on January 21, 1967 was professionally filmed for a future episode of the series, directed by Rafelson, called *The Monkees On Tour*. A wonderful document capturing the sights and sounds of an early Monkees concert, it featured a poorly-recorded live concert sequence which, despite being muffled by screams, still managed to convey the excitement they generated. Though subsequent tours would be more polished, the Phoenix show typified the freewheeling hysteria surrounding the Monkees. The episode's final touch was a gracious thank you to the Beatles for pointing the way.

Chapter Seventeen

SO MUCH HAD HAPPENED in so little time. Within three months, the Monkees had placed two number one singles and one number one album (with another one ready for release) on the charts, and had won kudos for their weekly TV series and their lucrative concert appearances.

The public slurped up everything the Monkees had to offer. Mania-starved preteens, many of whom had missed the boat on Beatlemania, channeled those nascent hormonal urges into a compulsive consumerism of all things Monkee. Anyone with any business acumen quickly swayed their allegiance to the group. Teen magazines, such as *Tiger Beat* and *16 Magazine*, replaced the Beatles' mustachioed mugs with the fresh faces of the Monkees on their covers. Lunch boxes, pencil sets, coat hangers—anything that a Monkees guitar logo could be attached to—began flooding the marketplace.

Outside parties, some reportedly on the shady side of business practices, wanted a cut. According to Rafelson, "Mafioso were coming into the office saying 'we're taking over Davy Jones' career and selling Davy Jones this and Davy Jones that.' You wouldn't believe some of the behind-the-scenes weirdness that went on. Muscle. There was a lot of muscle."

The power, the money and the glory began playing tricks on the minds of the inner circle. After all the disparagement in the press, insiders like Kirshner seemed a little too willing to wallow in a bit of self-adulatory praise. Tommy Boyce told interviewer Harold Bronson, "I felt a little embarrassed after a while knowing a song I wrote today would be number one around the world tomorrow."

While others basked in the glory of the moment, the Monkees were beginning to show signs of discontent. There were perks a-plenty—each Monkee, for example, had been provided a complimentary Pontiac GTO (the car that the TV show's Monkeemobile was based on)—but compared to the overflowing coffers of the three-piece suit set, they were making a pittance. Each member pocketed $450 per week for the TV show and a measly royalty on record sales.

Adding to that frustration was a lack of representation. Rafelson and Schneider were producers, but they lorded over the Monkees franchise like de facto management, making crucial decisions behind the group's back. There was no protection for Dolenz, Jones, Nesmith and Tork. When rumors, both true and false, circulated nationwide they had no adequate way of defending themselves.

Lacking a forum for their defense, the Monkees were reduced to bowling pins, knocked down, dragged out and then mechanically set back up again. Their silence, dictated by Raybert's press policies, was *prima facie* evidence they were stooges for "The Man."

The societal impact of music was being taken more seriously than ever. Thanks to the Beatles and Bob Dylan, it had become a critical facet in an emerging cultural war. The struggle for civil rights and protest over the Vietnam War provided the subtext of songs like Buffalo Springfield's "For What It's Worth."

The Monkees were on the wrong side of the battle. Even though the Buffalo Springfield were buddies of theirs (going so far as to thank the individual Monkees on the back cover of their album *Buffalo Springfield Again*) it did little to alter the public's perception of them as lightweights.

Anyone over the age of 15 would have been ridiculed for liking the Monkees. The consensus opinion was they were nothing more than a money-making enterprise with little or nothing to say—four indistinguishable puppets dangling from strings. Rafelson denied the accusation to *TV Week*: "I can tell you damn well they're not puppets. They're sensitive and intelligent—they have opinions on everything—they can speak for themselves."

But that wasn't quite true. The Monkees did have opinions but, up until then, they had not been able to express them. As long as the cash registers kept ringing, their corporate sponsors had no reason to let them. Far more damage could be done if one of the Monkees dared to say something topical about drugs or Vietnam. That just wouldn't wash in Walla Walla, so the muzzle remained intact.

Schneider, who handled the business end of the partnership, was particularly cautious, he later admitted: "I had a lot of desire to manage the way in which the press got a hold of them. It was like walking a tightrope all the time, because, on the one hand, we wanted to encourage the creativity of the Monkees but, at the same time, we wanted to keep it manageable so it didn't end up with a phone call that said 'you're canceled.' We were walking the line between industrial America, on one hand, and rebellion, on the other. What we stood for was the

Kirshner gets an earful from the two most popular members of the hit-making juggernaut.

rebellion, but at the same time, we were dealing with the real world. I was very personally desirous of manipulating the situation so that we wouldn't get our heads chopped off."

Raybert's hands-off press policy was a source of agitation for the scoop-hungry press. In an attempt to counterbalance the weight of their demands, Raybert became overzealous in their effort to bide time. Of all their ploys, none stooped as low as fake press releases that were being concocted. "Raybert wanted an atmosphere of mystique," Dolenz recalled. "They didn't want us to do interviews, so they arranged phony press conferences where they would send in their own reporters from Screen Gems and NBC…and we had stock answers to all these questions, many times funny ones, just to avoid the problems."

Ever-so-slowly, a power shift was underway. The success of the franchise meant the four Monkees could begin to exercise some clout. Each was a household name and together they were, in bean-counter parlance, "guaranteed box office."

The evidence was there on the weekly *Billboard* charts. "I'm A Believer" had been riding the top rung for an astounding 10 straight weeks. Against stiff competition such as the Rolling Stones' "Ruby Tuesday," the Beach Boys' "Good Vibrations" and the Beatles' "Penny Lane" and "Strawberry Fields Forever," the project was not only holding its own, it had snatched the brass ring.

Filming during the day and recording at night left little time for the quartet to pursue their ambition of becoming an authentic band. All that was about the change, however.

The first collective act of power of the four Monkees was to force Raybert's hand on press access: it was time to go public. Reluctantly, Rafelson and Schneider finally relented. Judy Stone from the *New York Times* was the first reporter to get a crack at the group. Aptly titled "The Monkees Let Down Their Hair," her article was hardly the sensational exposé Raybert feared. Screen Gems officials had cast a watchful eye over the proceedings. Despite the monitoring, some of the Monkees' pent-up frustrations could not be suppressed. "We're advertisers," Jones candidly admitted. "We're selling a product. We're selling Monkees. It's gotta be that way."

Tork leapt at the chance to unburden himself. Nearly going off the deep end, he told Stone, "If you want something really visionary and mystic, telepathy is the coming phenomenon. Nonverbal, extrasensory communication is at hand." As the blood pressure of Screen Gems officials slowly came to a boil, Tork dared to offer his opinion on the Vietnam War. "I stand for love and peace," he told the *Times*. "To my way of thinking, they're the same thing. But the man who said 'My country, right or wrong' made a slight error in judgment. My country wrong needs my help." His final comment was the most telling: "I guess I've got myself in enough hot water."

The *Times* article did little damage because it did not address the most hotly-debated aspect of the Monkees phenomenon—the making of the music. But that was about to change. The floodgates opened with the January 1967 issue of the *Saturday Evening Post*, an expertly written and researched piece of journalism by Richard Warren Lewis and perhaps the definitive behind-the-scenes probe of the group in its original incarnation. Lewis carefully dissected the scientific packaging of the Monkees with eyebrow-raising quotes from the four overworked, under-paid, much-maligned Monkees.

By far, the most damaging revelations were the acerbic comments of an embittered Nesmith. After months of vague, never-fulfilled promises from Kirshner, Nesmith now had a forum to air his grievances. Never a shy man when push came to shove, Nesmith took his case public and did not hold back. "The music has nothing to do with us," he confessed to the *Post*. "It was totally dishonest. Do you know how debilitating it is to sit up and have to duplicate somebody else's records? That's really what we were doing."

"Maybe we were manufactured and put on the air strictly with a lot of hoopla," Nesmith continued later in the article. "Tell the world that we're synthetic because, damn it, we are. Tell them the Monkees were wholly man-made overnight; that millions of dollars have been poured into this thing. Tell the world we don't record our own music. But that's us they see on television. The show is really part of us. They're not seeing something invalid."

For the first time, one of the Monkees was publicly biting the hand that was feeding him. The consequences were immediate. All the allegations and innuendo that had been passed on as rumor were being confirmed. Was Monkees music fake? Was it all junk culture being foisted on an unwitting public? Were they merely puppets for The Man? There were no longer any doubts—a member of the Monkees had said it himself.

Chapter Eighteen

NESMITH HAD SPILLED HIS GUTS to one of the most widely read publications of its day. For someone who distrusted the media—"the great American narcotic machine" as he later colorfully dubbed it—Nesmith had bluntly demonstrated he was quite canny about using it to serve his own interests.

He was now the ringleader of a rebellion, the one marshalling the troops and leading them into battle. What he desperately wanted was something authentic to happen in the completely artificial environment he found himself in. "I think, the idea that we would actually play as a band was frightening to them in some twisted way," Nesmith told the *Saturday Evening Post*.

Reportedly within the inner ranks no one was too thrilled by this loose-lipped display of candor, especially when the media pounced on the revelations like raw meat. "Michael blew the whistle on us," Tork later explained. "If (he) had gone in there with pride and said, 'We are what we are and we have no reason to hang our heads in shame,' it never would have happened."

The kind of brute honesty that Nesmith was peddling was diametrically opposed to the showbiz-friendly attitudes of Jones and Dolenz who considered themselves actors first, performers second and musicians a distant third. Even Tork, who shared Nesmith's ambition to have the cast members become an organic band, was taken aback by his methodology.

Tork was no less anguished by the "crummy game" of having to smile and pretend to play an instrument during a Monkees romp. "I think Michael and Peter were equally pained about their roles, although Michael may have been a little more aggressive than Peter," Schneider contended.

But rather than go public, Tork began retreating. Playing the fourth banana on the series, he was feeling the strain. "I was mortified that the records were being made without me. I felt humiliated, shunned and slighted," Tork recalled years later. "I would scream and yell and rave and they would scratch their heads."

Tork and Nesmith lead the other two into battle. Jones was the most reluctant of warriors.

Among the head-scratchers were fellow cast members Dolenz and Jones, both of whom would eventually, but reluctantly, relent. "Micky and Davy went along with us although they didn't understand because it's a different ethic entirely," said Tork. "Actors, when they make records, they just walk into the studio, and somebody's prepared the tracks and they sing over them. And that's the way actors make records—that's the way Davy made his record beforehand."

Envy was also playing a subtle role in Nesmith and Tork's pent-up ambitions.

"From Kirshner's point of view, Davy and Micky were the commercial elements in selling records and Nesmith and Tork were inconsequential," Schneider explained.

To achieve their aims, Nesmith and Tork needed to enlist, in terms of popularity, the top two Monkees, both of whom were initially skeptical, if not downright confused. "The drums to me were more or less a prop," Dolenz contended. "To Mike and Peter, however, the music mattered most. So every time they had to pander or compromise their music it really affected them deeply."

The bad blood between Kirshner and Nesmith was not an isolated case. Even the consummate pro Dolenz clashed with Kirshner in the studio. After a long night of recording, the frustrated Monkee stunned observers by pouring ice on top of the Golden Ear's head. "It was just Monkee pranks," Dolenz remembered with a laugh. "I guess he didn't find that as funny as everybody else did."

As the pressure increased, tempers frayed with greater frequency. The strain of taping weekly episodes, recording new music, and touring on the weekends was taking its toll. The fact that Nesmith and Tork were making noises about taking over Kirshner's role was, to Jones, a warning sign that things were going seriously awry. "Everybody started to want to do everybody else's job," he later recalled. "It was like the deck hands taking over the ship."

Chapter Nineteen

1966 HAD BEEN A TRIUMPHANT YEAR and, in terms of commercial prospects, 1967 was looking even better. But a Monkee rebellion seemed only a hair-trigger away. "Looking back, it was real tough to contain us," said Dolenz of the quartet's rapidly expanding egos. "It was like this little nuclear reaction that they'd started by their own design."

That nuclear reaction finally became a meltdown in Cleveland, Ohio. The night before, the group had played live to a rapturous crowd of over 15,000 fans in Detroit, their largest audience yet. But discontent within the ranks was about to simmer over. The question of artistic control was eating away at Nesmith and Tork, who were both hoping to claim a creative stake in the new recordings being readied for release.

In Cleveland, word filtered down that a second album, *More of the Monkees*, had been rush-released by Kirshner and was already available to the public. This was unnerving news—the group had not seen a copy of the LP, did not even know of its existence. With haste, one was duly purchased and brought back to the hotel.

Gathered together to examine their latest commercial product, the four Monkees gazed in disbelief at the front cover, a photo of the band dressed in garishly uncool clothes sold by the J.C. Penney department store. Each member had been paid $1,000 for what they thought was a promotional shoot; now, to their dismay and shock, the photo had become the cover shot of a record they knew nothing about.

It got worse. Flipping the album over, they read the back cover copy. In an astonishingly tone-deaf display of self-serving bluster, Kirshner's liner notes extolled the talents of his prized staff of songwriters before mentioning, and briefly at that, the names of the Monkees. It was a snub that was hard to take. "The back liner notes were Don Kirshner congratulating all his boys for the wonderful work they'd done, and oh yes, this record is by the Monkees," Tork later told *Goldmine* magazine.

Putting needle to vinyl, the four Monkees gathered close for a listen. Already furious at the betrayal, Nesmith experienced a meltdown as the album began playing. "I regard the *'More Monkees'* album as probably the worst album in the history of the world," he later growled to *Melody Maker*.

If Nesmith hadn't been a fan of "I'm a Believer"—the bestselling song in their catalog—he wasn't inclined to drink the Kool-Aid for the bestselling album in their catalog even though he received considerable royalties for his two original compositions.

The anguished protestations of Nesmith and Tork made no sense to Kirshner. He had already handed them checks for $240,000, a princely sum for any young pop star at the time. As far as Kirshner was concerned it was the public that mattered and they'd made their choice. From a dollars-and-cents point-of-view, *More of the Monkees* was a grand slam, the glorious zenith of the Golden Ear's accomplishments in the music industry. Hyperbole wasn't needed, this was the real deal—just in time for holiday sales Kirshner delivered an album with blockbuster appeal.

It was difficult to argue with the quality of the songs. There were two top-flight Boyce and Hart cuts sung with melodramatic fervor by Dolenz—the opening head-banger "She" and "(I'm Not Your) Steppin' Stone." Neil Diamond had delivered a twin set of winners: the whimsical torn-lover saga, "Look Out (Here Comes Tomorrow)" and the pop classic "I'm a Believer." Nesmith more than held his own with the hard-charging "Mary, Mary" and "The Kind of Girl I Could Love" written with Roger Atkins.

But the real star of the record wasn't Kirshner or the songwriters—it was Micky Dolenz. The album testified to the fact that Dolenz had blossomed into a major recording talent and the crucial link in Kirshner's hit-making machine. His delicate vocals on Goffin and King's "Sometime in the Morning" were a thing of beauty, full of personality and warmth.

Jones, on the other hand, had become a liability. His skin-crawling whispering on "The Day We Fall in Love" made discerning listeners lunge uncontrollably for the turntable stylus to skip the track as quickly as possible. It was matched, in sheer treacle, by the insanely bone-headed lyrics of "Laugh" ("laugh, when you lose all your money").

No, this wasn't *Rubber Soul* or *Pet Sounds* where every track was stellar. There were a number of audible production glitches. One of the best songs on the record, "Sometime in the Morning," suffered from muddy track reductions. It was slapdash.

The occasional dicey quality was due, in no small measure, to having nine separate producers work on the record. Kirshner stuck to his guns—he believed top-rank studio professionals coupled with great songs could outperform a real band every time.

The counter-argument to Kirshner's way was that session players, for all their flawless technique, never quite captured the sound of a real group meshing together. There was no cohesion or chemistry between one track and the next. Instead of allowing Nesmith to handle the instrumental end of his song "Mary, Mary," Glen Campbell was recruited for lead guitar. Campbell was no slouch, in fact he would later become a superstar in the music industry, but when the song was performed in concert by the Monkees it truly came alive.

The Monkees *were* inexperienced in the studio—tapes of a tracking session for "Mary, Mary" bore this fact out. As Nesmith tried leading his troop of amped-up bandmates to complete a vocal take, the non-stop shtick, particularly Dolenz's comic raps, were clearly impeding progress. Finally Nesmith exploded: "OK, really, honest to God, no shit—let's cool it!"

But Dolenz, Jones, Nesmith and Tork were stars and they had their pride. Listening to *More of the Monkees*, they experienced a collective sinking feeling. The crassly-commercial presentation could only add fuel to the fire concerning rumors about their supposed musical ineptitude. Cool factor? There was none— not one track that was edgy or challenging. The protest song of the bunch, "Your Auntie Grizelda," was an embarrassment. "He was pure vanilla," Schneider said of Kirshner, "and they were not, nor were we."

In the short term, it looked like Kirshner held the cards. He had veto power over issuing the final product and the full endorsement of executives of RCA Records. "The whole thing was a farce," he said of the Monkees' frustrations. "I mean it was ridiculous. I gave them each a quarter of a million dollars…and really they could have been more appreciative. Every record I put out was number one. The problem was that I was getting all the press and publicity which I didn't generate, but the music was a phenomenon—we were outselling the Beatles. The point of the matter was that I had a show to get out; I had albums to put out. It wasn't like we were failing."

This was true—the corporate wing of the Monkees project was succeeding beyond anyone's wildest expectations. Five million copies of *More of the Monkees* were in the process of being sold. The LP remained number one on the album charts for 18 weeks. Riding along shotgun was the debut LP which firmly held onto the number two slot. Combined, the first two records were number one on *Billboard*'s album charts for an astonishing 31 consecutive weeks—the same length as Michael Jackson's *Thriller*.

As a feat of mercantilism it was unrivalled, but Kirshner had betrayed the group by keeping them in the dark and a day of reckoning was approaching where they would exact their revenge.

Arriving back from Cleveland, the group marched straight into RCA's recording studio hellbent on making their own music. Nesmith's hand-picked producer, Chip Douglas, sat behind the mixing board as the group attempted recording Nesmith's sprightly-rocker, "The Girl I Knew Somewhere," along with Bill Martin's "All of Your Toys." Also in attendance was Screen Gems official Lester Sill who sent back reports to skeptical brass in New York.

A marathon seven-hour session ensued. The group, at first tentatively, assumed their positions with Dolenz drumming, Nesmith playing guitar, Tork switching off on piano and bass and Jones, the reluctant warrior, shaking maracas and banging on tambourines. After a rocky start, the unit began to gel, creating two tracks bursting with energy and spirit. They had pulled it off. Despite the obstacles, including one large Golden Ear, the four Monkees had fulfilled their ambition. They were now a recording act.

Chapter Twenty

SALES OF MONKEES MERCHANDISE—lunch pails, wool hats and bubblegum cards—had the bigwigs from RCA, NBC and Screen Gems smiling from coast to coast. The newly-minted franchise showed no signs of ebbing. "Their simple, appealing zaniness has snowballed into the biggest and fastest selling commodity since the Beatles," wrote *Billboard*. "The Monkees' brand of talent has inoculated the market with a welcome splash of high sales, whose ripples extend as far as soaring circulations for fan and music consumer publications."

Perhaps the most significant feather in their cap was conquering England. In a frenzy not seen since the Beatles, the Monkees reversed the tide of the British Invasion and became an occupying force over the English pop scene. In early 1967, the American pop phenomenon exploded with a rare intensity. "In the world's hit parades so long dominated by Liverpool and then London, the Monkees' rapid ascent to international fame and fortune, marks another major phase in the renaissance of American talent," *Billboard* wrote.

In a deviously clever bit of marketing, Dolenz, Jones, Nesmith and Tork took separate whirlwind UK publicity tours timed to promote the airing of the show. Native son Davy Jones caused the biggest stir of all. The near riot that met the shaggy-haired Monkee at Heathrow airport was reported by the *London Times* with an air of detached bemusement:

> "Tempers began to fray as the hysterical girls waving banners
> and balloons started to chant, "We want Davy." Screaming
> teenagers tore through the terminal building to try to catch sight
> of Jones. Others staged a sit-down protest on the roadway leading
> to the tarmac. Inside, police and airport staff struggled to get
> incoming passengers through the arrival doors which buckled
> under the weight of the girls pressing against them. Long after
> Jones had been driven out of the airport by a back road, the

Above: Jones' press tour of England caused the biggest tempest. Below: While in London, Dolenz met future wife Samantha Juste (pictured), the inspiration for "Randy Scouse Git."

Michael and Phyllis Nesmith. Their trip to London included a memorable stay with John Lennon.

teenagers refused to believe he had left. They blocked the airport staircases and drowned flight announcements by repeatedly chanting, "We want Davy." Five hours later, more than 200 girls were still running wild through the building. Eventually police regained control by threatening to turn the fire hoses on them."

By this time, Jones' popularity was so overwhelming that another young British singer named David Jones decided to change his name to David Bowie.

Not since Buddy Holly and the Crickets had an American act so tickled the aesthetic fancy of the British public. But, much like America, many a skeptical eyebrow was raised. *Melody Maker*, the dean of the British rock journals, reported schisms within the music community: "Oh, the bitchiness! Oh, the arguments! Oh, the rows! It's amazing how pop can still cause furor and uproar from one side of the Atlantic to the other. A mighty thunder of sledgehammers filling the air as the knockers get to grips with their latest self-appointed task—demolitioning the Monkees."

The magazine ran an open debate between supporters and detractors. Music industry insiders, such as Eric Burdon of the blues-purist Animals, were asked their opinion. Burdon, surprisingly, rose in defense of the Monkees. "They make very good records," he claimed. "I can't understand how people get upset about them. You've got to make up your minds whether a group is a record production group or one that makes live appearances. For example, I like to hear a Phil Spector record and

I don't worry if it's the Ronettes or Ike and Tina Turner…I like the Monkees record as a good record, no matter how people scream. So somebody made a record and they don't play, so what? Just enjoy the record."

Arriving in the midst of this fray, Dolenz asked "What's all the fuss about? Nobody criticizes Sonny and Cher for not playing on their records, or Sinatra for not playing all those 21 strings."

In a hurry to meet Paul McCartney in a prearranged get-together, Dolenz had blown off a recording session in New York and flown straight to London. "Somebody set it up for me to meet Paul McCartney and that was going to be the big Monkee-Beatle meeting," he later recalled.

Although he was a showbiz vet and a superstar in his native land, Dolenz was so star-struck about the prospect of meeting a Beatle that he brought along an autograph book for McCartney to sign. The informal chat began at a local disco and then moved on to McCartney's house, where Beatle Paul previewed the Fab Four's soon-to-be-released single "Penny Lane"/"Strawberry Fields Forever." Privately, McCartney made it clear his group had no issue with the Monkees. "He was very gracious and treated me like a peer, which I appreciated," remembered Dolenz.

If anyone knew what it was like to live inside the bubble of a music phenomenon it was McCartney. A fan-created tape recording from this period captures him cheerfully defending the Monkees though baited to do otherwise. "They're not really trying to be us," McCartney tells a fan, "but everybody keeps telling them they are. If the Monkees weren't around there'd be no one to watch on TV. Their program is better than most things on TV. You know, I like them. I really do, they're nice."

In a telling bit of insight, McCartney revealed "they're so worried now because everybody says, 'you're like the Beatles and that's crummy.'" He added a postscript straight to the band: "I like the show fellas. I dig what you're doing."

At the conclusion of the Beatles-meet-Monkees summit, McCartney extended an invitation for Dolenz to attend a Beatles recording session at Abbey Road's EMI Studios. When the dandified Monkee showed up in the latest Carnaby Road fashions, he was "so stoned and stunned" he could barely contain himself. "Hey Monkee Man," Lennon reportedly cracked, "do you want to hear what we're working on?" A slack-jawed Dolenz listened as the band recorded "Fixing a Hole" from the upcoming album *Sgt. Pepper's Lonely Hearts Club Band*. During a break, he was invited to tea. "And then they went right back to work," recalled Dolenz. "That's what they were; they were working lads."

An even bigger moment awaited Micky the Monkee. After taping an appearance on the British TV panel show *Top of the Pops*, he caught site of the gorgeous co-host of the program standing in the studio cafeteria. Her name was Samantha Juste and she hailed from Manchester, England, as did Dolenz's bandmate Davy Jones.

Juste was the epitome of '60s glamour, seemingly plucked straight from a fashion runway. The attraction was both immediate and mutual, swiftly leading to romance, a blossoming affair that became instant fodder for fan magazines.

Upon returning to the States, a love-besotted Dolenz wrote a daffy travelogue about his adventures in the UK, which he waggishly titled "Randy Scouse Git"— translated from British slang it meant "horny Liverpool bastard." The lyrics of the song made it clear Dolenz was head-over-heels for Juste. "She's mine, all mine," sang Dolenz about "the being known as Wonder Girl." With a thundering chorus ("Why don't you cut your hair?") it was a tour-de-force, the best song, bar none, that Dolenz would ever write.

Chapter Twenty-One

DURING HIS UK TRIP, DOLENZ TIPPED HIS HAND regarding his allegiance in the band's now-public feud with Kirshner—he sided with Nesmith and Tork. He was "annoyed with the recording set-up," he told *NME* and wanted an "all-Monkee production" to be the next single.

This was a significant development. Dolenz was the cash cow on Kirshner's farm. But the group's desire was not only highly ambitious, as things stood, it was highly unlikely. Much had happened while Dolenz had been tripping the light fantastic in Swinging London. The recording session he had skipped in New York had produced Neil Diamond's "A Little Bit Me, A Little Bit You," the A-side of the group's next single.

The secretive sessions would prove to be Kirshner's undoing. In terms of musical direction, Jeff Barry's bubblegum productions were the polar opposite of where Nesmith and Tork wanted to venture. But, of course, Nesmith and Tork were nowhere to be seen. Kirshner made sure of that. Acutely aware of the politics of the situation, Kirshner invited only one Monkee to attend these sessions—Davy Jones.

By far the most popular Monkee (he later claimed the ratio was 10 to 1 in his favor), Jones needed an identifiable song to match his popularity. Up to that point, the Monkees' three most recognizable tracks—the theme from the TV show, "Last Train to Clarksville" and "I'm a Believer"—had all been sung by Dolenz.

Unlike the other three, Jones had no problem with sidling up to Kirshner and playing nice. He was plainly eager to do whatever his corporate backers said he should do. A song written by Neil Diamond and produced by Jeff Barry—the team that had produced the smash "I'm a Believer"—would be his reward for playing the game.

Knowing full well how his bandmates were striving to break out of Kirshner's stranglehold, Jones' decision seemed, on the surface, a betrayal. Unquestionably, the lure of cold hard cash played an influential role. Despite being the star of the world's biggest act, Jones was complaining he hadn't seen bupkes. "So far we really haven't seen a penny of it," he griped to the *New Musical Press* and anybody else who would listen.

There were other mitigating factors. Jones had already made it clear he did not share his bandmates' ambitions. He considered himself a pro—good at hitting marks and reading lines. As far as Jones was concerned, there was nothing to be embarrassed about being a Monkee. He was reveling in the glory of it all. By embracing showbiz conventions, he had managed to escape the grit and grime of Manchester for Hollywood's glitz and glamour. Why rock the boat? Besides, entertaining was in his DNA. Whatever it took, it took.

"That's not what we were hired for," was Jones' argument. "We're actors playing the parts of rock and roll musicians. All of a sudden you want to do the music and write the songs?"

The fuss eluded him. It wasn't like Jones to mess up a good thing with self-serious prattle about fighting "The Man." Unlike his fellow cast members, he had no desire to impress the rock star friends who were a part of Tork's social circle like David Crosby, Cass Elliot and Stephen Stills. He might take a few tokes from the communal joint, but LSD enlightenment, revolutionary politics and organic hippie-ness were out of his league. Jones' league was showbiz. "When I open the refrigerator door," one of his standard lines went, "I do ten minutes because the light goes on."

Underneath the layers of ingratiating charm, there was an unflattering aspect to Jones' brand of charisma, a neediness which took the form of shameless showboating. His will to become famous and then stay famous betrayed an ego of Napoleonic proportions. If there was no subtlety to it, he did not seem to care. Without Jones there was no Monkeemania. The show had been built around him; therefore, he was a force to be reckoned with.

Jones had an undeniable talent for being on the scene. From playing the Artful Dodger in *Oliver!*—the first British musical to make an impact on Broadway—to being in the studio with Neil Diamond and Jeff Barry, the world's hottest record production team, Jones displayed an uncanny knack for being the right guy at the right place at the right time. In show business, timing was everything.

Given the circumstances it is easy to imagine the temptation Jones felt to do what Kirshner wanted. Groups in the mid-1960s rarely waited more than three or four months between releasing new vinyl. Finished musical product had to come from somewhere and, in the opinion of the Golden Ear, "all-Monkees" productions were not ready for prime time. Luring Jones into the studio to work with Barry and Diamond was Kirshner's easiest move. Jones was just a pawn in a bigger game.

Chapter Twenty-Two

AFTER THEIR EARLY SUCCESSES, the West Coast team of Boyce and Hart had been kicked to the curb by Raybert for producing music deemed insufficiently commercial. This gave Kirshner greater license to shift the Jeff Barry-produced New York sessions into overdrive.

Nesmith was "fit to be tied" about the New York sessions. They were three thousand miles away from his control and Nesmith did not like losing control. The deck, however, was stacked. Kirshner had no intention of allowing the group's recordings on the next single; in fact, it was already decided: the single had been promised to the team of Barry and Diamond.

A self-described "nervous wreck," Nesmith desperately needed a break from his pressure-packed life. A scheduled trip to London was just what the doctor ordered. With his wife Phyllis in tow, Nesmith left for his UK promotional junket. On a whim, after arriving at his hotel, Nesmith fired off a telegram to John Lennon signed "God is Love, Mike Nesmith." To his delight, an invitation arrived for the Nesmiths to attend a Beatles recording session. This wasn't any session: it was *the* session of 1967. On February 10, the Nesmiths strolled amongst the gathered glitterati invited to participate in recording the climactic orchestral flourishes of the Beatles' masterpiece "A Day in the Life" (a brief glimpse of Nesmith appears in the song's promotional clip).

Nesmith savored having "access into places where you don't get to go very often." Being invited by Lennon to spend the weekend with his wife, Cynthia, was the summation of this desire. The Nesmiths were taken by a driver to the Lennon's home in Weybridge, Surrey, where Lennon screened films ("Weird films—like art films," Phyllis Nesmith would later tell *Monkees Spectacular*) and played unfinished tracks from the Beatles album *Sgt. Peppers*. When Lennon asked Nesmith for his opinion of the music, the normally-verbose Monkee was flustered. "I just didn't have any way to talk to him," Nesmith later recalled, "because he was just rearranging my musical realities at the time."

Invigorated by his trip to England, Nesmith came back determined to up the ante with Kirshner. A showdown loomed, one that everybody, except Nesmith, seemed eager to avoid. A meeting was set up to visit Kirshner in his swank hotel suite at the Beverly Hills Hotel. When the day arrived it was probably no coincidence that Rafelson and Schneider were nowhere to be found.

Chip Douglas came along as a guest of the Monkees. Also in attendance, and someone who figured prominently in events that would soon unfold, was head of Colgems business affairs Herb Moelis, a Kirshner corporate henchmen later described by Nesmith as a "sidekick and thief" as well as a "little troll." Adding to the awkwardness of the scene, Kirshner's wife and mother-in-law were also on hand.

Kirshner opened with an ostentatious display, presenting the group with gold records for *More of the Monkees*. He was deliberately making it difficult for the group to press their case. Nesmith was undaunted. He came forward with a list of demands—they wanted to play their own music, choose their own music and have Douglas produce the whole thing. Kirshner could oversee, but not dictate, their musical direction.

Douglas remembers the uneasiness of the scene. "I was very awed by the whole thing," he said. "Suddenly, here I was in the driver's seat. It was very scary looking back on it. I felt like a little shrimp amongst all these lobsters."

Kirshner countered the Monkees' demands by handing the group demo tapes he wanted them to record (allegedly one of these songs was the future Archies smash "Sugar, Sugar"). "I'm glad I was there at the time. I probably saved the Monkees from having to do some *real* bubblegum," said Douglas.

Kirshner launched into another vainglorious sermon about the realities of the music business. Nesmith countered, "We could sing 'Happy Birthday' with a beat and it would sell a million records." When the increasingly-animated Nesmith issued an ultimatum—he would quit if the Monkees could not record their own music—Moelis reacted forcefully, waving papers and warning the truculent Monkee he'd better read his contract before mouthing off.

Nesmith snapped. Ramming his fist through the plaster-board hotel wall, he snarled to Moelis, "That could have been your face, motherfucker!" and then stormed out of the room.

Many years later, in a calmer frame-of-mind, Nesmith shrugged off his display of pugilistic prowess, stating, "I just lost my temper for a few moments." But clearly more was at stake. This was a matter of integrity for Nesmith—the status quo could no longer hold.

Dolenz and Tork were in Nesmith's corner; Jones, however, was torn. The least likely to act out was being forced to take a stand. As far as Jones was concerned, the Beverly Hills Hotel incident was a full-blown disaster. "Lester Sill and I walked out of that place," he remembered, "and I looked at him and he looked at me and I said, 'We're on the down now, aren't we?' He said, 'Yeah, this is the beginning of the end,' and it was."

Shortly afterwards, a blow-by-blow account of the explosive events appeared as a *TV Guide* cover story called "The Great Revolt of '67." In the accompanying article, Kirshner made it clear he had not, and would not, accept Nesmith's premise. His hit-making formula was performing exactly as it was designed to—it made hits. If anything, he argued, the Monkees were acting supremely ungrateful. He later claimed, "The Monkees were very temperamental guys. I had given them royalty checks for over a million dollars at a time—kids who previously had nothing."

Chapter Twenty-Three

THE LINES WERE DRAWN and something had to give. Ultimately, this decision rested in the hands of Rafelson and Schneider, who already had a stack of problems on their hands. The most prominent was a lawsuit that had been filed by David Gordon and David Yarnell, who were claiming Screen Gems had stolen the idea for *The Monkees* from their project *Liverpool, USA* and that Davy Jones had already been attached to the project. Jones was served a subpoena as a material witness. The suit was later settled out of court for a reported $500,000.

These and other problems were haunting reminders that, underneath the towering edifice of the world's hottest brand, the foundation of the enterprise was a fragile house-of-cards. Rafelson and Schneider were also in hot water with the Writers Guild of America, which decided in favor of pilot writers Paul Mazursky and Larry Tucker receiving screen credit and merchandising rights for having helped create *The Monkees*. "We never really understood why Bert and Bob, who were making a lot of money, wanted to screw us—especially since we were all on the same wavelength," Mazursky later wrote in his autobiography *Show Me the Magic*.

Adding to all these troubles was a bill for plastering over a hole in the wall at the Beverly Hills Hotel.

As for the battle with Kirshner, Rafelson and Schneider hoped to strike an accord. They needed to find a song the Monkees could call their own. "All of Your Toys" was a no-go since it lacked a Screen Gems publishing copyright but Nesmith's "The Girl I Knew Somewhere" had potential; with the producers' blessing, the group could reconvene in the studio with Douglas producing and, if the results were deemed worthy, the B-side of the new single was now theirs for the taking.

These were the words that everyone except Jones wanted to hear. The trump card was wielded by Schneider. "Another guy would have said, 'I can't let you do it boys, Kirshner would take us to court,' but Bert doesn't mind a fight," Tork said of Schneider. "He won't be threatened or bludgeoned. If he wants to do it, he'll go

Nesmith's collision with Kirshner turned into a wall-busting smackdown. Something had to give.

ahead and do it. And he wanted us to do it. That's what I love about Bert—he didn't goad us, but he certainly didn't deny us the effort."

Schneider was encouraged by the group's ambition. "I was totally in accord with their desires as long as it wasn't going to make it a flop," Schneider maintained. "If it was going to make everything a flop, then there was no point to it, it was just self-destructive. I was trying to run a middle course between eventually getting to where they wanted to go and Kirshner's approach, which was 'don't let them do anything.'"

On February 23, 1967, Dolenz, Nesmith and Tork returned to the studio to re-record "The Girl I Knew Somewhere." John London, a friend and former band

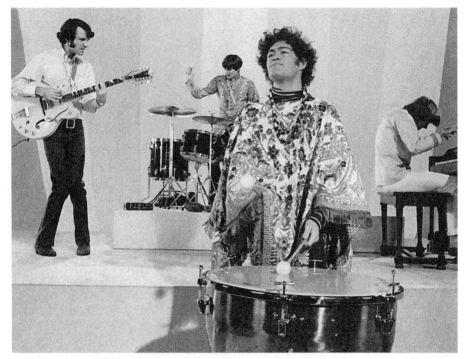

The Monkees triumphed over the odds to win their freedom but Kirshner got the "Sugar Sugar."

member of Nesmith's, stood in for the intriguingly-absent Jones (officially on vacation). Tork was delighted to have the opportunity to play guitar and contribute a lyrical harpsichord solo. "Boy, was that thrilling," he wistfully recalled. "It's a pretty good pop record. It's got a beginning, a middle and an end. It does all the things that a pop record is supposed to do."

Nesmith may have been the public face in the Monkees' rebellion but Tork was equally adamant about the Monkees getting a chance to prove themselves. "All we ever said was 'we want to be the musicians in the studio when we're making the album.' That's all we ever asked for. Kirshner, whose idea of control is 'everything in place!' saw this as the barbarians at the gates of the Holy Roman Empire and he wasn't having any of it."

This was true. Kirshner was not remotely interested in what the wall-smashing Nesmith and his bandmates were cooking up. Back at his New York offices, in an act of striking bravado and sheer obstinacy, Kirshner ordered the masters of the next single, "A Little Bit Me, A Little Bit You" be rush-released with Jeff Barry's "She Hangs Out" on the B-side. The masters of the new single were being sent to Canada at the exact same time the Monkees were in the studio recording "The Girl I Knew Somewhere."

It was a power move and nothing less—a decision, Kirshner later rationalized, that was necessary under the circumstances. "Eventually, I was going to let the boys do their own thing, but my standards were number one records and hits," he claimed. "And in all due respect to Peter Tork, if he came up with a song that was less than a pop hit, I was the guy who had the job to supervise them and I had to say yea or nay, and I had the creative power to do so."

Translation: Kirshner didn't need the Monkees. In fact, (except for Jones) he didn't like the Monkees. He just needed their voices and nothing more. With an infallible, but artistically bankrupt, method of fabricating records, he had every intention of maintaining control of his 15% royalty on every Monkees record. He also harbored a curious, and ultimately fatal, desire to upstage everyone else.

When word got around that Kirshner had deliberately ignored the edict to put the Monkees on the B-side, the record was hastily withdrawn from American distribution. His Machiavellian maneuver had backfired. Releasing the single without the group's consent was an affront, not only to the four Monkees but to Rafelson and Schneider as well.

In a stunning turn of fortunes for the high-riding publishing magnate, Kirshner was summarily fired. The trade papers breathlessly reported the news: the Golden Ear had been chopped off.

Lester Sill and Emil Viola were quickly recruited as Kirshner's replacements at Colgems. Their first act was to re-release the withdrawn single with Nesmith's "The Girl I Knew Somewhere" on the B-side. The record-buying public, eager for the latest Monkees sides and clueless about the internecine warfare sent "A Little Bit Me, A Little Bit You" rocketing up the charts where it peaked at number two. The flip side—the first Monkees-penned *and* performed composition on vinyl—fared respectably as well, charting as high as 39.

The two sides of the single revealed the philosophical polarity between Kirshner and the Monkees. The A-side was bubblegum that lost its taste right away, undeniably catchy but lacking the drive of Diamond's previous hit, "I'm A Believer." It was ordinary.

"The Girl I Knew Somewhere" did not have the production values of the A-side radio hit but it also didn't suffer from rote professionalism. It was a breezy slice of competent pop, far from perfect, but joyful and, above all, real. From Tork's adept keyboards and Dolenz's endearingly-wistful vocals to Nesmith's songwriting chops, it highlighted the group's individual strengths and a tangible sense of ensemble.

Slaying the Golden Ear raised the group's spirits. Jones, however, needed an extra boost.

Chapter Twenty-Four

THE MONKEES ORGANIZATION HAD NOT HEARD the last of Kirshner. On February 27, 1967, he filed suit in federal court against Columbia/Screen Gems to the tune of $35,000,000. Accusations of conspiracy and breach of contract were handled by Kirshner's lawyer, the formidable Edward Bennet Williams. Within weeks, Columbia/Screen Gems filed countercharges in federal court, issuing a statement that claimed "Kirshner caused or permitted to be issued self-adulatory publicity which was demeaning to the Monkees."

Other charges levied against Kirshner included the unauthorized release of the third single and an accusation he had withheld master tapes in a publishing royalty dispute prior to the show's debut.

Although the case made a big splash in the trade papers, it was quietly settled out of court many months later. Kirshner later hinted he won the biggest settlement in the history of Columbia Pictures. With typical braggadocio, he claimed "it was such a large settlement that I was not allowed to disclose the amount at the time." The exact details of the settlement never did emerge.

As the dust settled, the debate over Kirshner's role raged on. There was no doubt that Kirshner had usurped his authority by releasing the third single without authorization but the publicity he drew to himself was, in many ways, far more damaging. Kirshner's public logrolling shattered the very myth that had sold so many records—that the Monkees were a real group. This self-destructive policy is what ultimately led to his demise. "My feeling was fine," Rafelson said of Kirshner's role, "just don't take the credit for it because you'll eliminate half your audience—authenticity, integrity and a certain kind of pop truth being the slogans of the day."

Schneider, who dealt more directly with Kirshner, was less forgiving in his assessment. "The Monkees were much more oppressed by Kirshner's ego and his grabbing of all the credit in the papers than the rest of us," he claimed. "I didn't give a shit what he said, except that it damaged the group. My attitude was, 'this was all very successful so let's not rock the boat,' but Kirshner had an ego that transcended everything else. As a matter of fact, the press issue was probably magnified a hundred times over because of Kirshner. He wanted everybody thinking, 'hey, he's doing all this, not them.' In the end, it was very self-destructive because it heightened the whole press issue and it made them feel lousy."

Nesmith felt vindicated. Summarizing the argument he explained, "Kirshner kept saying, 'you can't make the music, it would be no good, it won't be a hit'. And I was saying, 'hey, the music is not a hit because somebody wonderful is making it, the music is a hit because of the television show. So, at least let us put out music that is closer to our personas, closer to who we are artistically, so that we don't have to walk around and have people throwing eggs at us', which they were."

Schneider concurs: "They were the butts of the attack, not Kirshner, not me, not Bob."

Kirshner, it seems, never did come to terms with the factors behind his dismissal. "They had just re-signed me to a 10-year deal and probably felt threatened by my earning so much," he later reasoned. "So, instead of being a mensch and calling me in and settling it by renegotiating my contract, which I would be happy to do... they fired me."

From hero to goat, Kirshner's run had been remarkably short. A few months prior to their clash at the Beverly Hills Hotel, the four Monkees had given their mentor a large photograph of themselves with an inscription that read: "To the man who made it all possible."

With the power of television and a bevy of talented songwriters and record producers, Kirshner had taken a non-existent group and created a wall full of Gold Records for them, one of the great coups in rock history. "I'm not trying to be cocky," he recalled years later, "but I think my track record proved that with selling over 500 million records, I knew how to pick songs. The whole fallacy was this: people were accusing us of fabricating and foisting on the public. Do you know how many takes they do for a movie scene? As long as you're entertaining people, I say what's the difference? We weren't fabricating anything."

Twenty years later, Kirshner was still fulminating. "You don't know the aggravation I had—it was like pulling teeth," he said. "When I put Micky on the lead, Peter wanted lead, Michael wanted lead. Somebody had to get a semblance of organization."

Bemoaning the vast riches he lost, Kirshner never quite recovered his domination in the field of song publishing. "The aggravating part is, I could have lasted with that group for another six years," he claimed in 2009. "They could have been trillionaires."

Regrets, he had a few. "I couldn't help but think how it could have lasted longer with the right people," Kirshner reflected. "There was a certain psychology and sensitivity that I felt I had—it's a certain magic, like a double play combination in baseball or like when you see the Lakers—it just works. And you don't break up that combination."

Chapter Twenty-Five

KIRSHNER WAS GONE, but the Monkees' troubles were far from over. The possibility that Jones might be drafted by the U.S. Army (he was considered a tax-paying U.S. citizen) hung ominously in the air in the spring of 1967. Little girls everywhere said a special prayer for their beloved Davy, who they feared might soon be a Monkee in the jungles of Southeast Asia. Fortunately, Jones managed to dodge the call-up due to the fact that he was the sole financial support for his father.

All four Monkees, in fact, were potential draftees and each managed to skirt out of military service in different ways. Nesmith had already done time in the Air Force, where he hadn't exactly distinguished himself; a childhood illness prevented Dolenz from serving; Tork, the peace-and-flowers hippie of the bunch, disqualified himself by informing recruiters (falsely) that he was gay.

Rafelson and Schneider exhaled a sigh of relief. There would be no Elvis-getting-a-buzz cut moment for the Monkees.

Even though controversy was shadowing every move the group made, their popularity had not abated. *Variety* reported *The Monkees* had been renewed for a second season. "The kids have done nice enough," they wrote, "to ensure at least another semester of Beatles-type film fun, and that might be all the producers need to clinch Ft. Knox honors for a long time to come."

But where was that gold? A painful reality was slowly dawning on the quartet's members: they had signed a horrendous deal. Financially it was measly pickings—a weekly stipend for filming episodes of the show, a paltry percentage of royalties on their recordings, and virtually no cash at all from the merchandising bonanza featuring their smiling mugs. The quickest, but not easiest, way to make quick money for the quartet was performances where the group split 30 percent of the concert gate. Given their hectic schedules, it was an exhausting option but they had little choice.

In the spring of 1967, after filming of the first season finished, they finally had six weeks to themselves. Hitting the beach was an option but there were other plans. Rather than kicking back and enjoying the fruits of their celebrity, they doubled-down on the bet of making their own music. The album they would make would be called *Headquarters* and, unlike the old Kirshner days, the four of them had creative license to pick the songs and provide instrumental accompaniment.

Headquarters marked a turning point in the group's history. The world's only made-for-TV-band had seized the reins of production. Now the question was: what would they do with them?

Clearly, the task at hand was daunting. "We were determined to play every little stinking note on every little track," was how Dolenz remembered it. But what was grueling for some of the members was enthralling for the others; in particular, Tork, who remembered the making of *Headquarters* as the happiest time in his tenure as a Monkee.

Tork approached the project as a musical purist. "The point of us doing it in the studio was that it was us and if anything happened, it would be us; it wouldn't be professional musicians competently doing their job," he explained.

The Monkees faced a giant hurdle. Competing against the likes of the Beatles and the Rolling Stones was difficult enough but they possessed a serious handicap. Beyond their friends and their dedicated fanbase, few were rooting for the newly-independent superstars to succeed. Jealousy was a by-product of success in Hollywood—the more you inspired it, the greater you had succeeded. The Monkees inspired a particularly-intense form of jealousy. Many industry insiders (like radio programmers who were essentially forced to play the group's records) were privately praying for their swift demise.

As the group toiled away making *Headquarters*, they were facing a seemingly-insurmountable challenge—to be taken seriously as musicians. While the public could be forgiven for their media-fueled animosity, it was plain to see many showbiz vets were envious of everything the Monkees were achieving—the hit records, the tours, the TV show.

As of June 5, 1967, there was something else to be envious about: Emmy Awards.

The recognition the Monkees so desperately sought from their peers finally arrived when *The Monkees* show took top Emmy honors for Outstanding Comedy Achievement for the debut episode *Royal Flush*. Jim Frawley also took home an award for directing.

Celebrating their Emmy Award as Jimmy Durante looks on. Take that, Gilligan!

In Frawley's acceptance speech he thanked "four very special guys" but instead of name-checking Davy, Micky, Peter and Mike, he thanked Harpo, Chico, Groucho and Zeppo—the Marx Brothers. However well-intentioned, the joke rubbed Tork the wrong way: "I thought, 'You know, buried in this remark is the seed of something most profound.'"

Credit, it seemed, would never go to the four Monkees; it always went to Raybert and their crew. The best the four guys could hope for was a modicum of respect. It was an elusive goal but there were some encouraging signs. Timothy Leary, a countercultural hero, made a surprise announcement: he was a Monkees fan. The former Harvard professor who famously encouraged youth to "turn on, tune in, drop out," wrote glowingly about the group's accomplishments in his 1967 book, *The Politics of Ecstasy*.

On his plane of perpetually higher consciousness, the guru of LSD enlightenment saw beyond the fashionable disdain of the times, commending the Monkees as exemplars of a new cultural vanguard:

"The average Mom and Dad, sitting gently in front of the television set, are unaware of the complex guerilla skirmishes raging in the streets outside the door between the kids and the menopausal society. The reflex instinct of distrust and suspicion of the establishment, the underground—Negroes, Mexicans, artists, Puerto Ricans, hippies, kids.

The youngsters see it. Skillful and experienced at handling the media and psychedelic drugs (on which they were nursed), they know how to react. Take, for example, the classic case of the Monkees.

Hollywood executives decide to invent and market an American version of the Beatles—the early, preprophetic, cute, yeh-yeh Beatles. Got it? They audition a hall full of candidates and type-cast four cute kids. Hire some songwriters. Wire up the Hooper-rating computer. What do the screaming teeny-boppers want? Crank out the product and promote it. Feed the great consumer monster what it thinks it wants, plastic, syrupy, tasty, marshmallow-filled, chocolate-coated, Saran-wrapped, and sell it. No controversy, no protest. No thinking strange, unique thoughts. No offending Mom and Dad and the advertisers. Make it silly, sun-tanned, grinning NBC-TV.

And what happened? The same thing that happened to the Beatles. The four young Monkees weren't fooled for a moment. They went along with the system but didn't buy it. Like all beautiful sons of the new age—Peter Fonda and Robert Walker and young John Barrymore and Young Steinbeck and the wise young Hitchcocks—the Monkees use the new energies to sing the new songs and pass on the new message.

The Monkees' television show, for example. Oh, you thought that was silly teen-age entertainment? Don't be fooled. While it lasted, it was a classic Sufi put-on. An early-Christian electronic satire. A mystic-magic show. A jolly Buddha laugh at hypocrisy. At early evening kiddie-time on Monday, the Monkees would rush through a parody drama, burlesque the very shows that glue Mom and Dad to the set during prime time. Spoofing the movies and violence and the down-heavy-conflict-emotion themes and fascinate the middle-aged.

And woven into the fast-moving psychedelic stream of

action were the prophetic, holy, challenging words. Micky was rapping quickly, dropping literary names, making scholarly references; then the sudden psychedelic switch of the reality channel. He looked straight at the camera, right into your living room, and up-leveled the comedy by saying: "Pretty good talking for a long-haired weirdo, huh, Mr. and Mrs. America?" And then-zap. Flash. Back to the innocuous comedy.

Or, in a spy drama, Micky warned Peter: "Why this involves the responsibility for blowing up the entire world!"

Peter, confidentially: "I'll take that responsibility!"

And Micky, with a glance at the camera, said, "Wow! With a little more ego he'll be ready to run for President."

Why, it all happened so fast, LBJ, you didn't ever see it."

Chapter Twenty-Six

PSYCHEDELIA WAS THE FLAVOR of the year. The Beatles, as usual, led the way with *Sgt. Pepper's Lonely Hearts Club Band*, an album simulating the ecstasy of an acid trip. Not far behind were the Doors, the Velvet Underground and the Jimi Hendrix Experience—dark, brooding bands inspired by the lyricism of Bob Dylan. There was also a new kind of throbbing raga-rock being offered by groups like Pink Floyd and the Grateful Dead.

Swept up in this tide of change were the biggest, best-selling band of the year: the Monkees. In just one year, they, and an entire youth generation, had evolved from innocent ersatz Beatlemania to bleary-eyed hippies letting their freak flags fly.

Shedding the mod uniforms and Gene Ashman shirts it was clear there would be no more bubblegum for these boys. But would the masses be enlightened by their metamorphosis? The question had not eluded the group's members. "I used to be a hippie. Tell me about a group like the Monkees and I'd sneer," Nesmith admitted to *Seventeen*. "I'm not that way anymore."

Never before or after would the group rally around a single project like they would with *Headquarters*. "It was a labor of love for all those guys. They really wanted an album of their own," recalled Chip Douglas, who produced the album under his real name, Douglas Farthing Hatlelid.

Beginning in March 1967 and extending through much of April, the Monkees undertook the painstaking process of generating an entire album's worth of original music. Their efforts (much of which can be heard on the box set *The Headquarters Sessions*—an exhaustive 84-track set that contains numerous outtakes and tracking sessions) were filled with moments of frustration, anxiety, and, occasionally, genuine inspiration.

The group's inexperience in the recording studio was clearly the largest stumbling block. "They could hardly play" was Douglas' assessment. "Mike could play adequate rhythm guitar, Peter could play piano but he'd make mistakes, and

Micky's time on the drums was erratic, he'd speed up or slow down."

Jones mostly sat around. Tork, sarcastically, recalled, "Davy's arm got tired. (He) played nothing but tambourine so he had his part down after the second take, and we would sometimes do fifty takes to get our basic track down." Bearing out Tork's evaluation, Jones remembered "it took us six valuable weeks to do it...God, it was grinding."

Nesmith, who had advocated strongly on the behalf of the others, privately harbored some doubts of his own: "I got the feeling, three-quarters the way through it...'Maybe it's better if we don't try to do this since we don't really work that well as a band.' But we had a good time. It was a lot of fun. And aside from just the workload of it we all felt pretty good about the songs we were making."

In Tork's mind, Nesmith had another agenda. "Mike wanted to produce his own records," he contended. "He wanted to have total control."

Despite the schisms, the Monkees went to great lengths to make *Headquarters* an authentic expression of their collective will. Raybert was literally bending over backwards to insure the Monkees' artistic aspirations were met. Douglas remembered, "The hierarchy, Bert and Bob, kept advising me not to play with the group. They wanted the guys to have their chance."

Eventually Douglas, a fine bass player, was allowed to contribute—and a good thing, too, because without his instrumental prowess it might have been an utter disaster. Instead, *Headquarters*, rather remarkably, cohered together into a legitimate musical statement. The endearing amateurism and heartfelt intentions of *Headquarters* mark it as one of the more fascinating rock documents of its day.

The very idea that four TV actors had won a chance to record their own music was noteworthy to begin with; the fact they succeeded, however modestly, was truly unique. Without overreaching their grasp, the album (which has risen in critical estimation over the years) turned out to be an enjoyable collection of earnest pop music which was banged out with wit and verve. The decision to leave in slips, goofs and guffaws on tracks like "Band 6" and the psychobabble of "Zilch" provided the proceedings with just the right dose of self-effacing humor.

The stand-out moment was Mann and Weil's "Shades of Gray" whose lilting piano riff, written and played by Tork, complemented Douglas' supple orchestration. Tork's singing style was never a strong suit ("I compare him vocally to Ringo Starr, he had questionable pitch," Douglas said of Tork's pipes) but he blended seamlessly with Jones on the classic Monkees track.

Do they play their own instruments? On *Headquarters* Nesmith and Tork happily did so.

Plainly, Tork was in his element. "For Pete's Sake," a song co-written with his roommate Joey Richards, was an effective slice of '60s utopianism which later became the closing theme song on *The Monkees* TV series. Nesmith also delivered a quota of quality songs including fan favorite "You Just May Be The One" and the country twanger "Sunny Girlfriend."

Not to be outdone, Dolenz nailed everything he sang, from the delicate "Mr. Webster" to the Little Richard-style rocker "No Time." The album closed on a high note, Dolenz's lunatic hybrid of music hall and thumping protest rock "Randy Scouse Git," the song which recounted his recent adventures in England.

The listenable quality of the final product was testament to Chip Douglas, who expertly stitched together fragments into finished takes. He was ably assisted by recording engineer Hank Cicalo. As a gesture of thanks to the latter, the group credited the song "No Time" to the studio engineer, even though the composition had been created by all four members of the band. This generous gesture resulted in a veritable windfall of royalties for Cicalo who, reportedly, bought a house with the earnings.

Unlikely as the prospect seemed, the brand had become a band. And, best of all, reviews were positive. *Melody Maker*, in particular, seemed to love the quartet's ambition to become an organic musical unit. "The Monkees are in a strange position. They came into pop backwards with a huge reputation custom-built for them," wrote the taste-making magazine. "It's a tribute to Dolenz, Tork, Nesmith and Jones that the Monkees are equaling the high standards of their competitors and are even moving ahead of them."

Within the inner circle opinions splintered regarding the overall quality of *Headquarters*. "The recording techniques are really, really more advanced now," Jones contended. "You can hear how thin it is and how puny we all sound."

Tork countered, "I think that album is a very young band with a lot of enthusiasm and promise and as such the album stands up today. It's not a mature rock band by any stretch but I think the music shows a lot of inventiveness and energy. I think it's a very good album for its time and place."

In many ways, the time and place could not have been worse. Only one week after the release of *Headquarters*, the entire music community would turn its ear to the Beatles' groundbreaking concept album *Sgt. Pepper's Lonely Hearts Club Band*, which rudely bumped the Monkees' handcrafted LP from number one on the charts. For several months, the two albums would vie for top honors with *Headquarters* invariably one notch lower than the Beatles' celebrated classic. Douglas readily admitted, "*Headquarters* seemed like amateur hour by comparison. It lacked heavy rock tracks."

Obscured by the universal acclaim greeting *Sgt. Pepper's*, the Monkees' bid for respectability vanished into the shadows. Three million copies of *Headquarters* were sold—no mean feat—but primarily they had been snatched up by their fan base, not the older fans they were hoping to reach.

The truth was bleak: as the four Monkees strived for artistic credibility, the ghost of the Golden Ear was going to haunt them. "They were determined to overcome that image," Douglas asserted. "But even when *Headquarters* came out, people were still asking me, 'is it true those guys don't play their own instruments?'"

Chapter Twenty-Seven

THE MONKEES NOW FACED ANOTHER CHALLENGE: touring. As Nesmith recuperated from a tonsillectomy in May, 1967, the group prepared for their upcoming performance at the Hollywood Bowl. The four Monkees were determined to put on a slam-bang live show and this time they would go at it alone, confident of their abilities. "In terms of putting on a show," Nesmith later told interviewer Harold Bronson, "there was never any question in my mind, as far as the rock and roll era is concerned, that we put on probably the finest rock and roll stage show ever. It was beautifully lit, beautifully costumed, beautifully produced. I mean, for Christ sakes, it was practically a revue."

The choreography of the show retained elements of their previous tour. After bursting onstage through mock Vox speakers and running through quick renditions of their more-popular songs, each member took a solo turn backed up by the opening band the Sundowners. Although the program often varied, the basic musical styles of the solo set remained the same: Tork plucked a folk tune on the banjo, Nesmith delivered an R&B cover, Jones offered up a hammy Broadway number and Dolenz charged through his elaborate James Brown collapsing "capes routine."

Like the TV series, a rapid pace was set and maintained throughout the show. Costume changes, comedy routines, and spontaneous quips kept the audience entertained. "Taking pictures of one another in weird poses, waving, jumping and feigning screams of ecstasy," was how the *New York Times* described the group's onstage shenanigans.

The climax of the show was a psychedelic rave-up complete with feedback, strobe lights and Dolenz flailing away on timpani drums on the song "(I'm Not Your) Steppin' Stone." The Monkees became one of the first major bands to experiment with psychedelic light shows, soon an obligatory part of every rock concert. Occasionally, a light operator would balk at the suggestion of waving a spotlight randomly—they considered it unprofessional.

Buffalo Springfield's Stephen Stills (left) hitched a ride on the Monkees' tour plane.

"Tours weren't quite as sophisticated back then as they are now," explained Bobby Dick, bassist of the back-up Sundowners. "A lot of reasons why is that you had these old-timers in the lighting department because of their union cards—they'd been union lighting men for thirty years. So if they were good enough for Lawrence Welk, they were good enough for the Monkees. So you had a lack of communication. They didn't like us because we were long-haired screwballs. It was the blue collar ethic against the faggot musicians."

Many of the innovations were lost in translation. "It wouldn't have mattered what we were playing and it seldom did," said Dolenz, alluding to tumultuous crowd reaction. "You couldn't hear a thing, which was too bad after all the criticism."

Public speculation about whether or not the Monkees played their instruments had not subsided. When asked about the rumors by a reporter just before hitting the stage, Nesmith replied, "Man, I'm about to step out in front of a stadium full of people, and if I can't play my own instrument, I'm in a lot of trouble!"

The summer tour of 1967 would be their most extensive tour as a full-fledged band. Under the aegis of Dick Clark, the powerhouse producer and host of *American Bandstand*, the tour would hit every major market, including New York and Los Angeles.

Up first was the Hollywood Bowl. With soul music icons Ike and Tina Turner hired as their opening act, the Monkees would need to be razor sharp as a performing unit to impress the skeptics. The pulled it off with aplomb. The only hitch occurred when an over-amped Dolenz somersaulted into one of the Hollywood Bowl's famous fountains, a definite no-no at the prestigious venue.

The very next day, still buzzing from the show, the group marched into RCA Studio A to record Goffin and King's "Pleasant Valley Sunday." Jones was missing in action. His unexplained absence hinted that a rift within the group had widened. Musically, his lack of participation didn't seem to matter. With Nesmith on guitar, Tork on piano, Chip Douglas on bass and "Fast" Eddie Hoh on drums, the line-up sparkled.

A few days later the same team reassembled to record a backing track to John Stewart's "Daydream Believer." It too was a winner. Against considerable odds and a tsunami of bad publicity, the Monkees were proving they could back up their claims and create hit music without the oversight of corporate suits.

Chapter Twenty-Eight

UP THE COAST FROM THE HOLLYWOOD BOWL, a major musical event was taking place—the 1967 Monterey International Pop Festival. With girlfriends in tow, Dolenz and Tork traveled to the watershed music event of the Summer of Love. What they saw would change them and the industry, as a whole, forever—a cavalcade of new and emerging talent including Otis Redding, The Who, Janis Joplin, the Jefferson Airplane, and the Grateful Dead joined a lineup featuring such popular hit-makers [or chart-toppers] as the Mamas and the Papas and Simon & Garfunkel, as well as sitar maestro Ravi Shankar, for three days of performances from June 16-18.

Bedecked in full Indian headdress and regalia, a resplendent-looking Dolenz watched in wild-eyed wonder as the Jimi Hendrix Experience—one of the breakthrough acts of the festival—bedazzled the crowd. A left-handed guitar wunderkind, Hendrix wooed the "love crowd" with walls of feedback. The Monkees drummer, undoubtedly as high as everyone else that night, had a peculiar flash of inspiration as he watched Hendrix: here was a performer who could open for the Monkees that even the most jaded of critics could not ignore.

"I didn't get it," Tork later confessed. "At Monterey, Jimi followed The Who and The Who bashed up their things and Jimi bashed up his guitar. I said, 'I just saw explosions and destruction. Who needs it?' But Micky got it. He saw the genius and went for it."

After the festival, at Dolenz's urging, the Monkees camp contacted Mike Jeffery, Hendrix's manager. Jeffery loved the idea. He knew, at the very least, that Hendrix's wild pyrotechnics were guaranteed to generate publicity. Recognizing an opportunity, he leapt at it.

And what about Hendrix? Several months prior, when *Melody Maker* magazine asked his opinion on the Monkees, his contempt was visceral: "Oh God, I hate them! Dishwater. I really hate somebody like that to make it so big. You can't knock

In a purple haze at the Monterey Pop Festival, Dolenz had a revelation about touring with Hendrix.

anybody for making it, but people like the Monkees?"

Had *Headquarters* inspired a religious conversion to Monkees fandom? The truth later emerged: nobody in the Hendrix camp, except his manager, wanted to go forward with the idea but once the contracts were signed it was too late to back out.

Hendrix made the best of the situation. At Tork's invitation, he came to stay at his notorious den of decadence in Laurel Canyon. It was Hendrix's first entrée into the emerging West Coast rock scene. During his stay, rock's latest sensation befriended David Crosby and Joni Mitchell, as well as scene-makers like his soon-to-be-girlfriend Devon Wilson (inspiration for the song, "Dolly Dagger"). It was an eventful visit. Hendrix even managed to find time to smash up Tork's Pontiac GTO.

Chapter Twenty-Nine

BEFORE THE SOON-TO-BE-LEGENDARY Monkees/Hendrix billing could begin, the Monkees traveled to France to film an episode of the TV series, *The Monkees in Paris*. As the group cavorted madly around famous Parisian landmarks, Rafelson sought to capture the pandemonium of Monkeemania in the style of cinema *verité*, but since the TV show had yet to air, hardly anyone in France knew who the Monkees were and, therefore, rather embarrassingly, there were no crowds going wild.

The reaction was quite the opposite in London. Thanks to their strategically placed publicity trips, the arrival of the Monkees was headline news. Like Americans loved cheeseburgers and fries, the British public loved a jolly old pop phenomenon.

The Monkees were all that and more. In the UK, everything they touched was turning to gold. Much to the group's surprise, a track from *Headquarters*—the Dolenz doozy "Randy Scouse Git"—had been released as a single in the UK. Its original title had been deemed offensive which necessitated a change; Dolenz, rather puckishly, renamed it "Alternative Title." Despite that generic name, "Alternative Title" became a massive hit, topping out at #2 just as the band arrived to make their first UK concert appearances.

The five shows at Wembley Pool, promoted by the Beatles' manager Brian Epstein, were greeted by British music magazines as the pop events of the season. Among the rock aristocracy who attended the shows was the Who's drummer Keith Moon and Brian Jones of the Rolling Stones.

The pressure to live up to expectations mounted. Once again the Monkees delivered. With Lulu as their support act, the group's performance generated critical raves. *Melody Maker* was particularly impressed by the smash-up climax. "With noise and screams," the reviewer wrote, "I suddenly realized the Monkees were actually freaking out properly, and much better than many of the much vaunted psychedelic groups."

The Monkees even embraced controversy—both Nesmith and Dolenz sported black arm bands in a show of solidarity for Mick Jagger and Keith Richards, who had been arrested in trumped-up drug busts.

After playing their last show at Wembley Pool, the Monkees (minus Jones, who was visiting with family) were guests of honor at a bash sponsored by Brian Epstein's NEMS Enterprise. The toast of the town who gathered at the trendy nightclub The Speakeasy included Paul McCartney, John Lennon, and George Harrison, every member of the Who, as well as music icons Dusty Springfield, Jeff Beck and Eric Clapton.

As the boisterous celebration rolled into the wee hours, decorum loosened as well. Tork recalled "George [Harrison] and John [Lennon] singing to the tune of Hare Krishna 'Micky Dolenz, Micky Dolenz, Dolenz, Dolenz, Micky, Micky.'"

Tork was already dosed to the heavens. "I had just done some STP which was an LSD-type psychedelic drug," he remembered, "and I mentioned it to John. So I went back to the hotel and I got some and popped one down his throat."

An impromptu jam session broke out with Harrison on ukulele, Tork on banjo, and Keith Moon banging on a table. Dolenz claims to have little memory of the event but clearly recalled what happened afterwards. "We all get hammered and I end up in this park just walking around at six in the morning—I hadn't slept all night—in my pure Indian Afghan leather bell-bottom things, tie-dyed silk from India…and I ended up walking in this park just to get away and just to kind of space out," he recalled in an interview from the documentary film *Hey, Hey We're the Monkees*.

Unbeknownst to the drug-addled Monkee, children on their way to school began recognizing him and soon surrounded him. He chatted amiably, singing songs, answering questions. The "great ethereal spiritual moment," as Dolenz described it, was shattered when police arrived, whereupon the spontaneous tribe became a mini-stampede of "kids running along and falling and crashing and grabbing." Once the glassy-eyed leader of the tribe had been safely escorted back to his hotel he ran up to the balcony to wave good-bye to his "children."

Only a few months before touring with the Monkees, Hendrix declared, "Oh God, I hate them!"

Chapter Thirty

THE ROLE OF MOOD-ENHANCING SUBSTANCES was having a dramatic effect on the behavior of the Monkees, both on screen and in public. "Of course by that time drugs were everywhere," Nesmith recalled. "But they were largely recreational drugs with little consequences as far as I could tell. They were always more recreational, like social drinking in a way."

Recovering from sheer exhaustion after their British escapades, the group canceled the opening date of their tour in Atlanta, Georgia. Instead, the festivities kicked off in Jacksonville, Florida. The Monkees traveled in style on their own airplane, complete with the Monkees' guitar logo, which jetted them across the country in first-class comfort. Coming along for the ride were the opening acts, the Sundowners, Australian singer Lynne Randell (who was linked to Jones romantically in the teen magazines) and the soon-to-be-notorious Jimi Hendrix Experience.

Police escorts met the group in order to protect them from potential mob scenes. The airplane, a huge four-engine turbo prop DC-6, became the Monkees' playpen in between gigs. The entourage would sneak to the back of the plane, where they would pass around joints and sip champagne laced with Hendrix's white lightning. No extravagance was spared. At a stop in Miami, the group chartered a yacht to throw a birthday party for Hendrix drummer Mitch Mitchell.

"One of the nice things about the Monkees," remembered Bobby Dick of the Sundowners, "is that they were true to their old friends. You don't always get that kind of camaraderie once someone makes it—that helping hand doesn't always come down from the top. It was nice to see that friendship made a difference."

Controversy loomed. Clearly, the double bill of the Monkees and Hendrix was a provocation. Not only were the two acts musically poles apart, so were their audiences. It was strictly soda pop versus psilocybin. But as a publicity stunt it was the stuff of genius.

"I'm positive that there must have been some concerns and skepticism raised,"

Eight miles high in their chartered Summer of Love tour plane, the Monkees partied like rock stars.

said tour promoter Clark, "because anybody could have seen that it was not a compatible coupling. They [The Monkees] were in the driver's seat—that's what they wanted—and the deal was made."

Tork confirmed the group's motivation, in part, was to have a close-up view of rock's hottest artist: "We went early to the show and listened, just to listen to what this man could do because he really was a world-class musician."

Nesmith was similarly enamored. "I went down in the sound check and I stood in front of the stage…I was just moved back physically about three feet. I thought, 'Well, this guy's from Mars, he's from some other planet, but whatever it is, thank heaven for this visitation.'"

Almost immediately it became apparent that Hendrix was in a no-win situation. The "death spot," as Hendrix later described it, meant being greeted at every show with impatient teenage girls screaming "Davy!" at the top of their lungs.

Hendrix countered with a sonic assault of his own. "Scaring the balls off your daddy music" was Tork's pithy description. Parents in attendance were none-too-amused by his amp-humping tactics. The cacophony of Hendrix's feedback orgies, mixed with his lascivious sexuality, was clearly too much for a teenybopper audience to comprehend.

"(Jimi) walked into the beast," recalled Nesmith with a smile, "There were twenty thousand pink waving arms. Every time he would say, 'Foxy,' they would say, 'Davy'…oh man, it was a seriously twisted moment."

"It was difficult for Jimi," corroborated Dolenz, "because the kids were there to see us. He didn't have much recognition at the time, so it was very strained as far as he was concerned. We had much more fun offstage than on, at the hotels and in the airplane."

One memorable offstage incident was reported in detail by Tork to writer Dave Zimmer: "We were in this hotel room. Jimi and Stephen (Stills) were sitting on these beds facing each other, just flailing away on acoustic guitars. In between 'em was Micky Dolenz, slapping his guitar like, 'slap, whacka, slap, whacka, slap.' And all of a sudden Micky quit. Then Stephen and Jimi stopped and Stephen said to Micky, 'Why'd you stop playing? Micky said, 'I didn't know you were listening.' So there's one for ya—Hendrix, Stills, and Dolenz."

Chapter Thirty-One

THE MONKEES/HENDRIX TOUR was not destined for longevity. Frustrated by the less-than-enthusiastic reaction at Forest Hills Stadium in New York, Hendrix reportedly flipped the crowd the bird and stormed offstage. With no malice towards the Monkees, he asked to be released from the tour after only seven shows. In order to cover up the circumstances behind his departure, a press release was circulated claiming that the Daughters of the American Revolution complained that Hendrix's stage act was too erotic. It was a classic put-on, a tongue-in-cheek joke, but, somehow, this thinly-guised ruse managed to go down as historical fact.

Tork believes "being thrown off the Monkees tour was probably one of the better things that ever happened to Jimi in his career." What did Hendrix think of the debacle? When asked by the *New Musical Express* about who would substitute for him, he responded, with characteristic sly humor, "I think they're replacing me with Mickey Mouse!"

For the rest of the tour, the Monkees paid tribute to Hendrix by performing a snippet of "Purple Haze." With or without him, they were still the hottest attraction on the concert circuit. Even the skeptical *New York Times* gave the group's Forest Hills show an enthusiastic thumbs up: "No one profiting from the millions being brought in on television, radio, gadgets and costume manufacturing need have worried about the investment in the Monkees. The audience protected them beautifully. From the moment the four personable young men bounced on the stage at 9:15 until they left an hour later, amid a psychedelic display on a screen and swinging giant spotlights on the audience, a shrill, ear-shattering stream of adulation pierced the air."

Doubts about the group's performing capabilities were laid to rest. As the tour traveled from venue to venue their behavior grew progressively wilder. It was the Summer of Love and the four Monkees shared their musical peers' willingness (eagerness?) to indulge in sex, drugs and rock and roll. In Chicago, the group was invited to visit Hugh Hefner's Playboy Mansion. They gladly accepted. Later, that same day, they were approached by an unorthodox set of groupies calling themselves the Plaster Casters who were on a mission to make plaster of Paris casts from the phalluses of their favorite rock stars.

The leader of this industrious gang, Cynthia Albritton (aka, Cynthia Plaster Caster) requested the Monkees participate in the offbeat art project. "We were sitting outside the Monkees' hotel," she later wrote in her biography. "One of the roadies saw the suitcase outside and had us brought up to the room. We were going to cast Peter Tork, who was notorious for walking around naked. There he was playing the grand piano, totally naked, and the Buffalo Springfield were also hanging out, except for Neil Young. I was about to open the can of dental alginates which I didn't know how to mix, and I split my middle finger almost in half. Luckily for me, because I didn't know what I was doing, Micky Dolenz personally tourniqueted my finger."

Onstage, the band was playing with greater authority. At the end of the summer tour, a decision was made to professionally record a series of shows in the Pacific Northwest. Decades later these performances (along with a Mobile, Alabama performance) would be released as a box set called *The Monkees Summer 1967*. Although crude by today's standards, the recordings capture the band at their "psycho-jello" best, raving it up in proto-grunge fashion. Especially notable were the scuzzy renditions of "(I'm Not Your) Steppin' Stone" and its extended freak-out jam sequence.

The live recordings provide aural proof the Monkees could thrash out an exciting live performance. A surprise highlight was Dolenz's deft drumming. The tapes also reveal a loosey-goosey atmosphere onstage. As Nesmith struggles to tune his guitar, Dolenz, ever the wiseacre, announces to the crowd, "This is called tuning. We're putting an album out of this pretty soon." In the background, Nesmith can be heard calling, "we tune because we care!"

The group was riding a hot hand. Their latest single, "Pleasant Valley Sunday"/"Words" quickly became the band's fourth consecutive million-selling single, peaking at number three behind the Beatles' "All You Need Is Love" and the Doors' "Light My Fire." Written by the ever-tasteful tunesmiths, Goffin and King, the breezy song was the group's first stab at relevancy. Tweaking suburban values may not have been a revolutionary topic but the production values were sterling and the performance was winning. "Pleasant Valley Sunday" was a perfect showcase for the Monkees' maturing sense of ensemble. The single's B-side, Boyce and

Hot rod hero Dolenz was a gadget-hound, purchasing one of the first Moog synthesizers.

Hart's atmospheric "Words," was a psychedelic raver that bore no relation to the material the duo had written for Kirshner.

As the Summer of Love reached its peak, seemingly every angle of popular culture had been cornered by the Monkees. Their presence was inescapable. Writing in her weekly column, advice columnist Ann Landers, the bellwether of mid-American mores, acknowledged the group's pervasive grip on mass culture. Landers fielded a question of etiquette at Monkees concerts:

> Dear Ann Landers: I am a fourteen-year-old girl who spent
> six dollars to hear the Monkees give a concert last night. It was
> one of the greatest experiences of my life. Something happened
> at the hall and I need to know if I was right or wrong. My
> girlfriend and I were screaming a lot which is only natural when
> the Monkees perform. A middle-aged woman about thirty was
> sitting in front of us. After the second number she turned around
> and said, "If you kids don't stop screaming in my ear I am going
> to scream in yours.—Monkee Lover

Yin and yang. Tork's public image of peace-and-love often clashed with angry displays in private.

Dear Lover: If you screamed in church or at the ballet, I would say the woman had a right to complain. But screaming at a Monkees concert is not only in order, it is practically compulsory."

Chapter Thirty-Two

FOR ONE LONG MAGICAL SUMMER the Monkees had ascended the throne of pop royalty. The *Billboard* album charts on August 26, 1967 confirmed they were in good company:

Sgt. Pepper's Lonely Hearts Club Band – The Beatles
Headquarters – The Monkees
Flowers – The Rolling Stones
The Doors – The Doors
Surrealistic Pillow – The Jefferson Airplane

Now that the critics had begun to ease up on them (if only briefly), the Monkees began to address a comparison that had dogged them from their early days: the Beatles. At first, the Monkees had bowed deferentially towards their predecessors. They not only bowed, they scraped: "They're the greatest. What can I tell you?" Jones told the *New York Times.* "If we can only be one-quarter as good…or maybe a tenth?"

One dizzy year later, Jones had changed his tune. "We're not the Beatles yet—we're not that good—but there's as much difference between our first two albums and our new one, *Headquarters*, as between the Beatles' first album and their sixth, *Rubber Soul*," Jones claimed to *Seventeen.*

If success had swelled the Monkees' heads, then it was up to Raybert to cool them down. "I remember times when the Monkees came in and said, 'we're bigger and better than the Beatles,'" recalled Rafelson. "I had to sit them down and say, 'now look, for God's sakes, don't get caught in this trap. You have a television show on the air every week and it's immensely popular but it's really the force behind your records.'"

So much had happened in so little time. From being virtual unknowns they had become jet-setting millionaire superstars partying with the Beatles, touring with Hendrix, riding around the country in their private airplane playing to ecstatic sold-out crowds.

As a by-product of the non-stop adulation, already-ballooning egos were beginning to inflate to the stretching point. As they did, a new prickliness emerged. Anybody outside the inner circle who tried to assert control over them was not to be trusted. The four members now scrutinized every move for its creative significance, believing their artistic sensibilities would no longer be compromised by the lure of filthy lucre. Or so they said. For the time being, they could afford the luxury of their conviction.

It seemed like nothing could stop them except themselves. Negotiations were underway for a Monkee movie. What more could they have asked for? But gradually, and perhaps inevitably, all sorts of personal schisms were emerging. In private, away from the set and the stage, the quartet was splintering.

It was an understatement to say they were four very different people. The teen heartthrob Jones, outwardly the most accessible and fan-friendly, had a peevish diva side of his personality. He could be standoffish. By his own admission, he considered himself "special" from an early age. Now he was a star and he acted like one. At the height of Monkeemania, Jones confessed, "I was a pretty cocky little guy."

Nesmith was practically the opposite of Jones; he shied away from the spotlight to the point of becoming reclusive. Despite his insistence that the Monkees cohere into a real band, Nesmith was often absent when the other three gathered for parties. That lack of camaraderie was noted by Jones. "We would all go back to Micky's house and swim in the pool or Peter's—Michael never joined any of that," carped Jones. "He was never, ever part of that little team. It was very rare you'd see Mike anywhere that we were. It always baffled me."

Dolenz, whose free-wheeling humor hinted at a carefree demeanor, was perhaps the most easygoing of the four. One flaw was a reluctance to assert himself in creative situations. "Micky's major character drawback in my book," Tork later claimed, "is that he is afraid to go where he has done well. (He) will not re-enter the territory where he has had a stroke, a flash, of inspiration."

Tork, himself, was a jumbled-up mixed bag, both ambitious and plagued by self-doubt. The empty-headed character he played on the television series had nothing in common with the keen, at times preening, intellect he displayed in private. "Peter actually had the toughest acting job," explained a sympathetic Dolenz, "because the character that Peter plays on the show is nothing like he is in real life."

Nesmith chafed at stereotypes: "The idea that I was this musician with a lot of talent but frustrated by three manufactured guys is nonsense." Accused by Jones of being "aloof," Nesmith described his pressure-packed years in the Monkees as "psychologically tough."

The itinerant-musician was now a rock star and Tork was ill-prepared for the transition. He embraced a version of the '60s lifestyle that later became the cliché: a dope-smoking, acid-dropping, bead-wearing, sexually-experimental vegetarian flower child. "Peter was my entrée into the world of bohemia," Dolenz claimed. "You know, he was a real bohemian and still is. And he always struck me as being pretty far out there."

But behind the scenes Tork could also be high-handed, obstreperous and quick to anger. His hippie ethos didn't always translate into peace and flowers. On one occasion, Tork decked Jones with a punch that was powerful enough to require stitches and a visit to the hospital. What caused the outburst? Tork's only explanation was they were "getting on each other's nerves."

They had one thing in common: they now had more money than they knew what to do with. "I made a lot of money, Lord have mercy. I made more than I thought there was in the whole world," Nesmith told *NME*, adding how he "bought all the superstar things. You know: a limousine with black windows and a mansion with guards and dogs, and furs and jewels."

Dolenz, an inveterate tinkerer, indulged his curiosity. He bought a special lighting fixture that corresponded to individual movements, noodled on an early Moog synthesizer purchased at the Monterey Pop Festival and invited friends to help him assemble a full-size gyrocopter in his living room.

All four were spending profligately, often to their detriment. Tork's hippie crash pad had become a financial sinkhole. A coterie of hangers-on and sycophants helped themselves to Tork's windfall. Years later, singer Jackson Browne recalled how Tork's expense account at a local health food store kept him and other struggling performers fed.

Despite Jones' constant whining about money he unwisely trusted business matters to others. Investments were made in his name including a vanity record label, a boutique in New York City and a new mall in Los Angeles. None of them turned a profit.

Chapter Thirty-Three

THE PRIVATE LIVES OF THE FOUR MONKEES, when there was time for privacy, were filled with all sorts of intrigue, details of which rarely reached the public. Had some of the more salacious information been disclosed, the group's good standing and public image would have been in trouble.

Of the four, Nesmith lead the most secluded life. His privacy was guarded by security fences and a snarling guard dog. "I was really off and working on my own—just completely by myself during the whole time. Which was really a pressure. Tough. It was psychologically very tough," he remembered.

Privately, Nesmith's marriage—a union, in his words, which had been "stormy from day one"—lay in shambles. Although Mike and Phyllis Nesmith were a highly visibile couple in teen magazines, always portrayed as lovebirds and exemplars of domestic bliss (Phyllis had become something of a minor celebrity thanks to the fan magazines), all was not well behind closed doors.

In interviews conducted for the 1997 documentary *Hey, Hey We're the Monkees*, Nesmith discussed the difficulty of the situation. "We never really had the time to let an emotional bond develop. We were two kids thrust into a situation and I was suddenly in a situation of having to make a living and raise a family and build a house and do all that kind of stuff. So I had the pressures of marriage but I didn't really have that bond of marriage. And what the Monkees sort of did, especially with all the groupies, was begin to make that marriage explosively disassemble."

An out-of-wedlock child he was having with photographer Nurit Wilde (a friend of Tork's who briefly appeared in an episode called *The Monkees in Texas*), was undoubtedly a factor in having the marriage "explosively disassemble," but this assiduously-kept secret was never disclosed to the public. Nesmith was an intensely private individual—few were privy to his private predicament.The most eligible bachelor of the bunch, Jones, was nearly as elusive as Nesmith when it came to full public disclosure of his love life. He had been linked romantically, in fan magazines, to Lulu, Sally Field and singer Lynne Randell but these were often ruses used to drum up publicity. Unknown to the fan magazines, the bankable heartthrob was already committed to a full-time relationship with Linda Haines.

Jones first spotted Haines at a welcoming party held for the Monkees' debut performance in Hawaii. The two struck up a long-distance relationship which turned serious when Haines decided to relocate to California. Not a word leaked to the scoop-hungry media. Astonishingly, Jones also maintained a total press blackout when Haines later became pregnant.

This was a deliberate attempt to keep Jones' predominately female fan base happy. He was the pin-up dreamboat who was going to take them to the prom (as he later did with Marcia on *The Brady Bunch*). With his orthodonture-perfect smile beaming down from photos plastered all over their walls, the adorable Monkee had become the object of their desires, the star of their daydreams, the fuel of their fantasies. Why spoil the fun, reasoned Jones and his backers, even if ethics took a backseat to business?

As the stakes became higher, Jones became ever-more fastidious about his reputation, as was his consigliere Ward Sylvester (technically, Sylvester was a producer on the TV show but his exact job description remained murky). Together, they crafted Jones' public image, straddling a tricky line. How to be hip but not too hip—that was the goal. Jones was at the Sonny Bono end of the spectrum of suspect hipsters.

Honesty and authenticity were among the catch-phrases of the day but Jones was a showman, not a rebel. He read *Variety*, not *Rolling Stone*. He was for peace (who wasn't?) but anti-war protests were out. Jones was always a duck out of water in a room full of hard-partying rockers. The Hendrix entourage barely concealed their contempt for him but, then again, their hippie ethic didn't sit too well with him (he would later publicly slag Hendrix for being a drug casualty). He spent time getting expensive haircuts and being fitted with the latest mod fashions. Wearing a tie, perhaps; wearing tie-dye, perhaps not.

There was a yawning gap between the teen-throb's wholesome image and the radical free-thinking libertines that Tork brought around; and, yet, ironically, with his long hair and questionable band mates, Jones was part of the youth movement in the eyes of the establishment whether he wanted it or not. Privately he disdained the prevailing values of the counterculture. At Tork's naked pool parties he and his girlfriend Linda Haines remained resolutely clothed. At the earliest opportunity

A faux-romance with Sally Field (left). Jones with daughter Talia (right).

they beat a hasty retreat.

"Peter was in another world—water beds, brown rice, Hare Krishna," Jones later recalled. "He was scary. I didn't want to go to his house. I thought I'd be in some sort of orgy or some sort of drug den. Scared the hell out of me."

Chapter Thirty-Four

A CIRCUS-LIKE ATMOSPHERE REIGNED at Tork's Laurel Canyon mansion. It had morphed into an Aquarian Age version of Hugh Hefner's Playboy Mansion, a never-ending party-out-of-bounds where every fantasy could be realized and often was. A police raid would have uncovered enough unsavory behavior to fill the scandal sheets for a year.

Musician Dave Van Ronk, a folkie acquaintance from Tork's Greenwich Village days, recalled the palace of decadence fondly. "I have no idea how many rooms were in that place," he reminisced in *When the Music Mattered.* "But there must have been twenty. Swimming pool, the whole thing. And it was wall-to-wall with crashed out hippies. In every room you had to step over zonked-out people, screwing couples, whatever…I was marveling to myself at the enormous amount of bread that was obviously just going straight down the tubes and at the enormous number of leeches and hangers-on that he had acquired and was more or less supporting with very good will. Nothing stingy about our boy Peter, by God. He was enjoying it."

Tork shared his rock star haven with friend Joey Richards (co-writer of "For Pete's Sake") and Stephen Stills. Many of the jam sessions that lead to the formation of the superstar band Crosby, Stills and Nash were held there.

A constant presence among the merry band of revelers was Tork's girlfriend Reine Stewart, a raven-haired beauty who had been introduced to him by Crosby (it was rumored Crosby had written the song "Triad" about a ménage à trois he and Stewart had participated in). In his autobiography, Crosby described Stewart as an "ecstasy coordinator" with a talent for rolling joints. Among her other talents was drumming in the spontaneous jam sessions that took place.

Singer Jackson Browne remembers visiting the Tork castle and getting an eyeful of Stewart in action. "(One) time Jimi Hendrix was up there jamming with Buddy Miles in the pool house, and Peter's girlfriend was playing the drums,

If these police officers knew about Tork's private life they might not have been smiling.

naked. She was gorgeous," Browne told interviewer Bruce Pollock.

Although Tork was hardly a poster child for the joys of monogamy, his relationship with Stewart was a long-term commitment. Together the couple would form the band Release and have a child together.

Dolenz's main squeeze, Samantha Juste, also possessed some musical talent. Back in England she lent vocals to a single called "No One Needs My Love Today." It wasn't a hit but, of all the Monkee girlfriends, it's probably fair to say Juste was the most socially adept. Unlike the other relationships in the band, the pairing of Dolenz and Juste was fit for public consumption.

It helped that Juste had a career in the media. When she left her high-profile hosting job on *Top of the Pops* to move into Dolenz's house in the Hollywood Hills, their romance became fodder for the press. Lovebird photos of the couple were splashed all over fanzines. Taking advantage of her stateside notoriety, Juste penned articles for the popular teen magazine *16*, including her experience at the Monterey Pop Festival.

Chapter Thirty-Five

THE UNIT THAT GELLED COLLECTIVELY on record, stage and screen never quite meshed offstage. Like other rock bands (the Beatles) or TV show casts (*Star Trek*) who were their contemporaries, the Monkees struggled to get along. When the mask of public fraternity came off in private, relationships were strained. Dolenz told interviewer Harold Bronson, "we were just crazy at this time because of the popularity and our egos...we were four of the most different people in the world."

From an outsider's perspective, the four Monkees seemed to have much in common. They all were in long-term relationships and shared professional goals. But by the fall of 1967, the magic was beginning to wear off. The unified band ethos of *Headquarters* was nowhere to be found on their upcoming album *Pisces, Aquarius, Capricorn & Jones, Ltd.*

Suddenly, and without explanation, recording sessions were no longer all-member affairs. Nesmith chose his own session musicians; Tork did likewise. The public, however, had no idea—whatever appeared on vinyl would be labeled "Produced by the Monkees."

Much like the Beatles on the *White Album*, the new work was the sum total of four solo careers. According to Dolenz, this divergent path was inevitable. "There has never been this group or brand consensus on anything," he explained. "With the Monkees, there's four lead singers, four groups, four captains with very, very distinct musical tastes. I was old-time rock and roll, Chuck Berry; Mike is some kind of electro-country pop or something—I don't know what he calls it—Peter was always into blues and down-home folk music; Davy's flat-out Broadway."

Chip Douglas, who marshaled the troops so valiantly on *Headquarters*, was losing his ability to make a group out of them. Some in-studio behavior was bordering on indulgent. Tork undertook epic recording sessions trying to get a proper version of his composition "Lady's Baby." With an ever-present entourage of hangers-on following him around, Tork, often in a drug-induced haze, started making over-the-top requests. If he wanted sound engineers to follow a baby around the studio with microphones in hand, that's what he got. But the prohibitively costly studio time was becoming the subject of group dissension and when the "Lady's Baby" sessions produced nothing worth releasing, Tork went into a funk.

Nesmith was more productive but no less indulgent. At the cost of $50,000, he booked 51 top-flight musicians to perform on an instrumental album of his songs called *The Wichita Train Whistle Sings*. The extravagant two-day session, featuring gourmet food catered by Chasen's restaurant, was a session musician's dream come true. "We were like kids in a candy store," explained drummer Hal Blaine in his biography *Hal Blaine and the Wrecking Crew*. "It was the greatest party I've ever been invited to."

When Blaine asked Nesmith why he was bankrolling the side-project, the profligate Monkee explained it was a tax dodge. "Uncle Sam was about to remove 50 grand from his pocket and, instead of paying the taxes, he decided to spend it on a raucous write-off," reported Blaine (Nesmith later denied these claims).

What did he get for his money? *The Wichita Train Whistle Sings* was nutty and daring and utterly obscure. Most likely, that's just the way Nesmith wanted it. The music, itself, was a bizarre fusion of genres. Big band treatments of Monkee tracks like "Sweet Young Thing" and "Papa Gene's Blues" had rendered the songs almost unrecognizable. Nesmith enjoyed a good lark. Immediately after the *Wichita Train Whistle* sessions, he joined his fellow Monkees as they traveled to Ojai, California to hash out ideas for their upcoming movie with Rafelson and Schneider. "Hash out" was an apt description of the trip. For several days, they smoked joint after joint in an effort to get loose and inspire each other to open up.

Nesmith remembered the sojourn fondly. "We were exploring some good territory and had some good laughs and coming up with stuff that was what I thought was genuinely funny," he recalled, "It was a good creative time, the best for me."

Coming along for the ride was a B-list actor named Jack Nicholson who had been brought in to coordinate the effort and eventually produce a script. With the group increasingly coming apart at the seams, they needed all the help they could get.

From the start of the project, the four Monkees demanded a stake in the creative process. "They had pretty swelled heads as the major pop stars of their time," recollected Rafelson. "They said, 'Fuck it, we don't need a director, we'll write our own movie.' Jack came to me and said, 'these guys are mad – they think they're Marlon Brando!'"

Nicholson injected new blood into the proceedings. His wicked sense of humor

The wrap party for the opulent session that produced Nesmith's *The Wichita Train Whistle Sings*.

and non-stop charisma greatly impressed the group. Nicholson, himself, was a virtual unknown. Even though he had been bumming around Hollywood for nearly a decade, he had very little to show for his career. The only measly crumbs on his resume were a brief star turn in Roger Corman's cult comedy *The Little Shop of Horrors* (an uproarious performance as an unhinged patient begging a dentist to pull his teeth out), along with screenplays for LSD exploitation movies *Psych Out* and *The Trip*. "Nicholson's acting career appeared to be over," writes Peter Biskind in *Easy Riders, Raging Bulls*. "After a decade of B pictures, he had barely made a dent."

Rafelson, always a keen judge of talent, saw great promise in the intensely irreverent actor. After a fortuitous meeting at a movie screening the two became fast friends. "I think the most fun I've had working with Jack occurred during *Head*," Rafelson contended. "It was a very carefree, strange and experimental film to make. We were both on a total acid trip, free of any rules."

Schneider loved Nicholson, who soon became a fixture on the scene. "Jack used to hang out at the Raybert offices," Biskind writes, "(and) had become good friends with Bert (Schneider). They went to Lakers games together, where Bert had

Above: On *Pisces, Aquarius*, the Texas twang of Nesmith, the purist folk of Tork, the music hall senti-
mentality of Jones, and the rock'n'soul of Dolenz finally gelled. Below: Chip Douglas instructs Jones
on vocals. "Daydream Believer" would be Douglas' last high-profile production and the group's final
number one single.

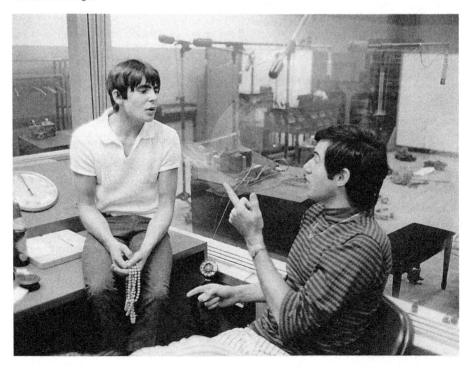

expensive, courtside seats, and ostentatiously sat through the National Anthem."

The Nicholson effect was immediate. "We all fell in love with him," claimed Dolenz. "We just thought he was magnificent. He was a very charismatic man."

As a tape recorder rolled, Nicholson encouraged the Monkees to contribute their concepts to the non-existent screenplay. Fueled by cannabis, they free associated ideas about what being a Monkee meant to them. "They just wanted to feel like they were participating," explained Rafelson, "and I wanted them to participate."

By the end of the weekend, most of the movie had been devised by talking extemporaneously into a tape recorder. Nesmith later described the meeting of the minds as "an intense, soul-searching weekend."

"When it came down to doing the feature, we all took our clothes off, everybody got naked for that," maintained Rafelson. "It's the exposure of the whole myth— 'let's come out and tell the truth about this whole concept of having manufactured and manipulated them.' Let it be a movie that made their statement on the mess of it all."

All four collectively agreed on one principle: it was time to shatter the group's image as goody-two-shoes pop idols. Rafelson and Schneider were only too happy to comply. The movie would be a vehicle for channeling everyone's frustrations. The working title was *Changes*. Eventually the cinematic venture would be renamed *Head* (a head, in the parlance of the 1960s, was someone who smoked pot). In Nesmith's opinion, the film represented the "most bona fide example of the Monkees' collective thinking." But, like so many efforts to achieve a unified vision, it would leave a bitter aftertaste.

Chapter Thirty-Six

THE GOOD VIBES OF THE OJAI ESCAPADES quickly dissipated as the group returned to the daily grind of shooting episodes of the TV show. There was, however, a bit of good news. *Pisces, Aquarius, Capricorn and Jones, Ltd.* was the number one album on the *Billboard* charts, the fourth consecutive Monkees LP to achieve this distinction.

Arguably, *Pisces, Aquarius* was the finest album ever produced by the Monkees, which was a testament to the talents of Chip Douglas, who managed to weave all the disparate elements into a cohesive artistic statement. Not everyone agreed. Nesmith (surprise) was unhappy about his lack of input. "This last album was completed in nine days," he told *Hit Parader* magazine about *Pisces, Aquarius*. "It's been cut in our own time between TV rehearsals and everything else. How creative can you be in that amount of time?"

Nesmith's prickly comments notwithstanding, *Pisces, Aquarius* was an inspired set of songs. The selections were light years away from the Brill Building bubblegum favored by Kirshner. The Nesmith-sung opening cut, "Salesman," (a swipe at the Golden Ear?) established a new tone. No longer "too busy singing to put anybody down," the group seemed content to pass judgment this time, signaling a different vision of the Monkees had arrived.

One track in particular, "Cuddly Toy," was downright naughty. Written by a bank clerk named Harry Nilsson, the song was about a deflowered groupie who gives in "without a fight"—a darkly malevolent tale of lost innocence hidden by a sprightly melody. The inclusion of the song was a breakthrough moment for Nilsson. Royalties allowed the fledgling songwriter to quit his job and devote himself full-time to a career in music (Nilsson's stunning nine-song demo session, arranged by Douglas for the group to listen to, is well worth seeking out on the Internet).

Pisces, Aquarius was stacked with off-kilter gems. "Daily Nightly," Nesmith's wild foray into psychedelia, was a bizarre stroll through the "phantasmagoric splendor" of Los Angeles. It was notable for Dolenz's swooping Moog synthesizer, one of the earliest appearances of the newfangled instrument on a pop record. Nesmith also contributed heartfelt vocals on Bill Martin's "The Door Into Summer" and Michael Martin Murphy's "What Am I Doing Hangin' Round?"

It wasn't all roses. Always the weak link in the musical chain, Jones brought things to a halt with the sappy ballad "Hard To Believe" (an enormous hit, curiously enough, in the Philippines) which he co-wrote with three songwriters.

Conspicuous by his absence was Tork, whose only songwriting credit was the novelty intro to "Pleasant Valley Sunday," a trifle called "Peter Percival Patterson's Pet Pig Porky." The long-gestating "Lady's Baby" had not been delivered and Tork's presence, in general, was non-existent.

Later, Tork expressed his disappointment that the "all Monkees" band ethic of *Headquarters* had fallen by the wayside. He wasn't interested in returning to the slick professionalism of the group's early recordings. Dolenz felt the opposite way, making it clear he did not miss the ardor of the recording process. "Micky didn't want to go back in the studio," Tork remembered. "Micky said—these are his exact words—'You can't go back, Peter.'"

Despite its haphazard construction, the use of hand-picked studio professionals, like renowned banjo picker Douglas Dillard, made it the most assured musical production to date.

Pisces, Aquarius represented a high-water mark. Shortly after the album's release, the group scaled new creative heights with the release of the single, "Daydream Believer"/"Goin' Down," their fifth-straight million-seller. The A-side, written by ex-Kingston Trio member John Stewart, was a classic slice of personable pop with an irresistible sing-along chorus. Of course, this being the Monkees, *somebody* had to be pissed off. In this case, it was songwriter Stewart, who complained Jones had, without permission, changed the word "funky" to "happy." Jones defended his decision: "Can you imagine me going out there now saying, 'Now you know how funky I can be?' It's not one of those words that improves with time."

The B-side of "Daydream Believer" was the group's most ambitious production to date, a show-stopping blues vamp featuring Dolenz's breathless scat-rap and a big brassy arrangement by Shorty Rogers. Sounding unlike any other track in the group's catalog, "Goin' Down" remains a treasured nugget among Monkees' fans.

If any further proof was needed they had reached the pinnacle, it was the prestige

Nesmith gives the thumb's down on a script. Episode-making had become "laborious" in Tork's words.

accorded to Nesmith's song "Different Drum" which became a hit when covered by the Stone Poneys. The group's vocalist Linda Ronstadt had transformed Nesmith's kiss-off tale from talking blues into a wistful torch ballad, creating a signature '60s pop moment in the process. Peaking at number thirteen on the *Billboard* charts, the single turned many a skeptical head in the direction of Nesmith, who, for all his fussing and fighting, had yet to strike gold with any of his original Monkees compositions.

An extraordinary year in the career of the Monkees was coming to an end. When every dollar was counted, the Monkees were named the top-selling band of 1967. Perhaps most impressively they had sold more records than the Beatles and the Rolling Stones combined. This was, they would soon find out, a feat that was impossible to duplicate.

Chapter Thirty-Seven

IT WAS NEW YEAR'S EVE, 1967, and Davy Jones and Peter Tork were in England, celebrating in style. They joined scene-makers Lionel Bart, the Svengali behind *Oliver!*, and Tork's GTO-smashing buddy Jimi Hendrix at the exclusive club The Speakeasy.

For the time being, the Monkees were still on the A-list. The Beatles threw a private party for Jones and Tork at their hotel. Afterwards Tork took full advantage of his Beatles connections, touring the new Apple store (which, despite its name, was not a place to buy computers and wireless devices—it was a boutique set up by the Beatles). While in England, Tork accepted a spontaneous invitation to play five-string banjo on George Harrison's *Wonderwall* soundtrack. "They certainly treated us with all kinds of cordiality," he later recalled. Several months later Tork reciprocated the hospitality by inviting George Harrison and Ringo Starr to stay at his Caligula-like mansion in Laurel Canyon.

What drew the Fabs to the Pre-Fabs? "We got reports that they admired us very much for the ability to go into the studio and make television day in and day out, that we were working studio actors," was Tork's explanation. "They said they couldn't do that. And when we met those guys, they acted like they respected us."

While in London, Tork requested and received a special screening of the Beatles' TV special *Magical Mystery Tour*. A few days later, when asked at a press conference about the direction of *The Monkees* TV series, he referenced the psychedelic Beatles film. "Did you see *Magical Mystery Tour*? That's what we like. We must go as far afield as possible," he told the assembled reporters.

Tork confessed that making the show had become "laborious," implying, creatively, the group had begun to chase their own tail. Dolenz concurred. "I was getting a little bored with doing the same show every week—even after only two years," he reported. "We'd met The Beatles. We'd been around the world. To come back to doing a half-hour TV show seemed like a bit of a letdown."

The second season of *The Monkees* presented a major set of artistic challenges: how to keep it fresh and different, how to keep the group's chemistry from imploding, and how to keep already-inflated egos from exploding. Weary of the pace and demands of their newfound fame, each member made their concerns known to Rafelson and Schneider.

In response, the producers made concessions. Instead of five days, episodes were completed in half the time. The format on the show also loosened—inside jokes, political swipes and outré humor began sneaking into the final edit with greater frequency.

"We improvised almost the entire show," Dolenz later boasted. Nesmith saw it differently. "The scripts provided a launching platform for the way we actually did it, which included some ad-libbing," he argued. "But we didn't make up the situations, we always went back to the scripts."

Improvised or not, the general atmosphere on the set was convivial. Perhaps too convivial. A goof-off room, adjacent to the set, had been built so the band could practice music and expand their consciousness. "It was wonderful," recollects Tork. "They built a great big refrigerated room where we could set up amps and play guitars without the sound creeping back into the soundstage."

The clubby atmosphere was accented by billowing clouds of marijuana smoke. The influence of cannabis—red eyes, fractured smiles, spacey behavior—was impossible to ignore. In certain scenes they were clearly high as kites. "There's a couple of times when I watch the show and I think, 'I think I was stoned there,'" remembered Dolenz with a laugh. "I can tell that maybe after lunch I'd gone up in the rafters and had a couple of hits."

Jones, while hardly a reticent participant, believes smoking had a detrimental effect. "Grass does kind of slow you down a little bit," he explained. "You know, mellow you out. So maybe the edge had gone."

Rafelson and Schneider turned a blind eye to the shenanigans. With a movie in the works they needed to keep their charges placated, a tricky task. Chilly relations—especially between Nesmith and Tork—required keeping the four headstrong pop stars physically separated. Raybert came up with a novel solution: each of the four was assigned a special dressing room with a system of color-coded lights to alert them when they were needed on the set. "Let me explain why they were made," said Dolenz. "Because we had nowhere that they could contain us. They were more like cages."

High times on the set. No one on television at the time was higher than the Monkees.

In many ways the four dressing rooms mirrored the quartet's individual personalities. Tork's room was decked out in hippie regalia with musical instruments strewn willy-nilly. Jones sported a traditional Broadway-like dressing room with huge mirrors and lights as well as photos and congratulatory telegrams. "He could look at himself in the mirror 24 hours a day," joked Dolenz, whose own set up included a shag carpet, candles and a few pillows. "That was my little nest—a womb, maybe, is more appropriate."

Nesmith's dressing room was characteristically offbeat and more than a little freaky. Psychedelic black lights refracted off shiny inside-out cellophane cigarette wrappers that papered the walls. Along with a string of Christmas lights that had been

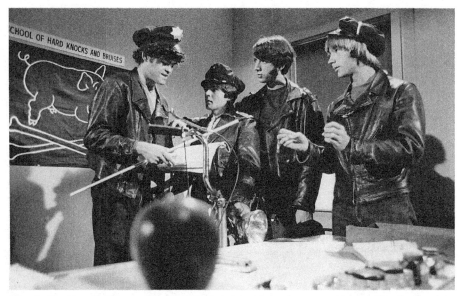

School of hard knocks. "There were six fights," Tork claimed—one between each pair of Monkees.

hung, Nesmith devoted a wall to hundreds of safety pins. "Mike's was the strangest," Dolenz remembered, "and of course Mike is strange."

Strange was a good description of the group's appearance in the second season's roster of episodes. Their physical appearance had changed. Dolenz was suddenly sprouting a curly afro that earned himself the nickname "Fuzzy." Nesmith's mutton chop sideburns grew to the size of Chia Pets. Tork, in general, looked scruffier, growing a freak-folk scraggly beard. As usual, Jones was the most fashion-conscious and fastidious. Adorable little Davy took to wearing love beads with his paisley-printed shirts and crisply-laundered Nehru jackets. Stoned or not stoned, he always managed to look sharp.

Shedding their first season uniforms—those natty Gene Ashman shirts—the four cast members now looked disconnected, like individuals artificially joined at the hip. There were reasons they were losing the plot. Factoring in their private lives, which were becoming increasingly tumultuous, the amount of traveling, lack of sleep, and constant partying, may explain the lack of cohesion. And then there were the egos. Everywhere they went a fuss of some kind was being made. "It was slowly burning a hole through the center of our brains" is how Dolenz put it. "We were full of ourselves, no question about it. You know, who wouldn't be?"

Chapter Thirty-Eight

IT WAS "GETTING HARD TO ACT," Tork explained. Their original roles playing hard-luck musicians united in their desire to achieve success was now out-of-date.

Nesmith agreed. "I knew at the beginning of the second season that was the beginning of the end of that whole thing and that there was no way that this was going to be sustained; it was too intense."

Drugs were making an impact. Experimentation with psychedelics— a part of the rock star repertoire at the time—had a deleterious effect. "There was one very real acid trip I took and they had to shoot around me," Tork later told *Goldmine* magazine. "We had this Hawaiian thing and we were supposed to be wearing skirts and I just said, 'that's too much.' So I shined on them for a day."

Nesmith, who shined on several episodes over artistic differences, came up with a colorful metaphor to describe the decay. "The whole Monkees thing had become bloated with its curious position in the landscape of television," he explained. "It was like something that was starting to wash up on the shore having been at sea too long."

In the process of flaming out, the Monkees burned their most brightly. The last dozen original episodes produced for the TV series were full of groundbreaking, risk-taking, comic ingenuity. A closer look at these episodes reveals an amazing run. It starts with the exquisite four-part *a capella* rendition of "Ríu Chíu" that caps off the personable holiday episode *The Monkees Christmas Show*. The following week's episode, the clever spoof *Fairy Tale*, featured a bravura turn by Nesmith in drag, playing the haughty, foul-tempered Princess Gwen. For fans of Nesmith's droll humor, this episode was a highlight. "Oh, God, Michael was so good in that," remembers Tork of *Fairy Tale*. "It's really Michael's finest hour as an actor. I think he should have gotten an Emmy for it, for that one part."

Nesmith, ironically, was all but missing from the following week's episode, *The Monkees Watch Their Feet*. His only appearance was the opening teaser segment where, flanked by two soldiers, he announced, "this evening Raybert Productions and Screen Gems, with its usual lack of cooperation from the National Broadcasting Company, is pleased to present this special report from the Department of UFO Information." Featuring comedian Pat Paulsen, a deadpan satirist who was running for President in 1968, as the episode's narrator, *The Monkees Watch Their Feet* featured a lunatic plot about invading aliens.

The show turned even giddier the next week with *The Monstrous Monkee Mash*. Particularly notable was an extended outtake sequence featuring Dolenz and Nesmith botching take after take and breaking into hysterical stoned laughter. After seven tries, an uncommonly-giggly Nesmith manages to utter the gag's punchline—"Save the Texas Prairie Chicken." Where else on network television could you find such madness?

Audiences expecting to tune into a good-natured Monkees romp were left scratching their heads. Canned laughter, the staple of sitcoms at the time, had been eliminated about halfway through the season. Was it a joke at the end of *The Monkee's Paw* when Tork ruminated on the death of the hippie movement? It was certainly uncommon, to say the least, to hear a major pop star pontificating about such matters on a major TV network. Surrounded by his bemused bandmates, Tork's rap—bemoaning the fate of the peace movement due to "bad publicity"—was used as the episode's "reality tag." The remarks revealed Tork was no slouch, as he presciently predicted the counterculture would be co-opted by commercial forces. "The establishment will take it over and put down the people that originated it," he told the camera without a trace of irony (there *was* a certain irony, of course, that a member of the most commercial band of its time would be making this statement).

The following week was perhaps the most accomplished episode of the entire series: *The Devil and Peter Tork*. In a plot cleverly mirroring the fortunes and circumstances of the Monkees in real life, the episode depicted Tork striking a Faustian bargain with the devil (played deliciously by Monte Landis), selling his soul in order to purchase a golden harp, only to have Nesmith, in an unexpectedly dramatic court sequence, win it back for him. *The Devil and Peter Tork* summed up every progressive element that was unique to *The Monkees*—innovative plotting, strong character identification and a willingness to take risks. However, censorship issues over the use of the word "hell" (hard to believe but true) delayed the episode from airing. It was later nominated for an Emmy Award and deservedly so. There was nothing of its kind on television.

Airing next was *The Monkees Ride Again,* the last full Monkees episode to wrap before movie production began. Unlike *The Devil and Peter Tork*, it was a

Uncharacteristically-goofy Nesmith on the set of "The Devil and Peter Tork," one of the series' best.

tossed-off, forgettable affair—but it was notable for producer Bob Rafelson's brief cameo appearance as the "World's Oldest Flower Child."

The next episode, *The Monkees in Paris* was Rafelson's last in the director's chair. Breaking the fourth wall of comedy at the outset of the episode, the Monkees whine and moan about having to film yet another hackneyed comic routine. "You've seen one Monkees episode you've seen all the Monkees episodes," gripes Nesmith to an on-screen Jim Frawley. After a group huddle they announce they're off to Paris. The action cuts to France (this is the episode that features the Monkees pretending to run from their non-existent French fans).

In order to appease the temperaments of their headstrong stars, Rafelson and Schneider were encouraging greater creative license over the show, an invitation which included the possibility of directing an episode. Both Dolenz and Tork took them up on the offer. Tork went first with *The Monkees Mind Their Manor*, a competent, if unremarkable, installment.

Rafelson and Schneider were also inviting each member to hand-pick a guest star to make a cameo appearance. Jones' choice, Charlie Smalls, appeared in the closing tag of *Some Like it Lukewarm*. In a genial exchange, Jones engaged Smalls, who later wrote the musical *The Wiz*, in a conversation about the rhythmic

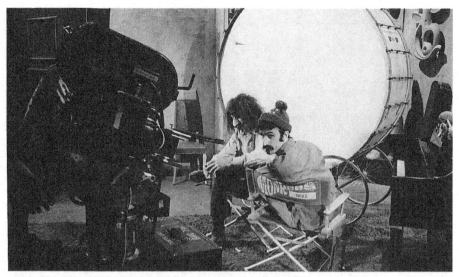

Underground musician Frank Zappa (right) later made a cameo appearance in *Head*.

differences of soul music and rock and roll (years later, Paul McCartney and Stevie Wonder would follow suit on the cringe-inducing "Ebony and Ivory").

Nesmith's invitation went out to Frank Zappa. Depending on your point of view, Zappa's cameo on *The Monkees Blow Their Minds* was either a creative peak or the ultimate in self-indulgent arrogance (or, of course, both). Appearing only in the opening sequence, Zappa, a celebrated underground musician, reversed roles with Nesmith in a bizarre mock interview, trading snarky jibes about the Monkees' "banal and insipid" music. The skit ends with Nesmith conducting a sledgehammer-wielding Zappa as he destroys a car to the tune of "Mother People." By anyone's definition it was odd stuff.

And finally Dolenz's directorial debut, *The Frodis Caper*, the last original episode of *The Monkees* to air. The inspired lunacy of this surrealistic tour-de-force—involving a pulsating eye that freezes TV viewers to their sets—was yet another high water mark. Closing out the run was Dolenz's choice for guest star, the moody folksinger Tim Buckley.

The sum total of the last 12 episodes found the Monkees on a creative high. The autonomy they had been granted had allowed them to express every aspect of their artistic desires without fear of corporate recrimination. This was the same fearless attitude they would present to the public in their upcoming movie.

Chapter Thirty-Nine

JUST BEFORE THE PRODUCTION OF *HEAD* BEGAN, Rafelson and Schneider received jolting news: Dolenz, Jones and Nesmith were going on strike. The issue: screenwriting credit. In a surprise move, Tork refused to join the work stoppage. "I felt it was another power play by Mike," Tork later told *Mojo* magazine. "It was strange, because I was raised a labor progressive. If ever there was a guy who understood the dynamics of labor organizing, it was me."

Nesmith believed the brainstorming sessions in Ojai entitled the group to have screenwriting credit alongside Nicholson and Rafelson. Reportedly, he hid tapes of the Ojai sessions in the trunk of his car as the dispute escalated. To advocate their case, the threesome enlisted the services of Jerry Perenchio, a powerful Hollywood agent (and future billionaire owner of Univision).

An accord was quickly struck—one that was a Pyrrhic victory for Dolenz, Jones and Nesmith. The threesome would not receive screen credit but they would get an extra thousand dollars for their creative contributions. It was a "horrendous" amount, Jones later recalled, "and they were reluctant to give us that."

Hard feelings lingered after the settlement and those repercussions were felt on the set. Hardly bosom buddies to begin with, Nesmith and Tork were now barely on speaking terms. Tork stood behind his conviction, even if it meant being a scab. He did not believe the group deserved writing credit: "Bert allowed a little trade-off and gave them a face-saving concession. But I got paid *nothing* for *Head*. I was given a piece of the action and it died. I'm not bitter."

Dolenz felt Tork's lack of participation "took the wind out of the sails of our opportunity," but years later, he changed his tune about the screenplay. "Jack got writing credit and rightly so, because he did actually script it," he contended, "but it was a real collaborative effort between us and Bob and Bert and Jack."

Nesmith eventually came around as well. "If you want to say whose vision the movie was, it was Jack Nicholson's. Jack is beyond world class, he's one of the

The gang, with Jack Nicholson, preparing for the live performance *Head* sequence filmed in Salt Lake City.

greats. He's always had a remarkably creative, astute, impeccable sense of taste. What he brought to Ojai was what ultimately became the parameters of the movie."

Nicholson provided a calming influence on the set. "Working for Rafelson is very difficult," claimed Tork. "He was not to me an artist's director. I was saved by the fact that Nicholson was on the set...and Nicholson, I think, is a master."

The positive vibes that marked the group encounter in Ojai were now so frayed that by the start of the shoot Rafelson and Schneider were harboring serious doubts about the film's viability. Rafelson recalled, "Bert kept saying, 'look, for all your life you've talked about making a movie. For God's sake, why do you want to make the Monkees' movie?' And I said, 'because it's an incredible thing we've all been through, let's put it on film.'"

What was the movie about? "We were trying to make a film we'd appreciate without network censorship problems," said Schneider. But no pithy explanation seemed possible. Simply put: there was no plot line, no protagonists, no clear-cut point to the whole thing. *Head* was a loosely connected series of sketches glued together by a darkly malignant comic vision.

The Monkees movie was well beyond anything the group had ever attempted. It was closer to an abstract European art movie than *A Hard Day's Night*. Inquisitive members of the press visiting the set were offered various interpretations of what was transpiring. Nesmith told a reporter the movie had "a very deep plot but it won't be readily apparent if you see the picture only once." Rafelson claimed it wasn't a comedy but then countered "it's funny."

"The Monkees are keeping the story a deep, dark secret" wrote *16 Magazine* but, underneath the non-committal answers, there was confusion. Of all the Monkees, Jones was the most mystified. "The *Head* experience has always baffled me," he later said. "I never understood it."

To underscore the incomprehensibility of the movie they were making, Dolenz jokingly offered bogus plot points to gullible journalists. "Part of the story concerns an itinerant parrot salesman in Florida who tries to get us to buy a warehouse," he tweaked *NME*, adding, "it also involves square basketballs."

Chapter Forty

THE CHANGING FORTUNES OF THE MONKEES in many ways mirrored the shifting currents in the culture. The giddy day-glo days of 1967 had darkened and, by 1968, the optimism of LBJ's Great Society was overshadowed by an escalating war and urban unrest. The "Summer of Love" had been followed by a year of hate. Riots plagued inner cities and civil discontent escalated. Martin Luther King, Jr. and Robert F. Kennedy were assassinated.

Amidst all the world's problems, no one had much use for a bunch of frolicking Monkees. By 1968, the public's taste for pure pop was fading. The heavier sounds of Iron Butterfly's "In-A-Gadda-Da-Vida" and Steppenwolf's "Born to Be Wild" reflected the mood of the times.

Dolenz, Jones, Nesmith and Tork did not mourn the downward spiral of their popularity. "They were tired of being bubblegum. They weren't bubblegum types as individuals," Rafelson contended. "Now that the word had gotten out that the Monkees were not responsible for their own music, the older kids said 'fuck the Monkees, let my kid sister watch them. I want to listen to Jim Morrison and Jimi Hendrix, not ersatz Beatle records.' And I think they took that to task."

The group had grown disdainful of their audience as well. Nesmith discussed his view of the fan base to writer Jerry Hopkins. It wasn't a very flattering assessment: "We end up with the 11-year-olds who don't get along with Mommy and Daddy. They're not articulate."

After *Head* wrapped, the cohesive unity of the project gradually unraveled. Instead of banding together, the quartet split into four factions. Each was seeking to achieve their artistic aims. Nowhere was this more evident than the group's music. "The Monkees albums became Micky and his vision, Mike and his vision, Peter and his vision, Davy and his vision," explained Dolenz.

Nesmith took full advantage of the recording studio. Absent his bandmates, he created demos for many of the songs that would later show up on his post-

Monkees records. Chip Douglas, whose services were no longer needed, recalled that Nesmith "mainly wanted to do his songs. If he could have done a whole album of his songs he would have been happy. He could be congenial and cooperative and get everybody playing on his two or three cuts and then he'd disappear."

Nesmith had a lot on his mind. On February 4, 1968, just as *Head* began shooting, his wife Phyllis had given birth to their second child, Jonathan. His third child came along a few months later on August 24, 1968, when Nurit Wilde gave birth to Jason Nesmith.

He wasn't alone in his troubles. Jones was being sued for five million dollars by his former manager Hal Cone, the man responsible for setting up a vanity record label and other cottage businesses. "I let other people handle my money," Jones admitted ruefully years later. "Bad investments were made." Happily for Jones, Cone was later found guilty of theft, forgery, receiving stolen property and conspiracy.

Clinging ever-more tenuously to his teen idol status, Jones discovered he was no longer "The Face." That now belonged to Bobby Sherman, another Ward Sylvester client. Sherman's gleaming smile had begun replacing the most popular Monkee on the coveted covers of trend-conscious fan magazines; ironically, he had been the recipient of a huge career break when he guest starred on an episode of *The Monkees*.

Chapter Forty-One

THE FOUNDATION OF THE FRANCHISE was starting to crumble. Despite a sterling track record, music producer Chip Douglas, like Boyce and Hart before him, suddenly found himself on the outside looking in. The Monkees felt his services weren't necessary—they could produce themselves.

A new single was needed to follow up the chart success of "Daydream Believer" but nothing was ready for release. Scouring the vaults for scraps to throw the public, Colgems came up with "Valleri"/ "Tapioca Tundra."

The A-side was a propulsive Boyce and Hart rocker that had been sitting in the cans for over a year. The evolution of the song was, in many ways, more interesting than the song itself. Hart remembered, "Donnie (Kirshner) kept telling us to write a girl's name song. So early one morning Tommy woke me up and said, 'I just told Donnie we wrote this great girl's name song and that we'd play it for him in a half-hour, so get up.' So I got up, took a shower, got in the car and on the way over there Tommy started playing some chords and shouting out as many girl's names as he could think of. Finally, we came up with the name Valleri. So by the time we knocked on Donnie's door, all we had was the word Valleri and a set of four chords. Donnie thought it was a smash."

"Valleri" had been relegated to the vaults while the Monkees' rebellion played out. After it appeared on an episode, two separate DJs in Chicago and Florida who taped the song began airing it, resulting in an avalanche of requests that Colgems release it. The story, never corroborated, sounds dubious. But it did allow Boyce and Hart to go back into the studio to cut another version, adding a beefy horn arrangement alongside ace sideman Louie Shelton's classical guitar licks.

The Monkees were far from happy about the single's release. In fact, they were sufficiently incensed to demand Boyce and Hart remove their names from the production credits and substitute theirs. Nesmith took the opportunity to slag off their latest hit, publicly declaring "Valleri" the "worst song of all time" (alongside

The vaudeville shuffle "D.W. Washburn" was out-of-sync with the signature Monkees sound.

his other "worst of all time," *More Of The Monkees*). Despite the controversy, "Valleri" went all the way to number three on the charts. It was the sixth and final million-selling Monkees single.

The B-side, Nesmith's "Tapioca Tundra," was a meandering tune. His disconcerting habit of naming a song with an arbitrary title having nothing to do with the lyrics was an artistic conceit that reeked of pretension.

Unfortunately, Nesmith's tendency to lapse into stream-of-conscious poetic babble would be fully realized on the next Monkees LP, *The Birds, The Bees & The Monkees*. A mediocre record to begin with, *The Birds, The Bees & The Monkees* was practically sabotaged by Nesmith alone. Such half-baked offerings as "Magnolia Simms" and "Writing Wrongs" made Jones' thin originals seem like Gershwin by comparison.

The new songs were the clearest indication yet that the Texas-born troubadour had given up on his bandmates. Nesmith music wasn't Monkee music—it was Nesmith music being played by anonymous session players. As for the audience, well, it often seemed he had little use for them as well. The humble pop ditties previously penned by Nesmith were slowly being replaced by irritating sonic experiments that strayed unconvincingly into avant-garde territory.

He wasn't alone. The normally trustworthy Dolenz was guilty of over-singing

World-weary Monkees meet the press on their tour of the Far East, their last together for nearly 30 years.

"Zor and Zam," ramming home the song's anti-war message with the subtlety of a sledgehammer. Sadly, a stripped-down version featured so effectively in the Dolenz-directed episode *The Frodis Caper* was supplanted with a gratingly overblown production on *The Birds, The Bees & The Monkeess.*

The Monkees' fifth long-player suffered many such lapses in quality control. Its twelve tracks lacked the spark of *Headquarters* and the shine of *Pisces, Aquarius*, although a few gems, like "Auntie's Municipal Court," a rousing rocker featuring double lead vocals by Dolenz and Nesmith, and Boyce and Hart's clever "P.O. Box 9847," managed to slip into the mix. Although credited as the first full album production by the Monkees, Tork was *persona non grata* without a vocal or song to his credit. His only contribution was playing piano on "Daydream Believer."

It was becoming increasingly obvious that without Chip Douglas at the helm, the Monkees' music lacked an overall uniform vision. *TThe Birds, The Bees & The Monkees* was chaotic and unconvincing. It may have moved a million units and hit number three on the charts, but, more than anything, it was a sign of decay. The moment for unity between the four had passed.

An even bigger disaster was waiting. The group's follow-up single, "D.W. Washburn," was not only the first single that failed to crack the Billboard Top Ten but, more crucially, it was out of sync with the signature Monkees sound.

The minstrel-styled toe-tapper written by Jerry Leiber and Mike Stoller, recorded effectively by the Coasters, was marred by Dolenz's ham-fisted vocals and a production which dragged. Lester Sill, the group's musical supervisor, later admitted releasing "D.W. Washburn" had been his single greatest mistake during his tenure with the Monkees.

Judging from music sales, Monkeemania was heading for a precipice. "The minute the television show went off the air," Nesmith later claimed, "the Monkees records meant nothing."

Chapter Forty-Two

NEWS HAD CIRCULATED: NBC WAS PASSING on another season of *The Monkees*. Was the show canceled or dropped? It didn't seem to matter to most of the inner circle. "We knew we had squeezed it dry," admitted Jim Frawley.

Judging from appearances Rafelson and Schneider were not upset. "They were happy to take a pass on another season," claimed Tork. "They didn't like us—I mean, we were a pain in the ass. We did things that I look back on now with horror. They wanted outlandish people and they got us and they had to pay the price and I think they got sick of it."

Rafelson concurred. "We weren't greed freaks," he asserted. "We had proved what we set out to prove. I think that when the TV show went off, a little of the bloom was off the plant—it didn't have that force."

The tried and true format of the show—Davy meets girl, Monkees sing a song, Davy gets girl, Monkees sing another song—had grown stale. The producers knew it and NBC knew it.

But not everybody else knew it or acknowledged it. "We ended the show because the Establishment wanted it to go on exactly the way it was and we didn't," Dolenz fumed to *Melody Maker*. "The Establishment, of course, controls the money, but we knew that the series had to grow or die. They didn't want it to change."

Tork also regretted the sitcom's short shelf life. "Personally I wish we would have gone on and done a third and fourth and fifth season, because I think we were just coming into our own. But I think that our ability to cut up was finally getting to the producers and they were beginning to want to wash their hands of us."

On September 9, 1968, a repeat episode of *The Monkees* marked their last appearance on prime time. The following week, *I Dream of Jeannie* took over their coveted slot.

All chips were now riding on the movie *Head*. In days and months leading up to its release the project teetered at the edge of disaster. The mood between all the major players had turned poisonous. The light had gone out of Tork's eyes. He sported an increasingly unkempt beard, looking nothing like cheery bass player from the early days. The most notable sign of Tork's indifference was his decision to stop recording music after the disastrous "Lady's Baby" sessions.

Things weren't much better in the Nesmith camp. He and wife Phyllis were now estranged. Their on-again, off-again marriage had been rocked by his affair with Nurit Wilde.

Out-of-wedlock children were still a scandal in the late 1960s. The fact that Jones and Dolenz also had children on the way, even though neither was married, was a potential hornet's nest of bad publicity. For Dolenz, that status became moot when he tied the knot with girlfriend Samantha Juste on July 12, 1968. As for Jones, everything was still hush-hush.

Just as Monkeemania lost its luster in the States, the four Monkees lit out for the Far East for a series of live performances. The experience seemed to buoy their spirits. Their tarnished image at home meant nothing abroad. In Australia mob scenes greeted every public appearance and SRO crowds awaited them. Fans seemed not to care if Peter wore a beard (although Jones later admitted he was "kind of put out by it") or if the group as a whole seemed slightly jaded by the adulation.

From Australia, they traveled to Japan, where they would perform their last full band shows for nearly 30 years. "By that time we were playing really good," Nesmith said of the Japan shows. "This was the best we ever played. I mean, we were playing prime cut, grade A, blast-the-back-wall-down rock and roll."

Tork fondly recalled the group "hitting the pocket" while playing the song "Sunny Girlfriend" in Japan. "We were on the road in Osaka and we caught fire. Davy comes waltzing over to me right in the middle of this wonderful thing and yells, 'We're gonna form a group!'" The show in Osaka was professionally taped for broadcast in Japan. An audio bootleg bears out the group's enthusiasm for their performances but sadly the videotapes were lost and never recovered.

Not everything was hunky dory on the trip. Rumors about Jones' private life had begun circulating in the foreign press, which was much less reticent about prying into Jones' relationship with Haines. Even though their daughter Talia was born on October 2, 1968, a day after the group arrived in Japan, Jones awkwardly denied the blessed event when asked direct questions by journalists.

Overall, the tour had been a triumph but when the group landed back in Los

A symbolic leap artistically, *Head* was a cinematic kiss-off to the monster they had created.

Angeles, more bad news awaited them. Despite sell-out appearances at every stop, the tour lost money. This was a bitter pill to swallow, especially for Jones, who seemed to never forget a financial slight.

With no network TV profile to publicize their activities, the band was becoming yesterday's news. When Nesmith was busted for sporting a shirt made out of the American flag, no one, beyond the fan magazines, bothered to mention it. After two years of full-on press attention, the Monkees suddenly couldn't buy publicity.

"*The Monkees* was going off the air about the time *Head* was being wrapped up," recalled Tork in *Mojo* magazine. "So we didn't do anything in the public eye for months—we toured Japan and that was it—and the public forgot about us. The Monkees were a TV-driven group. TV is a medium for short attention spans, and if you don't keep them fed, they're gone."

That was the nature of celebrity—when your fifteen minutes were up, they were up. The Monkees seemed indifferent. In interviews, they began talking about the experience of being in the group in past tense. For anyone who cared to listen, they made it clear they were sick and tired of their flaccid phenomenon.

One magazine was relishing their state of affairs—*Rolling Stone*. Ironically, the counterculture taste-making rag found it in their hearts to offer some belated praise to the dying enterprise. "By definition, the Monkees are in another world," the magazine wrote in their expose on the LA scene, "but they are honest people, after all, and do fit in the scene quite well."

The ungrateful not-quite-dead franchise had an answer for critics kicking dirt on their graves—a movie that expressed everything the Monkees wanted to say and nothing anybody wanted to hear—called *Head*.

Chapter Forty-Three

"IT DIED A DEATH YOU WOULDN'T WISH on your worst enemy." That was Peter Tork's assessment of *Head*, the movie to which the Monkees had pinned their career hopes. A box-office bomb of the first magnitude, *Head* was rejected on almost every level. It boasted perhaps the worst PR campaign ever devised, a tidal wave of derogatory and abusive reviews in the press and, worst of all, inspired complete and utter public indifference.

Until *Head*, every single product with the Monkees name on it had returned its investment, usually many times over. But the transition from small to big screens broke the franchise's winning streak. This was their Waterloo.

Arty, obtuse, confrontational, deliberately non-linear and seemingly aimless, *Head* achieved one distinction above all others: it was collective career suicide on a grand scale for everybody (and nobody) to see.

"It was unfortunate," said Nesmith of the film's failure. "It made me feel that this was a hole out of which there was no way to collectively climb. The environment was too hostile."

In its own dark, foreboding way, *Head* captures the end of the Monkees phenomenon with kaleidoscopic intensity. Compared to the depressing *Let it Be*, the documentary that chronicled the break-up of the Beatles, "it exposed much of what all rock groups went through but nobody had the guts to say," Rafelson, the film's director, contended.

When it came to *Head*, no one could accuse Rafelson of copying the Beatles. Films like *A Hard Day's Night* and *Help!* had sanitized the sexuality of the Beatles, portraying them as humorous and huggable lads, whereas *Head* went straight for the jugular. In a series of jagged vignettes, the group attacked its burdensome plastic image, seemingly gleeful to inflict the wounds.

Instead of portraying themselves as the good-guy heroes of their TV show, the Monkees acted like selfish ingrates—engaging in a kissing contest with a groupie,

In *Head*, the Monkees were no longer the good guys; in fact they were barely likeable.

spelling out the words "W-A-R" at a football game, taking bets on whether a troubled girl will jump to her death.

Ridicule and disgust follow them in scene after scene. "The song was pretty white," comments Frank Zappa after Jones' faux-vaudevillian dance route. "Well, so am I," responds Jones, "what can I tell you?"

The *coup de grace* was a merciless parody of their own TV theme which found them chanting:

You say we're manufactured.
To that we all agree.
So make your choice and we'll rejoice
In never being free!
Hey, hey, we are The Monkees
We've said it all before
The money's in, we're made of tin
We're here to give you more!

From the very first frame to the last, *Head* was a giant symbolic leap off the bridge. Throughout the film, the protagonists never control their destiny. Tork is tackled by Green Bay Packer football star Ray Nitschke, Jones is pummeled in the boxing ring by former heavyweight champion Sonny Liston, and Dolenz finds himself crawling in the desert dying of thirst.

The key moment in the film finds the group stuck in a black box, trying to devise a strategy for escaping. Nesmith whines and points fingers and Tork babbles nonsensically, mimicking an Indian mystic he's just met. Finally, in cartoon superhero fashion, a cocksure Jones kicks through the wall and punches his way to freedom.

The scene, like the movie, turns its claustrophobic gaze inward. As a savage work of art, *Head* is practically unrivaled. By portraying the Monkees as real people, not happy-go-lucky performers and casting an unrelentingly harsh light on its stars, it goes farther than any other rock movie would—or perhaps should.

What seems obvious in retrospect is how much the jaundiced, cynical, self-lacerating antics were out-of-synch with the fan base's expectations. The four characters beloved by millions, the shaggy-haired silly Monkees who were "too busy singing to put anybody down," were nowhere to be seen. And so was the audience.

Head laid an egg at the box office, recouping only $16,111 of its $790,000 budget. Considering what a bomb it was, it must have warmed the hearts of Columbia Pictures executives to hear Tork, in one of the movie's signature moments, offering Jones wisecracking advice that "nobody ever lends money to a man with a sense of humor."

Chapter Forty-Four

HEAD EVENTUALLY ACQUIRED A DEVOTED CULT FOLLOWING but even its most ardent admirers will admit it's maddeningly oblique, a movie whose parts are greater than the whole. For example, the electrifying in-concert performance of Nesmith's "Circle Sky" is evidence of the Monkees' ability as a self-contained musical unit but there is no follow up; therefore, it is lost in the shuffle.

Moments of visual ingenuity pepper the film. Dolenz blows up a Coke machine with a tank, the group bursts through the scenery of a Western as it is being filmed, and, most memorably, they find themselves playing dandruff in actor Victor Mature's hair.

As an exercise in stream-of-conscious psychedelic filmmaking, *Head* is an impressive achievement but, thematically, it is difficult, if not impossible, to pinpoint what exactly is going on. One particular bit of dialogue—the rambling thoughts of a factory tour guide—captures the pervasive world-weary tone of the film. "Pleasure, the inevitable by-product of our civilization; a new world whose only preoccupation will be how to amuse itself," the tour guide lectures, adding, "the tragedy of your times, my young friends, is that you might get exactly what you want."

What *did* the Monkees and Raybert want from this idiosyncratic exercise in self-flagellation? Why did they want to destroy the carefully-groomed image of world's most successful pop group? More importantly, if neither of those parties could answer these questions, how did they expect an audience to relate to the movie?

It later emerged that Rafelson had suffered a last-second crisis of confidence. "At this time I thought the name Monkees was an anathema to the public," he explained. "I was right. In fact, when the film opened the first night in the Village, people came storming out and demanded their money back because they found out the Monkees were in the picture."

There was a reason audiences were surprised. Prior to the film's debut, Rafelson tried to lend some hip credibility to the project through a bizarre promotional campaign that intentionally excluded the Monkees. The advertisements featured the balding head of John Brockman—an obscure Marshall McLuhan acolyte whom they were friendly with—with the tagline: "What is *Head* all about? Only John Brockman's shrink knows for sure!"

"Someone should have hit the buzzer at that point," argued Nesmith. "Excuse me! You know, the Monkees were white hot and to not put them on the marquee just was loony. I didn't understand why they didn't do that."

The nadir of the publicity campaign was the movie trailer. No scenes from the actual film were shown—only flashes of words like "commercial" and "paid" along with Brockman's static blinking face. "*Head* is the most extraordinary Western, comedy, love story, mystery, drama, musical, documentary, satire ever filmed," a phony-sounding narrator promised.

"They got very esoteric," Tork later told *Blitz* magazine. Rafelson, in particular, was smitten by the influential media theories of McLuhan, who famously coined the term "global village" as well as the meme "the medium is the message." McLuhan had argued that an advertisement that used a "noisy, redundant barrage of repetition" would "gradually assert itself."

Taking McLuhan's message to the advertising medium, Rafelson hoped to skirt the very real problems he faced. The Monkees *were* anathema to a large segment of the public. Adult audiences wouldn't be caught dead in a theatre running a movie by the beyond-contempt Monkees. However, by debunking and lampooning their prepubescent appeal, the film alienated the very audience that had supported the group in the past.

"I certainly knew it wasn't going to be 'let's clamor for Monkees' and bring in the seven-year-olds," asserted Rafelson, "because you don't have them starting off committing suicide in the movie if that's what you want to accomplish."

Desperate to drum up publicity before the film opened, Rafelson and Nicholson cavorted through the streets of New York City plastering stickers of Brockman's head wherever they could, trying to stir up trouble. Confronted by police officers and briefly detained, the duo were disappointed to discover nobody in the press seemed to care.

The night of the movie's premier, an invite-only party was held. In attendance were Andy Warhol and Peter Fonda (future star of Raybert's next movie, *Easy Rider*). The public finally got a chance to see the film on Wednesday, November 6, 1968, one day after Richard Nixon had narrowly defeated Hubert Humphrey in a bitterly contested presidential election. The timing could not have been worse.

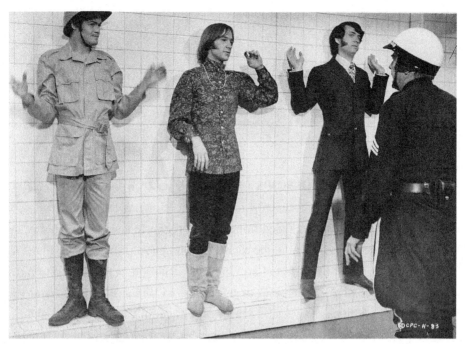

Guilty of what? *Head* did not provide any answers, only questions.

In an acutely political year, the mood was not conducive for a deeply weird movie called *Head*.

Early reviews were vicious. Some critics were repulsed by the seemingly-gratuitous snippets of war footage including the graphic execution of a Vietnamese soldier (amazingly, the movie was rated G for general audiences). Other writers, including a cranky Pauline Kael, perceived such moments as smug and flippant commentary on the most-pressing issues of the era. Kael, the *New Yorker*'s eminent critic, was unsparing in her criticism of *Head*, writing "the doubling up of greed and pretensions to depth is enough to make a pinhead walk out."

Even positive notices tended to include backhanded compliments. For example, Renata Adler, writing in the *New York Times*, theorized it "might be a film to see if you have been smoking grass…or if you are interested in what interests drifting heads." Adler offered faint praise for the Monkees' efforts: "the fact that fame was stamped on them by hucksters as it might have been on any nice four random, utterly undistinguished boys—makes their performance modest and almost brave."

Chapter Forty-Five

DUE, IN PART, TO NICHOLSON'S REPUTATION as an A-list celebrity, *Head*'s reputation slowly outgrew its anemic box office receipts. As the years went by, as other rock movies of the era faded from raucous romps to staid period pieces, the Monkees movie gained traction, the cachet of cult appeal. When the hit film *Five Easy Pieces*, directed by Rafelson and starring Nicholson, was released to much fanfare in 1970, Roger Greenspun of the *New York Times* admitted "*Head* was better than most critics allowed…in retrospect, (it) doesn't seem all that bad."

A showcase revival in 1973 found *Los Angeles Times* film critic Charles Champlin nearly gushing with praise: "Seen again, you wonder how the critics and the early audiences could have missed the film's fierce visual energy and perhaps even more the film's tart, iconoclastic point of view."

Once guilty of association with the Monkees, *Head* was absolved through its association with Rafelson and Schneider's prestigious BBS Productions, whose zeitgeist-defining films included *The Last Picture Show* and the Academy Award-winning documentary *Hearts and Minds*.

The belated acclaim that elevated *Head* to cult classic came too late to satisfy the four Monkees. Tork, in particular, was devastated by the film's reception. He would leave the group shortly thereafter. "It's too bad," Tork said. "It's a movie that I know with the right promotion would have made a much bigger splash."

Despite the accolades, Jones never changed his mind—he just didn't get it. "That was us searching for a little bit of credibility," he said of *Head*. "We should have made something like *Ghostbusters* or a nice fun Monkee movie."

The film's instant obscurity meant the accompanying soundtrack was all-but-ignored by the public. That was a shame—the album contained some of the best music the Monkees ever made. The musical centerpiece was the stunning "Porpoise Song," a psychedelic nugget written by Gerry Goffin and Carole King featuring a majestic arrangement by Jack Nitzsche. There was also "As We Go Along" with

The Monkees strike a familiar pose. The group rarely agreed on anything.

celestial guitar work by Ry Cooder and Neil Young. Several Monkees' originals were also noteworthy. Tork contributed two solid efforts, "Can You Dig It?" and "Long Title: Do I Have To Do This All Over Again?" while Nesmith delivered the dynamic "Circle Sky" with its prescient lyric, "yes, it looks like we made it to the end."

Presiding as a musical supervisor over the soundtrack was Jack Nicholson. Mixing snippets of dialogue and sound effects, Nicholson achieved a rich collage effect stylistically similar to the visual kitchen-sink construction of *Head*.

How did Nicholson feel about *Head* after the fact? Rafelson, who maintained a friendship and working relationship with the legendary actor, claimed he remained a loyal fan. "Jack loves *Head*," Rafelson told *Mojo*. "He still quotes lines from the film to me on a daily basis. 'Howzabout some more steam?' or 'Everybody's where they want to be.'"

In a 1970 profile written by Rex Reed for the *New York Times*, Nicholson made his only known comment about the film. "*Nobody* ever saw that, man but I saw it 158 million times. I *loved* it," he said. "Filmatically, it's the best rock and roll movie ever made. I mean, it's anti-rock and roll. Has no form. Unique in structure, which is very hard to do in movies."

Rafelson and Schneider also expressed an abiding fondness for the movie despite its disastrous reception. It was "my favorite of all our films" Schneider later

The TV special *33⅓ Revolutions Per Monkee* rehashed *Head* to lesser effect.

told the *New York Times*.

But the truth—a bitter truth for the four Monkees—was that he and Rafelson had much bigger plans that didn't include them. Their next production, a biker movie starring Dennis Hopper, Peter Fonda and Jack Nicholson, launched the duo into another stratosphere. Funded by money made on the Monkees, *Easy Rider* was the counterculture hit that *Head* wanted to be. By the time *Easy Rider* was receiving acclaim, *Head* was already a distant memory. As far as Rafelson and Schneider were concerned, the Monkees were over and done.

"We were quite satisfied to see the movie be the last thing the Monkees ever did," revealed Schneider. "That was really what the goal was—that this was the cap and then we're finished and if we can destroy the group in the process of making the movie, all the better."

The cruelty of this ambition only slowly dawned on the four Monkees. "People always interpret it as the Monkees' swan song—suicide and good-bye. It's not so," argued Nesmith. "We were on a roll. We were at the top of our form, at the height of our popularity with a network television show, we were cooking. Now, with this motion picture deal, this would set us apart—it would make us a valid member of the community. We were going to boogie across the silver screen with a series of movies… who knew it would be a swan song? It wasn't designed that way."

But Rafelson confirmed Schneider's ambitions. "In a way, it was my farewell to the Monkees," he admitted. "I mean, the movie begins and ends with them committing a kind of symbolic suicide."

"They wanted it to tank," Tork later recalled with barely-concealed bitterness. "Publicity for the TV show had been perfect, but the *Head* campaign couldn't have been better designed to ensure the movie would flop."

It was difficult to believe Rafelson and Schneider were no longer looking out for the interests of their former protégés. The same producers who had chosen them from auditions and nurtured them to stardom were now looking to wash their hands of them.

Looking back, it seems perfectly obvious. Rafelson knew audiences weren't interested in an art-house film by a prefabricated rock group. Even the film's title was a joke, a puerile pun so the duo could say on future promotional campaigns "from the guys who gave you *Head*."

Initially, the betrayal may not have been apparent, but over time it became quite clear. This was a wound that never fully healed. And while there is little doubt that *Head* accomplished what it set out to do—to counter allegations the project was artistically bankrupt—it is equally clear this attempt at vindication came at a very large cost to the four Monkees themselves.

Nesmith looking spiffy in his Nudie suit. "It just didn't have any heart," he said of *33⅓*.

Chapter Forty-Six

THE MONKEES FOUGHT VALIANTLY AND HONORABLY to reverse their fortunes and convince a skeptical public that they really did have something to offer. The obstacles, however, were too great. To nearsighted pop purists, the chapter had already been closed—the Monkees represented nothing more than a fast-buck and cash-in on Beatlemania. No apologies were asked and no quarter was given. They were a disposable pre-fab four, intended only for teenyboppers. And that was that.

As for the fans, they were growing up and moving on. An article in the *NME* titled "Year of the Monkee Crash" summed up the state of affairs. The group had dropped from the bestselling act of 1967 to the twenty-fifth bestselling band of 1968. The word was out: the Monkees were finished.

The desolate state of affairs was mirrored, to almost comic effect, by another headline, this one from the *New York Times*: "Rising Filipino Terrorism is Led by 'Monkees.'" The article explained that a Communist insurgency group in the Philippines nicknamed 'Beatles' because they concealed automatic weapons in guitar cases were doing battle with counterinsurgency guerillas nicknamed 'Monkees.'

You couldn't make it up.

For all intents and purposes, the Monkees were irrelevant by the end of 1968; *Head* had stiffed, the TV show was no longer on prime time, sales from Monkees records were plummeting and the group's camaraderie was close to extinction.

One contractual obligation remained: a TV special entitled, *33⅓ Revolutions Per Monkee*. It, too, would prove to be an arduous, unsatisfying ordeal.

Work began on the special only two weeks after the dispiriting debut of *Head*. The mood wasn't improved by the fact that a union strike at NBC forced the ambitious production—featuring chroma key, a new video technique—to be moved to the ill-equipped MGM Studios.

For Dolenz, the production of *33⅓ Revolutions Per Monkee* was an "absolute nightmare...Bob and Bert were no longer interested at all. They never even showed up."

Billed as a "psychedelic salute to the evolution of man and his music," the one-hour variety show, if anything, was even stranger than *Head*. Directed by Jack Good, a British TV veteran known for creating innovative rock revues (one writer described him as "the D.W. Griffith of pop style"), *33¹/₃* utilized the test-tube origins of the Monkees to mock and deride the artful pretenses of pop music.

It was perhaps *too* high-concept. "I remember feeling a little bit uncomfortable about the whole manufactured Monkee thing," Dolenz said of Good's intentions. He also felt reducing the Monkees' roles to bit players in their own special was insulting "because by this time we were a pretty shit-hot little band."

The master of ceremonies was Brian Auger, leader of prog rock outfit the Trinity, and his lead vocalist Julie Driscoll, a steely blues singer in the mode of Annie Lennox. Preaching demonically about the evolution of music, Auger introduced the band: "Here they come, idolized, plasticized, psychoanalyzed and sterilized...the Monkees!"

The special strikes a wildly inconsistent tone from the get-go. Nesmith's clever split personality on "Naked Persimmon" is followed by Tork's eye-rolling display of incense-and-peppermints hippie mysticism, "(I Prithee) Do Not Ask For Love," which is followed by a seemingly-endless sequence of abstract modern dance. There was only one bona fide highlight among the measly pickings and that was the sight of three pianos stacked one upon another featuring three bona fide legends of rock and roll: Jerry Lee Lewis, Fats Domino and Little Richard. Providing a sudden jolt of energy to the moribund special, a rollicking medley of respective greatest hits is performed. Joining the jamboree, incongruously enough, are the four Monkees dressed up as a greased-hair, zoot suited Doo-Wop quartet who manage to belt out credible versions of '50s rock hits "Little Darlin'" and "At the Hop."

Momentum is built but squandered as the one-hour special closes with a performance of Nesmith's "Listen To The Band." What could have been a signature swan song moment—a valedictory statement that was empirical evidence they'd pulled it off and become a band—devolves, instead, into a pointless freak-out jam session featuring the Buddy Miles Express and a bunch of scruffy dancers pulled off the street.

At least one critic loved it: George Melly. "What made this film worthwhile," wrote Melly in his influential pop essay collection *Revolt Into Style*, "was that it

Tork quit after completing *33⅓*. Dolenz, Jones and Nesmith carried on as a threesome.

demonstrated with a certain brilliance how yesterday's revolutionary can turn into today's reactionary. Good's enthusiasm is reserved for rock 'n' roll: sexy, extrovert, good dirty fun. When pop went highbrow, it lost him. I dare say *Sgt. Pepper* was his Waterloo, and he uses this film to make this point with considerable panache. The Monkees were originally computerized into existence as plastic Beatles but have become, not only adequate performers, but discontented with their lot. Good used this discontent as the vortex of an inventive piece of nostalgia and attack."

Not everyone shared Melly's enthusiasm. "There's no humanity, there's no compassion," claimed Nesmith. "(No) sparkles in the eyes, nothing. It was all kind of chopped and put together. And then by the time it was all said and done, I looked at it and it was cacophonous to me. It just seemed like noise. So I just never made any attempt to relate to that special, outside of being a party to it and getting paid for it. I just wrote it off...I think that was really the downslide. *33¹/₃ Revolutions Per Monkee* just didn't have any heart."

NBC executives guaranteed the bizarre extravaganza would be buried. After waiting nearly six months they aired the program head-to-head against the Academy Awards on April 14, 1969. The real surprise is it aired at all. One can only imagine the poor souls casually flipping the dial during an Academy Award commercial break, only to catch sight of robotic-dancing Monkees with cogs and gears projected behind them chanting "I'm a wind-up man."

Chapter Forty-Seven

FOR TORK, *33¹/₃* WAS THE FINAL STRAW. During filming he gave notice—he was leaving the group. The official reason—the PR spin—was that Tork was going to form his own band. The motivation went deeper, however. "There I was, you know, racked with self-doubt," he later revealed. "Do I really deserve to be here? And then, being a member of a synthetic group. I suffered from the criticisms— 'those no-talent schmucks from the street'—while in the meantime I wasn't able to make the music I thought needed to be made."

The announcement was greeted unsentimentally by the others. Nesmith, for one, wasn't going to cry crocodile tears for a bandmate he could barely stand. "It was no surprise that Peter left," Nesmith later told *NME*. "There were no arguments. About eight or nine months ago we discussed it, and I agreed that the time was right."

Public assurances aside, Nesmith had every reason to be piqued. Tork had quite clearly trumped him by quitting first. In his usual stubborn manner, Nesmith decided to carry on like nothing had happened. He would not cede control to Tork or anybody else—he would quit the group on his own terms.

"There was nothing to quit," a less-than-charitable Jones said of Tork's departure. "The band was finished, the TV show was over; everything was finished." Dolenz shared this assessment. "We were all very interested in our own individual egos and our own individual careers at that point."

How would the Monkees, minus Tork, revive a dying franchise? That was the question that lay in the bank balance. Fortuitously for the remaining three, *The Monkees* began airing as re-runs on Saturday mornings. This meant new music could be dubbed over the original Monkees romps. Lucky or not, Dolenz, Jones and Nesmith could continue to tour, record, and make money.

It was immediately apparent there was one crucial difference. In their present incarnation they were no longer innovative forces pushing boundaries. At best, the three remaining Monkees were seasoned entertainers performing evergreen pop ditties; at worst, they were peddling the cheap nostalgia of their fast-fading glory.

For decades to follow, tours would be launched and records would be made but the evidence was overwhelming—the Monkees as a creative force had peaked. To Jones, the reason was perfectly obvious. "As far as I was concerned," he said, "the Monkees was finished when Peter left."

In interviews conducted in 1969, Nesmith claimed the remaining trio had become closer buddies in the wake of Tork's absence. There was evidence to the contrary; however, as all three began recording separately from each other with their own hand-picked studio musicians.

The name of the game was contractual obligations—the trio owed Colgems albums of all new material. When enough tracks were ready the aptly-named *Instant Replay* was released. Although there was no shortage of Monkees' original compositions, only Jones' excellent "You And I" (with blazing guitar by Neil Young) carried any sense of urgency. Nesmith provided the interesting cocktail ballad "Don't Wait for Me" which he had recorded in Nashville with top shelf session musicians. It was passable. Dolenz, on the other hand, could only manage the meandering self-indulgent drivel of "Shorty Blackwell."

Instant Replay was an instant relic. Lukewarm sales—it barely slipped into the Top 40—were a sign of things to come. Did the Monkees care about these diminishing returns? Outward appearances said no. "At the time we got so fed up, we didn't give a damn what people thought," Dolenz remarked of the post-Tork period.

Perhaps to prove the point, the band released a two-sided turkey as their next single—Boyce and Hart's "Tear Drop City" backed by Goffin and King's "A Man Without a Dream." It was later revealed the A-side had been sped up 9% from an old Kirshner-era master tape to make it sound punchier. They needn't have bothered: the public ignored the song, which was a useless retread of "Last Train to Clarksville."

In the face of diminishing prospects, RCA should have locked the recording studio's door and canceled all the credit cards; however, instead of dropping their suddenly stone-cold premier act to concentrate on other Colgems artists like Hoyt Axton (who later wrote a chart-topping gem for Three Dog Night called "Joy to the World"), the execs, lacking all wisdom, re-upped the group's contract. Finally and officially, the trio had been granted the artistic license they had sought but it was a classic case of too little, too late—nobody wanted to buy the new recordings.

Chapter Forty-Eight

FOR THE FIRST TIME, THE MONKEES had a proper management deal. Brendan Cahill and David Pearl, both of whom had worked behind the scenes on *The Monkees* TV series, took over their managerial responsibilities. Getting high-profile network TV guest shots was their primary focus.

The Monkees prepared to hit the road with an ambitious revue featuring backing accompaniment by Sam and the Goodtimers, a slick R&B unit that had supported Ike and Tina Turner. It was an odd but interesting choice. Nesmith later described the musical mix as "rhythm and bubblegum."

Dolenz remembered, "We stood in front of this all-black, real hot rhythm and blues band. It was great except that all the tunes started having a little bit of an R&B feel. Everything started sounding like Otis Redding. The kids must have thought we were nuts but we had a great time."

While the Goodtimers funked it up, the Monkees knocked out soulful renditions of their greatest hits. They also performed an array of cover songs including "For Once in My Life" and "Johnny B. Goode."

Ticket sales were tepid. The tour kicked off before 5000 fans at the Pacific Coliseum in Vancouver, Canada on March 29, 1969. Instead of being the tumultuous sensations playing to crowds of 15,000 as they had in 1967, the Monkees were facing half-empty halls and sometimes worse. The numbers kept dwindling as the band trekked across the American heartland, playing only to the die-hard faithful. Dolenz later admitted the tour "was like kicking a dead horse. The phenomenon had peaked."

Amidst the gloom were a few brief shining moments of their former glory. One such moment arrived in May when the trio traveled to Nashville for a taping of *The Johnny Cash Show* at the Ryman Auditorium, home of the Grand Ole Opry. This was a prestigious gig for the attention-starved stars and they took full advantage, singing a lovely version of Nesmith's "Nine Times Blue" and joining the Man in

Black for "Everybody Loves a Nut." Afterwards, Cash graciously invited the group over to his house for a night of Southern home cooking.

Other high-visibility TV appearances followed including a highly-anticipated guest spot on *The Tonight Show* with Johnny Carson. What could have been a credibility-boosting appearance turned into an embarrassing debacle when Dolenz, seemingly star-struck by Carson's presence, hogged the spotlight by rambling on nonsensically about cough syrup and holograms to whatever else popped into his (addled?) brain. Jones and Nesmith could only watch and bristle.

Other network appearances on *Hollywood Squares*, *The Glen Campbell Goodtime Hour*, *The Joey Bishop Show* and *Rowan and Martin's Laugh-In* were wonderful opportunities to extend the Monkees brand name but the exposure did little to stoke the public's appetite for more Monkee product. This became abundantly clear after taping their appearance on the *Tonight Show* in New York City. Bitterly disappointing news awaited them: their scheduled return engagement at Forest Hills Stadium had been canceled at the last second due to the lack of ticket sales.

One last ray of hope was the group's new single, the quality of which had briefly renewed optimism within the ranks. The A-side, Nesmith's elaborate prog-country anthem "Listen to the Band" was a tricky tune that addressed the group's state of affairs. Pointedly singing about playing "a song and no one listens," the soon-to-be-solo Monkee dropped unmistakable hints about his new direction. "I think I can make it alone," he sang with a country drawl. Despite a punchy brass section, catchy melody and innovative arrangement, the single could not buy any chart action. The flipside, "Someday Man," a breezy ballad written by Paul Williams and sung by Jones, was particularly notable for being the first time a Monkees song did not carry a Screen Gems publishing credit. On its own merits, it made a slight dent on the chart and helped launch Williams' career.

Chapter Forty-Nine

IT WAS ALL OVER except for the funeral. The next single "Good Clean Fun"/"Mommy and Daddy" sank without a trace. Nesmith's "Good Clean Fun" was, in essence, a solo single with the name Monkees on it. It was pedestrian. The B-side, Dolenz's "Mommy and Daddy" was even worse than that—it was a pretentious mess. Both sides had been written by a Monkee—that was notable— but what did it matter when the single only barely managed to eke into the Hot 100?

Undaunted, the group soldiered on like three Don Quixotes for a series of shows in Mexico. One of the performances took place at cavernous Plaza Monumental stadium in Jalisco—a bull ring. Attendance was sparse. It was a long way from the Hollywood Bowl.

Bad news kept arriving in droves. A proposed British tour had been canceled. Only a few commitments—a handful of live dates and a new record—remained. Jones later recalled the last days of the tour as "one of the darkest hours of my life. We got out there and gave everything we have—that's something we always do— but afterwards, I couldn't help but wonder if it was all over for us."

The new album, *The Monkees Present*, represented Nesmith's last bow. A slight improvement over *Instant Replay*, it featured the recent singles and another fine selection from songwriter Michael Martin Murphy, "Oklahoma Backroom Dancer." Judging from the meager sales, however, the end was near.

The final performance for Dolenz, Jones and Nesmith as a trio occurred on November 30, 1969 at a concert scheduled for the cavernous Oakland Coliseum. As if to give a dead horse one last kick, *Rolling Stone* sent reporter Ed Ward to cover the non-event. With only a few thousand fans in attendance, Ward didn't have to work hard to land a few jabs. "I was thoroughly confused," he wrote of Nesmith singing "Johnny B. Goode" backed by the Goodtimers. "They really did think they were doing an R&B Show."

After the show, Ward interviewed the disillusioned threesome at their hotel room.

Both Tork and Dolenz lost themselves in substance abuse after their solo careers stalled.

Dolenz spilled his guts. "Look, the Monkees is the name of a TV show. I was hired to play the part of a rock-and-roll drummer, but what I am is an entertainer trying to reach an audience of eight-year-old girls. I'm no more a Monkee than Lorne Greene is a Cartwright." It wasn't the last time Dolenz would reach for that metaphor.

Nesmith was done. He had been preparing for a solo career for some time, woodshedding new material with his brand spanking new country-rock outfit, the First National Band, but first he had a score to settle with Screen Gems. Buying out his contract cost him well over $100,000 in unpaid wages. Nesmith gladly sacrificed the money. "You don't have to be blind to see a sinking ship," he told interviewer Harold Bronson. "I think if the four of us had stayed together as time had turned around that maybe we could have ended up with another television show and perhaps done something meaningful. I didn't want to. I didn't enjoy working with the other fellows. And Screen Gems had exhausted their money-making machine."

With Nesmith gone, the two remaining Monkees—Dolenz and Jones—doggedly carried the torch. They quickly discovered they were showbiz nonentities. To fulfill their contract, the duo were given a paltry $20,000 to record vocals for an album being prepared by Jeff Barry called *Changes*. "It was a snow job," Jones sniffed years later, and he was right: the tracks had already been prepared for a failed Andy Kim record. With Barry at the production controls, the two Monkees lent their voices and some last shreds of dignity.

The single "Oh My My"/"I Love You Better" was vapid bubblegum. Like the album it appeared on, it sank without a trace.

The death spiral was over by early 1970. All it had taken was a disastrous movie, a low-rated TV special, three bland albums, four so-so singles and a sparsely-attended tour with an R&B band to make it official, but the deed was finally done—the former hottest act in the world were kaput.

"I should have gone back to the stables," Jones said of his post-Monkees career.

Chapter Fifty

THE MONKEES WERE GONE and forgotten. Their fans had moved on and grown up. They boxed up their memories of Davy and the gang and sent them to out-of-the-way corners in attics and basements.

The lucrative pre-teen market turned its attention to the latest ephemeral pleasures. Hits like "Sugar, Sugar"—produced by (ahem) Jeff Barry for (ahem) Don Kirshner—were selling to a new generation of teenyboppers who also avidly followed a new musical sitcom called *The Partridge Family* starring a new teen idol named David Cassidy.

Being an ex-Monkee in the fast-food cultural wasteland of Hollywood was a prison the four erstwhile stars would find hard to escape. "It's like a blind man running for President," was how Nesmith described the prospects for his solo career in the early '70s. "I think you're gonna have to be a little bit better than the next guy to overcome that one handicap. I consider being a Monkee a serious handicap in terms of the serious music listeners. I consider it to be an asset in terms of merchandising value. So I greet the whole thing with mixed emotions."

Never close to begin with, the four Monkees splintered into four directions. Occasionally their paths would cross (Dolenz, Jones and Tork played a one-off show in Van Nuys, California in 1970; Tork produced a Dolenz solo single) but they were, for all intents and purposes, personally and professionally divorced.

And, yet, they had much in common, sharing a whole set of problems and predicaments; each in a marriage that would eventually end in divorce, each experiencing financial difficulties of some sort. More acutely, all four were haunted by the ever-present specter of their Monkee past.

Only Nesmith managed to forge a credible recording career. A trilogy of influential country-rock records he recorded with the First National Band—*Magnetic South*, *Loose Salute*, and *Nevada Fighter*—briefly generated quite a critical buzz. "Mike Nesmith? Why the hell not?" asked *Rolling Stone*, calling

Loose Salute "one of the hippest country rock albums in some time."

With a team of crack session players at his disposal, including steel pedal whiz Red Rhodes, Papa Nez forged a new musical path, showcasing an eclectic mix of country swing, roots music, Latin jazz and quirky iterations of the American songbook. As always, it was a "different drum" for the proudly idiosyncratic performer. Stylistically, his mash-up was similar in breadth and dedication to Gram Parsons who planted a similar crop of "Cosmic American Music" with the Byrds, the Flying Burrito Brothers and two critically-acclaimed solo albums.

Nesmith and Parsons (who died of a drug overdose at age 26 in 1973) were contemporaries but Parsons attained name-drop status that eluded Nesmith. "A Gram Parsons for television fans," was how *Village Voice* rock critic Robert Christgau dubbed Nesmith's music. "The Jimmie Rodgers of the Sunset Strip."

Christgau's backhanded swipe was fairly typical of the press Nesmith garnered. He had a perception problem. Fans of "I'm a Believer" were not necessarily predisposed to emotionally-probing ballads like "Propinquity (I've Just Begun to Care)."

Decked out in a Nudie suit, the lanky Texan gave off a "stone country" vibe but that label rested uneasily with a performer who refused to be pigeonholed by any one artistic construct. When he appeared on *American Bandstand* to play the hit song "Joanne," he deliberately downplayed the tender ballad's country roots. "I don't know whether it's country or not," he told host Dick Clark with a shrug. "It's what I enjoy playing."

He faced an uphill battle. Other groups such as the Nitty Gritty Dirt Band (which covered "Propinquity") were successfully mining similar territory but didn't have to tackle the preconceptions Nesmith faced. Except for England, where he maintained a devoted cult following, his albums were not shifting the kind of units that impressed RCA executives. Perhaps to jab those same executives, Nesmith sardonically dubbed his fifth album *And the Hits Just Keep on Comin'*. He could see the writing on the wall. Being taken seriously and achieving popularity were two vastly different things. Nesmith was in a bind. If he slagged off his accomplishments with the Monkees he risked alienating fans. If he played up his past, he would be accused of pushing nostalgia. Instead, he carved a middle course, never denying the act that brought him fame and riches but never capitalizing on it either.

Lingering resentment did occasionally surface in interviews. "They couldn't pay me enough money for the abuse I had to take about the group not playing on the records," he told *Disc* magazine in 1970. "That's why I had no compunction about accepting the royalty checks. No sir!"

But Nesmith was careful to never put down his former comrades. And if someone dared to call him the "smart Monkee," as Christgau did in the *Village Voice*, he was ready for a smackdown. "There are two common and, to me, repugnant notions about the Monkees," he said in a 1985 interview. "Number one, that I was the only one who had any talent, which is patently absurd. It's as unfair and as unkind as it is stupid. The other one is that I was the only musician. Peter was a much more skillful player than I was by some orders of magnitude."

Chapter Fifty-One

IF ANYTHING, TORK WAS HAVING A HARDER TIME than Nesmith being taken seriously. "After I left the Monkees, I went through an identity crisis right away. I called up Dick Clark and said: 'Put me on the road.' He said: 'Get a hit record; nobody will recognize you.' I went, 'What?' That was so staggering to me that it completely stopped me cold. I thought 37 promoters would be dying to have me perform," he explained.

Tork's band, Release, which featured girlfriend Reine Stewart on drums and Lowell George (later of Little Feat) on guitar, came tantalizingly close to having a song on the hit soundtrack to *Easy Rider*. But Bert Schneider, the movie's executive producer, refused to throw his ex-employee a bone.

It was the first in a series of big blows. "I was a very young man, and I lived through all that hoopla without a care," Tork later told the *Washington Post*. "I thought it would last."

Feeling guilty for the financial rewards that had come his way, Tork over-compensated in the most self-defeating way possible, embracing a hedonistic lifestyle that ensured money would disappear as quickly as possible. "Like the fixated person I was then, I went from one thing to another. I had to try everything: flower power, dope, orgies, fast cars," he later told writer Bruce Pollock in *When the Music Mattered*.

Nesmith understood Tork's predicament. "A lot of people asked us, 'how did you get through the thing without going stark raving mad?' Well, the point is we didn't. Peter had it more pronounced," he told interviewer Harold Bronson. "He was a very tired person."

Tork's financial troubles began to mount. "I spent my money grandiosely and other times I gave it away in abject humility. And what taxes didn't take went to unscrupulous persons of one stripe or another," he later explained.

His infamous rock star castle, paid for in cash, was foreclosed on to pay other debts. Tork became an itinerant traveler, skipping from town to town, looking for musical opportunities that never panned out.

Boyce and Hart, like a lot of Monkees songwriters, became famous in their own right.

Tork wasn't alone. Jones told the *NME* that he, too, was broke. Far-flung investments, including the high-profile fashion boutique Zilch in New York City and a shopping mall called The Street in Los Angeles, had sunken into bankruptcy. "I got ripped off," Jones later admitted.

As an entertainer Jones still had the goods—that old "impudent natural charm" first noted by the *New York Times*. He had his looks, his most marketable product. But nothing panned out. Logically Jones would have returned in another weekly TV series. He did manage to land highly-coveted guest spots on popular TV shows including *Rowan and Martin's Laugh In*, *The Tonight Show*, and *Love, American Style*.

He even won himself a place in cheese-pop history by starring as himself on a legendary episode of the TV sitcom *The Brady Bunch* called *Getting Davy Jones*. The episode's ludicrous plot twist had the ex-Monkee saving the day for Marcia Brady after she boasted that Jones had agreed to perform at the school prom. The insanely hokey installment of the kitsch classic prominently featured plugs for "Girl," Jones' latest single, but despite the exposure, the light-in-the-loafers ballad failed to register on the charts. Neither did his solo album.

Reportedly, the head of Jones' label Bell Records, Clive Davis, had become frustrated by Jones' inability to break a hit record. When Davis, a music industry legend, requested the struggling star open for fellow label-mates Tony Orlando and

Dawn, Jones peevishly refused, thinking the Vegas-style pop act was beneath him. Jones later admitted rejecting Davis' proposal was a foolish move. "It was weird," he said of his post-Monkees experience. "It was sort of like, 'But I am the king!' There was no place to go, nothing to do."

Dolenz followed a path similar to Jones. He recorded unsuccessful singles and recuperated from the ordeal. "There might have been a year or so where I just like fell asleep to recover," he later joked.

When he wasn't sleeping, Dolenz was partying hard. His social circle extended to the Hollywood Vampires, a loose conglomeration of decadent rock stars constantly on the prowl for naughty fun. Their booze-and-cocaine antics would become the stuff of legend. Dolenz happily joined these roving bad boys, stumbling around with the likes of Alice Cooper, Keith Moon, Ringo Starr and John Lennon (whose misadventures with the gang were later dubbed "The Lost Weekend.")

Comically noting the vast amount of marijuana he was smoking at the time, Dolenz later dryly quipped "they have a statue of me in Colombia, contributing to the gross national product, you know. I must have smoked about four hundred acres."

Dolenz fit comfortably into the wild early-'70s LA rock scene. His contemporaries, including drinking buddy and close friend Harry Nilsson, recognized and respected the former Monkee for his musical gift. That's probably why Frank Zappa offered him a job drumming in the Mothers of Invention. Dolenz later admitted he should have taken Zappa up on the offer.

When he wasn't self-medicating, Dolenz was scrambling for a payday. Gigs were becoming few and far between. "For a while there I wondered if I could still chew gum and walk at the same time," he later told *Q* magazine. He provided voices on Hanna-Barbera cartoons and won a few guest starring roles on TV shows *Adam-12* and *My Three Sons*. After he auditioned for the role of Fonzie on *Happy Days* he found, to his bitter disappointment, he didn't have a chance of landing the coveted role. Casting directors only saw Dolenz as a drummer in a rock and roll band.

The experience of being typecast after a popular role was nothing new for a veteran TV actor. The Achilles heel for Dolenz was that he retained his real name on *The Monkees* TV show. There was no way to be an ex-Monkee when everybody already knew your name.

Dolenz and Jones united with Boyce and Hart to record and tour in the mid-'70s.

Chapter Fifty-Two

THE PUBLIC'S INABILITY TO SEPARATE the ex-Monkees from their former personas seemed to be an insurmountable career obstacle. In essence, they had been branded for life. But their ex-producers had no such problem. Rafelson and Schneider were riding high as kingpins of the "New Hollywood" scene.

Relations between the four former cast members and the two producers were practically non-existent. Accusations, feuds, and never-resolved rifts lingered. Things got frostier when Dolenz and Jones banded together to sue for merchandising rights. Claiming they had never been fully compensated for the five percent royalty on all Monkees products sold, the duo were seeking twenty million dollars in damages but ended up settling out of court for a paltry $50,000.

When Rafelson and Schneider made it abundantly clear they had no desire to be associated with ex-Monkees, it was hurtful. "I just felt like an orphan at the end of the Monkees series," Jones said of the betrayal. "I felt from the energy and time I'd put in for Bert and Bob and the other execs—you know, that I could have gotten a phone call."

It must have been galling for Jones to find out Schneider had been so imbued with communal spirit that, after producing the countercultural cash cow *Easy Rider*, he had given a tiny percentage of the film's considerable profits to the movie's cameraman Laszlo Kovacs.

It was *Easy Rider* that catapulted Rafelson and Schneider into the big leagues. According to author Peter Biskind, "the impact of *Easy Rider*, both on the filmmakers and the industry as a whole, was no less than seismic." Suddenly, the producers of a contemptible flash-in-the-pan pop phenomenon were the toast of the town with power, money, access, and a cutting-edge reputation.

Bankrolled by Monkees profits, *Easy Rider* was hailed as a turning point in the development of independent American cinema. Once again, Rafelson and Schneider were at the epicenter of a cultural moment. Their newly-formed company, BBS Productions, founded with partner Steve Blauner, had a six-picture deal with Columbia Pictures and a plush four-story building at 933 North La Brea which became the mecca of New Hollywood's radical chic. "A hangout for a rag-tag band of filmmakers and radicals of various stripes," is how Biskind described it. "There was no hipper place in Hollywood, no hipper place anywhere."

The press fawned over BBS, usually ignoring or barely acknowledging a minor biographical detail in their resume called the Monkees. In 1970, Rafelson won international acclaim for directing *Five Easy Pieces*. He was now an auteur. Schneider began dabbling in underground radical politics.

On the opposite end of the spectrum, the four Monkees were struggling to make ends meet. Unlike Rafelson and Schneider, they were burdened with the legacy of Monkeemania. Every misperception about the project was something they had to answer for in public. It was as if the four of them—Jones, Dolenz, Nesmith and Tork—had cooked up the whole thing.

Rafelson and Schneider never denied they had been using the Monkees as a launching pad—it was the way they walked away that stung. "I hate to think there was some devious ulterior motive," Dolenz said about Raybert's disassociation from the project, "but there may have been and that's what hurt us. It didn't hurt them, the producers, but many years later, of course, we're the ones that took all the shit for it."

There were many bitter pills to swallow. Jack Nicholson, a nobody before *Head*, was now a superstar thanks to *Easy Rider*. When Rafelson directed him in the acclaimed *Five Easy Pieces*, both the actor and director received Academy Award nominations. Schneider was hailed for his conscientious artist-friendly approach as an executive producer. When he won an Academy Award for the anti-war documentary *Hearts and Minds*, his hackle-raising acceptance speech, which included a greeting from the Provisional Revolutionary Government of Vietnam, inflamed the right wing and sealed his reputation as a countercultural hero.

The ex-Monkees were on the outside looking in as a parade of A-listers thronged to the altar of Rafelson and Schneider. That was bad enough. Watching their songwriters become household names added insult to injury. Neil Diamond was now a spangled-shirt pop icon, Carole King's *Tapestry* was a Grammy-winning blockbuster, Harry Nilsson had become a rock superstar, and Boyce and Hart scored a Top Ten hit with "I Wonder What She's Doing Tonight." Even yeasty David ("Saturday's Child") Gates was making millions with the flaccid soft-rock outfit Bread.

And what of bogeyman Don Kirshner? The well-connected Golden Ear managed to carve out a credible career, beginning with the cartoon group The Archies. "The Monkees were not plastic enough for Don Kirshner," Tork later joked, "so he went straight to the Archies, who were not going to give him any s-dash-dash-dash." A studio group in all-but-name, the Archies' signature song "Sugar Sugar" was a bubblegum hit of monstrous proportions. Later Kirshner successfully launched the rock band Kansas and hosted the popular late-night variety program *Don Kirshner's Rock Concert* (the brutal wits at *Saturday Night Live* had a field day satirizing his painfully-stilted introductions).

Eventually the Monkees and their creators grudgingly gave Kirshner credit where it was due. "He had a tremendous sense for what was commercial," admitted Schneider, "and was able to take his producers and get the best out of them."

The Monkees fought passionately to free themselves of Kirshner's stranglehold but, not everyone, including Bobby Hart, was convinced firing him paid off. "At that point their musical career started to decline," Hart said of Kirshner's departure, "because they didn't take advantage of the high-caliber professionals they had at their disposal. They started using their friends and their songs instead. They could have had the same kind of run the Beatles had if they had fallen into the machinery and done it the way it was planned—hire all the best in every category to take care of everything, the publicity, the sponsors, the television and the live shows."

No doubt Kirshner agreed with this assessment. Despite all his latter-day success, he never quite recovered his mojo after the Monkees, at least in the world of song publishing. "It was a very bad experience," Kirshner recalled about his lawsuit. "I lost my whole company and had to do it all again. It wasn't very pleasant."

Of all the Monkees, Davy Jones was the only one Kirshner remained fond of. "Davy was very special to me," he claimed. "I read one of his depositions and he gave me credit for the whole thing. The others guys were either nervous or resentful about it."

Apparently Jones' feelings for Kirshner were not mutual. "Donny Kirshner was a bitter, twisted person," a more-blunt-than-usual Jones decried to the *New York Post* in 2009. "He had as much musical talent as a lettuce."

A "very hurt" Kirshner remarked Jones' comments had "floored" him.

Chapter Fifty-Three

THE FOUR EX-MONKEES BEGAN TO BOTTOM OUT professionally. None fell as far as Tork. Drifting between offbeat musical ventures and short-term employment, the directionless former TV star was arrested and jailed in 1972 after being caught crossing the border from Texas to Mexico with "three dollars worth of hashish."

It turned out Tork was lucky. Texas state courts were notorious for locking up drug offenders and throwing away the key. Instead he received special leniency as a first time offender, serving only three months in an Oklahoma-based Federal reformatory prison. "They realized I was not a criminal type, and they let me out," he told the *Los Angeles Times*.

Once free, his life spiraled between addiction and unemployment. "I found myself in a boardinghouse with my daughter in a room for twenty-five dollars a month, sleeping on a mat on the floor," he later told an interviewer. For a time, he taught English. His musical career was non-existent. "I had nothing to show for it in the outside world," he claimed. "No commercial success whatsoever."

Alienating himself from friends and family, he became a full-time alcoholic. "Being an entertainer in my case was deeply involved with it," Tork said of his bout with the bottle. "One of the features of alcoholism has to do with isolation. You feel you're not worthy of anybody's company. It's called 'arrogant doormat syndrome' and I had it."

By the mid-'70s, Tork was not the only ex-Monkee in desperate need of a career break. In 1975, a meeting between all four was held, the first since the break-up, to consider reuniting. Offers from McDonalds and the *Midnight Special* TV show were on the table but Nesmith balked, demanding they do a movie instead. The possibility of launching a tour was also rejected by Nesmith, who made it clear he would refuse to play the old Monkees hits if such circumstances ever did come to pass.

Dolenz and Jones sensed correctly that an untapped audience existed for their act. They teamed up with songwriters Tommy Boyce and Bobby Hart to record an album for Capitol Records under the name of Dolenz, Jones, Boyce and Hart. It didn't make much of a mark on the charts but when the quartet toured American amusement parks as "the guys that sang 'em and the guys that wrote 'em," they were greeted by adoring fans at every stop.

Despite Dolenz breaking his arm hang-gliding and being forced to perform in a sling, the foursome toured internationally and became the first American band to play in Thailand. A live album recorded in Japan was later released by Capitol. For Jones, returning to the stage was both a blessing and a relief. "I'd just been divorced so I wasn't feeling too clever—I was very unhappy," he remembered. "And it was good for me to get on the road."

The innocent fun of the Monkees had an audience, not just dedicated fans but a whole new generation who were watching the show in reruns. A greatest hits collection released by Arista Records in 1976 had become a strong back-catalog seller. At the very same moment, a new critical consensus was beginning to emerge and gain momentum.

"It's become quite commonplace to profess admiration for the Monkees, even fashionable in certain radical pop revisionist circles," reported Ken Barnes in 1976 in *Who Put the Bomp*. "There are fanatic collectors avidly tracking down every last manifestation of Monkees arcana (even unspeakable Davy Jones solo singles), the two-season run of TV shows has been exhumed and put into syndication, and when Micky Dolenz and Davy Jones joined with their former head songwriters Tommy Boyce and Bobby Hart to perform at amusement parks in Summer 1975 audiences (a startling proportion 15 or under) went wild over them."

On July 4, 1976, in the closest thing yet to a Monkees reunion, Tork joined Dolenz, Jones, Boyce and Hart onstage at Disneyland. It had been ten years since *The Monkees* debut and the group once dismissed as prefabricated pap was beginning to see new glimmers of interest. Thanks to disco and punk, the notion that pop music was a con job—a calculated effort to both please and provoke—was gaining traction. If you made the right moves, the theory went, you could subvert the mainstream culture and make money at the very same time.

The Monkees had created a template for pop phenomena that others sought to emulate. One of the most prominent was Malcolm McLaren, a London-based Svengali who was in the process of forming punk's pioneering Sex Pistols. As a self-styled agent provocateur, McLaren tipped his cap in the Monkees direction, even name-checking the group in the film *The Great Rock 'n' Roll Swindle*. Seeking to manufacture shock and outrage among the British public, McLaren viewed the high-level media manipulation of the Monkees as one of his guiding principles. In case anybody missed the point, the Pistols played a snarling cover version of "(I'm Not Your) Steppin' Stone."

McLaren and the Sex Pistols were not alone in their esteem. The Ramones shared a high regard for the Brill Building pop of the Monkees, and when punk became new wave, emerging performers like Elvis Costello and bands like the Feelies and Squeeze pledged their affection as well. Many cited the group as a formative influence. Michael Stipe, lead singer of indie darlings R.E.M., insisted his band would not enter the Rock and Roll Hall of Fame until the Monkees had been inducted (even though R.E.M. did show up it was the thought that counted).

There was no longer a stigma attached to being a Monkees fan. Their influence was undeniable. Every virtual band that came along could trace its origins to the Prefab Four—from Gorillaz to the Banana Splits, everyone aped them. Manufactured confections like the Partridge Family, Menudo, the Runaways, the Spice Girls, New Kids on the Block, the Backstreet Boys, 'N Sync and Big Time Rush kept coming and going.

Interest in the Monkees' music had broadened as well. From power pop to bubblegum, the Monkees sound could be detected in any number of bands. Tributes, in the form of cover songs, emerged. Overnight reality TV sensation Susan Boyle sang "Daydream Believer," and hip-hop pioneers Run-DMC recorded a bizarre version of Nesmith's "Mary, Mary." Groups discovered performing the music of the Monkees was a guaranteed crowd-pleaser. Both U2 and Coldplay slipped Monkees covers into their concert sets.

Chapter Fifty-Four

AT THE END OF THE 1970s, a new trend was emerging in the music business—the use of promotional video clips. As anticipated by *The Monkees*, music was increasingly turning into a visual medium.

Innovative examples of this new medium were being produced by an ex-Monkee living up in Northern California—Michael Nesmith. Having been asked to make a promotional clip for the song "Rio," which had become a moderate hit in the UK, the always-happy-to-experiment Nesmith grabbed all the cutting edge video technology he could get his hands on. The result was a whimsical mini-musical filled with wit and verve, clever montages, light comedy and even a few dance steps (the Papa Nez shuffle?).

The video for "Rio" represented a huge change in fortunes for Nesmith whose prospects for a recording career had dimmed with each passing year. Even diehard fans were slightly flummoxed by the ambitious agenda of Nesmith's multimedia project *The Prison*—the over-the-top concept album required you to read along as you listened.

"Rio" represented both a comeback and a breakthrough. By reaching back in time and borrowing the pacing and invention of old Monkee romps, Nesmith tapped into the emerging potential of promotional video clips. By updating the medium into a more-visually sophisticated kind of entertainment, he stumbled onto something big.

Always an artist in search of his next move, Nesmith happily found his métier. Pacific Arts, the Monterey, California-based indie label he started after RCA dropped his contract, began devoting itself full-time to video production. There was no mistaking Nesmith's conviction that music videos were the future. "You feel like you're in the presence of a power that's bigger than everything you've ever come in contact with," he said of video's potential. "I'm talking about a sociological phenomenon."

Michael Nesmith: Renaissance man, media maven, and a Monkee.

With the groundbreaking "Rio" video clip in rotation on new cable TV networks, Nesmith sensed an opportunity to exploit the new medium, just as Raybert had once grabbed onto the idea of making a rock and roll sitcom. He devised a half hour pilot series called *Popclips* which programmed back-to-back music videos and found a willing sponsor in the new Nickelodeon cable channel. After *Popclips* began airing, Nesmith decided to pitch an even-bigger idea: a 24-hour music video channel.

Improbably, the formula Nesmith devised—a host introducing musical acts—was not dissimilar to what his old nemesis was up to on *Don Kirshner's Rock Concert*. In an irony that was probably lost on both of them, Nesmith and Kirshner were converging on similar ideas at the same time. Apparently the hole in the wall separating the two visionary misfits had been quietly patched up. In a generous gesture, Kirshner consented to air Nesmith's videos for "Rio" and "Cruisin'" on two episodes of Rock Concert.

Dolenz, Jones, Nesmith and Tork in the mid-1980s, just before the MTV-inspired revival.

Nesmith's religious-like fervor as a proselytizer for the power of music videos would prove visionary when Warner Communications decided to transform his idea into a music video network called MTV. Just as Nesmith predicted, the public response to the video channel was overwhelmingly positive. A new musical revolution was underway, thanks in large measure to his foresight. Almost overnight Nesmith's Pacific Arts became a hotbed of video production. Perhaps more importantly to him personally, his standing as an artist soared.

When his mother Bette passed away in 1980 she reportedly left a $25 million inheritance of Liquid Paper profits to her only child. Nesmith was free to pursue his artistic aims without constraints. He found a creative outlet in many of the same avenues the Monkees had pursued—music, comedy, even live performances—but unlike the first go-around he now seemed to be enjoying himself. His follow-up to "Rio" was a song called "Cruisin'" featuring a catchy synthesizer riff (quite similar to Rick James' future hit "Superfreak") and another great video clip. He was on a roll.

In one sense Nesmith was going back and making everything right, proving he could have a good time while satisfying himself artistically and intellectually. As he went from strength to strength, plaudits came his way. In 1981, he was awarded the first Grammy Award for Video of the Year for his self-produced hour-long special *Elephant Parts*, a blend of music and comedy that coalesced all of Nesmith's talents into one entertaining bundle.

It was nice to see Papa Nez lightening up. "There is a common misrepresentation out there that I have some sort of hostile feelings towards the Monkees," he said in 1985. "The only bad feelings I have about the Monkees are the stupid questions I get asked about it—questions of gross misinformation. But as far as the Monkees experience in my life, I had a good time. As far as the Monkees fans, I like them quite a bit."

Regarding his image as the volatile Monkee, Nesmith denied his personality had been purely antagonistic. "I don't think I was an angry young man," he explained. "I was self-conscious, nervous and ambitious. All those things transformed into a severity of countenance."

Seemingly no longer beleaguered by his Monkees past, Nesmith's life came full circle in 1985 when NBC began airing his variety show *Michael Nesmith in Television Parts*. There he was, back on NBC, singing his own songs and acting silly for the camera. Although short-lived, the series was notable for giving early career boosts to unknown performers like Jay Leno, Jerry Seinfeld, and Whoopi Goldberg.

Nesmith had firmly established his credentials as a forward-thinking man of the future who embraced the impending computer revolution without reservation. A good fifteen years before mainstream acceptance he was talking about downloading off the Internet. "I don't see some big technological juggernaut coming through and running roughshod over the values and treasures of mankind," he explained in 1985. "What is happening is that we're getting tools, which enhance our own powers, so the power of the individual is just becoming larger and more enhanced."

From outward appearances it seemed Papa Nez's Monkees persona was now well behind him. But in a bittersweet irony, MTV, the network he had for all practical purposes invented, was about to turn his carefully-groomed public image as a Renaissance Man into something far more familiar to mainstream audiences and there was nothing he could do about it.

Chapter Fifty-Five

AS 1985 WOUND DOWN, DAVY JONES was playing Jesus in a British production of *Godspell*, Peter Tork was performing in small East Coast clubs with his band The Peter Tork Project, Micky Dolenz was producing and directing British television shows, and Michael Nesmith was working on a variety show for NBC.

1986 would mark the 20th anniversary of *The Monkees* series debut. The significance of the anniversary had not been lost on Bert Schneider. For years, Schneider had been plotting a stateside Monkees revival, shrewdly realizing a full-scale comeback required the TV series re-appearing on cable television. After negotiations with several cable channels, the successor-in-interest of the Monkees brand name struck a deal with the hottest network of all, MTV.

The masterstroke was Schneider convincing MTV to abandon their regular music video format on February 23, 1986 to air a 22 1/2-hour marathon of all 58 episodes of *The Monkees*. Not only did the marathon attract the largest rating in MTV history, it kicked-off a full-scale revival of Monkeemania.

By luck or fate, a project that had always been ahead of its time had found its moment. MTV, in the 1980s, was a cultural phenomenon, elevating video-savvy performers like Michael Jackson and Madonna (who once admitted a childhood crush on Micky Dolenz) to heavy rotation superstardom where they shared airtime with only-in-the-'80s trifles like Wang Chung and A Flock of Seagulls.

For the Monkees, lightning had struck again. In 1966, the group arrived with a brilliantly packaged response to a genuine phenomenon, the Beatles. In 1986, they returned to a culture awash in nostalgia and aching for non-programmed, pre-digitized fun. Ironically, 20 years later, the Monkees could authentically deliver the goods.

"The fans yet-to-be were all there," Schneider explained in 1988. "They were ready, but you can't do anything without the exposure." He added, "Why shouldn't it work again? The shows were funny, the songs were good and the guys were

That was then, this is now. Dolenz, Jones and Tork became the top concert attraction of 1986.

talented. Something of quality has the capacity to transcend the immediate culture. Of course I'm prejudiced."

Most of MTV's viewers had never heard of the Monkees but they liked what they saw and were already demanding more. Programmers at MTV, more than happy to comply, began running daily episodes of *The Monkees* along with *Monkee Minutes* that kept viewers up-to-date on the group's evolving plans.

Fortuitously, a tour was already in the works. Promoter David Fishof, whose offices were one floor below the headquarters of MTV, had been plotting the Monkees return to the stage. The erstwhile sports agent, a near-doppelgänger of Don Kirshner, discovered tapping into Baby Boomer nostalgia paid off handsomely. His 1985 "Happy Together" tour with the Turtles had drawn large audiences. Realizing the Monkees could easily duplicate this feat, he tracked down Tork, who embraced the idea during a backstage visit to a Turtles show.

According to Tork, Fishof did not entirely grasp what he was latching onto with the Monkees. "David Fishof didn't know about the Monkees," he claimed. "He was cloistered away in some Orthodox household and didn't even know about the Monkees, barely heard about it. Didn't watch television, didn't listen to pop music. So he didn't know what he had. He was ready to put us in 500-seat clubs until it exploded on him and then we were playing to 6,000 and 10,000."

Fishof and Tork flew across the Atlantic Ocean to persuade Jones and Dolenz to reunite and cash in. Jones was eager for the opportunity. He was a Monkee, first and last, and proud of it. "I'm not stuck with it," he said in a 1984 interview. "I feel it's up to me to be responsible to the people that inquire. When these little kids ask me, 'You weren't in the Monkees, were you?' you can't say 'Piss off, I don't want to talk about the Monkees.'"

Ever-ready for another round of adoration, Jones had toured Japan steadily for years, singing the old hits and soaking up the screams. With Fishof's tour looming, Tork joined him for a warm-up tour of Australia in February 1986.

Dolenz refused to join them at first. Having finally established himself as something other than an ex-Monkee by directing in the UK, Dolenz was wary of slipping the albatross back around his neck. After moving to London to co-star with Jones in the theatrical adaptation of Harry Nilsson's *The Point*, Dolenz had cultivated a reputation for directing quality children's television programs. He remarried, had kids, and said good-bye to the rock and roll life that nearly consumed him. "I just didn't have the desire," Dolenz said of his semi-retirement from the stage. "I had been doing it for so long, 20 years or more by the end of the Monkees, that I had no desire to be an actor or a singer anymore."

There was another obstacle—a rift with Jones that had yet to be resolved—that factored in Dolenz's reluctance to reform. The two hadn't spoken in years.

But it was tempting, too. The dead Frankenstein had been jolted back to life. MTV had sealed the group's reputation and confirmed its legacy, conferring credibility that was a long time coming. "It was nice to have a confirmation that there was something valid there," Dolenz later recalled, "that the show had stood up after all those years; you could still watch it and get something out of it."

How could he pass it up? The opportunity was too good. Dolenz signed on.

Three Monkees did not make a true reunion, however. The missing Monkee, Nesmith, was, from the start, a highly unlikely candidate for a valedictory tour. Contrary to popular belief, he did consider it. "Peter called me up and asked me if I would do it," Nesmith later recounted, "and I told him yes, I would do it and it sounded like fun but that I had a very small purse of time."

Rafelson and Schneider happily reunited with the four chosen ones backstage at the Greek Theatre.

When push came to shove, Nesmith refused to commit. "The time got closer and it became more and more clear that this thing was going to be popular and they began adding dates—it had gone from four or five dates to over 200. I was in the middle of filming a motion picture, *Square Dance*. I was running a business and starting up another motion picture, *Tapeheads*. The idea that I could go out and take out six to eight months was just not possible."

Chapter Fifty-Six

WITH THREE MONKEES IN HIS CORNER, Fishof took the last necessary step to embark on a tour. He licensed the Monkees name and the trademark guitar logo from Columbia Pictures for the entire year of 1986. Bizarre as it seemed, the individual members still had to get permission to use the word "Monkees" for promotional purposes. The Coca-Cola Company, which owned Columbia Pictures at the time, owned the license. Remarkably, Fishof landed the rights for a paltry $3500. "Boy did he luck out," said Tork of Fishof, adding ruefully, "Boy, did I ever make myself a terrible deal on that process."

In the meantime, everything looked rosy for Monkeemania Mach II. Responding to the astronomical ratings, MTV continued airing daily episodes of *The Monkees*.

With a tour in the works and the series back on nationwide TV, one element remained in doubt and it was the same old problem: music. Fortunately, the legacy of the Monkees' original recordings was in capable hands; Rhino Records, a reissue-oriented label out of Santa Monica, California, had presciently licensed the entire catalog. The reformed Monkees could not rely on old material alone, however, so Tork and Dolenz, without Jones' blessing, rushed into the studio with producer Michael Lloyd to create three new tracks for Arista Records' best-of compilation called *Then & Now...The Best of the Monkees*.

Jones was far from happy about this development. "I'm very angry about Arista coming in and cashing in on our project," he told an interviewer. "They have no interest in the Monkees' career beyond this year; they just want to sell old records. And I think Micky and Peter were trapped into that Arista way of thinking."

Curiously, and more than a little ironically, one of Jones' objections was the fact that Dolenz and Tork had abdicated creative control over the music, essentially allowing themselves to be given the same roles they had played on the first Monkees recordings. "We're forty-year-old guys and up," Jones carped. "We can't be holding our blankets and sucking our thumbs anymore. We've got to experiment."

In the creative sense, Jones was right—the three tracks that emerged from the sessions were a mixed bag. The best of the bunch was the upbeat single, "That Was Then, This is Now," a lightweight pop confection originally recorded by the Mosquitos. Boasting a symbolic title that aptly summed up their situation, the catchy single stunned music industry insiders by becoming a Top 20 hit—the first by the Monkees in over 18 years. The second track, "Anytime, Anyplace, Anywhere," was noteworthy for reuniting the Monkee duo with songwriter Bobby Hart, who co-wrote it. The third and last track was dreadful—a leaden cover of the old anti-drug anthem, "Kicks," written by Barry Mann and Cynthia Weil.

Whether it was fair to include these songs on a greatest hits package or not, and Jones argued bitterly that it was not, *Then and Now...The Best of the Monkees* went on to sell over a million copies. Was Jones still smarting from being unceremoniously dumped by Arista in the mid-'70s? He didn't say. But his petulance was clearly on display. Every time "That Was Then, This is Now" was performed, Jones would mysteriously disappear from the stage.

Old resentments still lingered, simmering beneath the surface of their upbeat public profile. Fans had no idea; in fact, they were totally smitten. For years, a "paisley revival" had been brewing; a castrated and distinctly '80s version of the '60s. The new motto, in the Reagan Age of "Just Say No" was pass the fashion, hold the ammo. This revival stressed the benign side of the '60s psychedelic styles and music while casting aside its more threatening aspects, drugs and civil disobedience. The biggest new musical act of 1986 was the Bangles, who perfectly bridged the gap of '60s style and '80s sensibilities. Was it any surprise the Bangles were huge Monkees fans?

Chapter Fifty-Seven

IF INTEGRITY HAD TO TAKE A BACK SEAT TO PROFITS, as Jones contested, there was hardly time to have a fist fight over it—it was time to get ready to play. In early May, 1986, Dolenz, Tork and Jones convened at Kiamesha Lake in New York's Catskill Mountains to choreograph and rehearse their impending 100-city tour. Before kicking off the festivities, the trio held a press conference at the Hard Rock Café in New York City. No longer the fresh-scrubbed faces of their televised youth, they displayed quick wit and nervous energy as photographers snapped away. When asked why they were re-grouping, all three replied in unison, "money!"

Nesmith's absence was noted but the missing Monkee provided a look-alike, life-size blow-up replica of himself to deflect attention. The resulting wisecracks neatly sidestepped the question—how legitimate was a reunion of the Monkees without the guy in the wool hat?

When the tour opened at the Tropicana Hotel in Atlantic City on May 30, 1986, all doubts were laid to rest. A sold-out crowd showered their love on the act. They did not care whether Nesmith was there or not. "The fact that Michael Nesmith opted out of this reunion tour," *Variety* wrote in their review of the show, "seemed to have had little effect on the audience or on the concert itself. Remaining members, Micky Dolenz, David Jones and Peter Tork, sounded just fine without him, coming through with a show that was lively."

For critics of the band it was time to swallow hard—the Monkees were getting rave reviews. "The Monkees are a legitimate rock and roll band," wrote *USA Today*. "They're also entertaining, something that can't be said about some of their '80s counterparts. The Monkees are a hard act to follow."

Opening acts on the tour included '60s pop cohorts Herman's Hermits, Gary Puckett and The Union Gap, and the Grass Roots. None could compete with the slick, Vegas-like revue staged by the Monkees. The show featured a non-stop barrage of costume changes and comic shtick. All of the Monkees' major hits were included but the real knock-out punches were Dolenz's sprightly renditions of "She," "Goin' Down," "Randy Scouse Git," and "No Time." Onstage, Dolenz had lost nothing—his voice was strong and his stage presence was commanding.

An air of recaptured glory hung over the proceedings. A sing-along version of "Shades of Gray" was the highlight, provoking a sea of arm-swaying and lighter-waving, as well as a few misty eyes. A good percentage of the audience was too young to understand the song's nostalgic lure. According to music market researchers at *American Demographics*, half were under 18. This uncommon mix of parents and their kids was a rare commodity at rock concerts at the time.

For Fishof, the young demographics and positive reviews were great news. His showcase act was the hottest ticket of the summer. Originally booked as a short run of small amphitheaters, the tour began playing larger capacity arenas and stadiums. Concert attendees were spending generously at the merchandising stands. Monkeemania had stormed back with a vengeance.

Chapter Fifty-Eight

WHAT HAD BEGUN AS A SIX-WEEK QUICKIE turned into a seven-month behemoth, the top-grossing tour of the year. "The '86 reunion was amazing," Dolenz later recalled. "It wasn't until 1986 that I realized what an impact the Monkees had on the cultural landscape of American pop culture."

The Monkees were often at a loss to explain their across-the-board acceptance. Even the member with the greatest distance, Nesmith, was stumped. "It still remains as mysterious to me as it was 20 years ago as to just exactly why this thing has such sizzle to it," Nesmith said in 1988. "There is something that people who like it are getting from it and there is something that the four of us on the television screen were putting out that's just working on some level that's completely hidden to me. But it was working on a level that was completely hidden to me 20 years ago and long before it gained public acceptance. I understood it was working, I just didn't know why—still don't."

Three weeks into the tour, curiosity got the best of Nesmith. On June 22, 1986, disguised in a "fat suit" and in the company of actress Winona Ryder, he sat with the fans at Arlington Stadium in Texas watching his former bandmates perform.

"There were several things that went through my mind, but none of them were peculiar or odd or unnerving," said Nesmith. "The first thing that went through my mind was Micky was really good and it was too bad that he was behind the drums. He should have been the front man all along. The second thing was that I wished that we could have existed at a time where we could have performed with a band like they were doing now. It would have taken such a great load off of us and enabled us to give the kind of show that the guys ultimately put together. And the third was sitting up in the stands with the fans and watching the thing, I realized there was an extraordinary amount of love that was exchanged. It was a real genuine experience. There was a real appreciation from the fans and there was a real return from the guys to the fans. It was good, high-energy, first-rate concert giving."

On the set of "Heart and Soul," the video MTV refused to play.

Backstage, Nesmith reunited with Dolenz, Jones and Tork after the concert. It was the first time in 10 years they had all been in the same room. Amidst the hugs and congratulatory toasts, plans were solidified for Nesmith to drop by at a future concert. Not all members were bowled over by that prospect. "I didn't particularly think that it was a great idea," an increasingly cantankerous-sounding Jones told *CREEM* magazine. "We've got a set show. There's three of us and we're on a sold-out tour. And you just really don't need anyone coming and taking the limelight."

The model of discretion in the past, Jones had become an effusive interviewee, apt to say whatever was on his mind. Now sporting a giant mullet, the hairdo du jour, he was a loose cannon in an otherwise well-oiled media assault.

As the event approached, Jones softened his stance and the date was set for a full reunion on September 7, 1986. Five days before the official 20th anniversary of *The Monkees* debut, the four former pop idols shared a stage at the Greek Theatre in Los Angeles for what might have been the briefest reunion in pop history. At the end of the concert Nesmith strolled onstage for the encore. A deafening roar greeted him. After a group hug, the foursome charged through two of their classic numbers—"Listen to the Band" and "Pleasant Valley Sunday." At the conclusion, the four smiling performers locked arms around each other's shoulders and "Monkee walked" off the stage. The improbable comeback was complete.

Bob Rafelson and Bert Schneider joined the festivities backstage where the mood was ebullient. "A great moment—really amazing," Dolenz told TV cameras. Only Jones seemed to be smarting with resentment. "Mike would have to obviously do a few work-outs in the gym if he wanted to come back on again. He's 20 years older and a lot fatter," he snidely cracked. When pressed, Jones finally did admit it was "nice" having him onstage.

Later, in a better mood, Jones recalled "the highlight of the whole tour was when Mike walked on the stage at the Greek Theatre. That, to me, was the highlight. That was the Monkees. Micky Dolenz, Mike Nesmith, Peter Tork and Davy Jones. Those are the Monkees."

In the opinion of a few observers, that is where the Monkees revival should have ended—at the top of the showbiz heap, gleefully thumbing their noses at the naysayers and counting their piles of cash. The trio had plenty of plans for 1987 however: more tours, and, above all, more money.

Chapter Fifty-Nine

BUZZ ABOUT THE GROUP BEGAN TO DISSIPATE after the Greek Theatre reunion, but Monkees business was far from over. MTV continued to milk the phenomenon for all it was worth. All three Monkees were invited to appear as guest VJs. The 22 ½ hour marathon was re-aired. A half-hour documentary entitled, *I Was a Teenage Monkee* went into rotation. Video cassettes were released of the original TV series, which had returned to syndication in nearly 100 markets.

Perhaps the most extraordinary example of their comeback's commercial impact was having seven albums charting on *Billboard* at the same time—Arista's *Then and Now* package, the original first five LPs and, most incredible of all, *Changes*, the Dolenz/Jones knock-off that didn't even dent the charts in its original 1970 release.

After selling two million records of the original LPs, Rhino Records began an exhaustive *Missing Links* reissue campaign which eventually exhumed almost all of the group's unreleased recordings. Of particular interest was the lost B-side from 1967, "All of Your Toys." Even "Lady's Baby," the so-called "most expensive song ever produced," was released from the vaults.

Far less interesting, and in a career sense far more disastrous, was *Pool It!*, an anemic collection of new Monkees tracks whose glossy '80s production techniques instantly dated it. Rush-released for their impending tour, *Pool It!* boasted a deeply disturbing cover shot of three shirtless Monkees wading in a swimming pool. The music, itself, was a disappointment on every level. Even the album's executive producer, the group's long-time supporter, Harold Bronson, admitted the recordings had not met his expectations. "I envisioned the old Monkees records updated and made contemporary," Bronson explained, "but I think their songs were not as good as 20 years ago. In all fairness, most hit records aren't as good as they were 20 years ago. Still, there wasn't enough of the Monkees personality in them."

There was a reason they lacked personality. In an act of mutual petulance, so reminiscent of the past, all three Monkees refused to sing on each other's tracks. The result was a disjointed album of bland, half-baked, practically anonymous pop music.

Although a few cuts, including the single "Heart and Soul" were tolerable, others were simply throwaways. Jones' contribution, "She's Movin' In With Rico," deserved special recognition in the all-time Monkee clunker department.

Chapter Sixty

IF 1986 HAD BEEN ANALOGOUS to the peak years of Monkeemania (1966-67), then 1987 was reminiscent of the downfall (1968-69). Once again, the spontaneous popularity of the project was gradually replaced by a more calculated attempt to crank out product and cash in. The group's harmony dissolved into personal enmity and ego clashes, creative impulses and sound judgment were sacrificed in favor of cynical gestures. Most importantly, a great wave of popularity dissipated into a much smaller cult of faithful followers. And, of course, what would a Monkees comeback be without a slew of lawsuits in its wake?

The warning signs were evident in the first weeks of 1987. Promoter Fishof, who was now doubling as the Monkees' manager, scheduled a live performance by the band at an MTV Super Bowl event. But the heavily publicized appearance was canceled at the last second when Jones announced he'd left the country for a family reunion.

MTV executives were fuming and retribution was right around the corner. The Monkees' video for their single "Heart and Soul" was nowhere to be seen. Lee Masters, the president of MTV, denied the group had been blacklisted. "We aren't playing the clip because we just don't feel the band works for us anymore," Masters told the *Los Angeles Times*. "They just don't have any legs. The whole phenomenon was a novelty—and for us, it's over."

Without the promotional push of MTV, "Heart and Soul" stalled on the charts. The shallow "Pool It!" barely climbed into the Hot 100. Meanwhile, attendance on their 1987 tour was trending downward. That was a pity because the show was a multimedia tour de force with film footage, props, costume changes, comedy routines and a set modeled on *The Monkees* TV show. Despite having Weird Al Yankovic, the king of novelty songs, as their opening act, ticket sales were average at best, and by tour's end they found themselves performing to half-empty houses. The only thing missing was Sam and the Goodtimers.

The second wave of Monkeemania had run out of steam and so had the Monkees. "When you're 20 years old, nothing much bothers you," an exhausted Dolenz conceded to the *San Francisco Chronicle*. "These days, the traveling can really wear you down."

Years later Dolenz was more succinct in recalling his memories of the tour. "I'm living out of a bus; it's ruining my family and destroyed my marriage. Peter and David and I are at each other's throats," he remembered, adding with a mischievous grin, "but I made a shitload of money."

They had played to 1,500,000 fans over the span of two years, a spectacular achievement. But what about the future? Would they ever escape the now-you-see-us-now-you-don't world of the oldies circuit?

1988 brought the answers. Plans for a Broadway play, a feature-length movie and a Christmas album never materialized, the possibility of a new Monkee record seemed remote at best, their former manager Fishof was suing them for uncollected commissions and, despite a successful tour of Australia, the group's camaraderie had spiraled downward.

No longer reticent to air his grievances in public, Jones went on a rampage, dishing dirt about his fellow Monkees. "They take themselves too seriously, I believe," Jones railed to *16 Magazine*. "From the very beginning, Peter didn't think he could do his own thing and still be on the Monkees shows."

Jones saved his venom for Dolenz. "We were never great friends off the screen or personally, but we work well together. You know, *The Sunshine Boys*. I mean, that would be an incredibly perfect show for Micky Dolenz and I to do, 'cause really we hate each other."

As usual, as the mania decreased, the revelations increased. Among the documents issued by Fishof in his lawsuit against Dolenz, Jones and Tork were allegations that Jones had caused irreparable harm to the group's relationship with MTV. "When MTV has asked Davy to be a guest VJ, he made an outlandish request for $5,000 to appear when even major acts eagerly appear for free," Fishof told the *New York Post*. "When he finally agreed to guest VJ he came in for work drunk."

The reason Jones left the stage during "That Was Then, This is Now" was also revealed. Since he made no money off it, he refused to perform it.

Chapter Sixty-One

HAVING RE-ESTABLISHED THEIR BRAND IDENTITY as performers, Dolenz, Jones and Tork fielded offers for roles on TV and theatrical productions. Jobs previously non-existent were now coming their way. Nesmith also benefited from the renewed interest. By showing up at the Greek Theater, he not only regained the good will of Monkees fans but revised his media image as the angry Monkee who was now above it all. Thanks to his many songwriting credits, Nesmith also reaped significant financial rewards. He even entertained the idea of reuniting with his erstwhile bandmates. "I think it would be fun, if the guys wanted to, to go out and do four or five dates a year…and given enough advance notice, I could square away the time to do that," said Nesmith.

On July 9, 1989, the Monkees were awarded a star on Hollywood Boulevard's Walk of Fame. The day before the ceremony, Nesmith joined the trio for a set at the Universal Amphitheater in Los Angeles. He performed two solo hits, "Joanne" and "Cruisin'," and played along good-naturedly when Jones made jokes at his expense onstage. "Where have you been?" asked Jones as the missing Monkee sauntered onstage. "I've been looking for my hat," was Nesmith's crowd-pleasing reaction.

Backstage the celebratory spirit was not matched by Jones, disgruntled as usual about being upstaged by Nesmith's appearance. He also complained publicly and loudly that the group had not rehearsed properly. The bitchiness did not end there. He moaned about Dolenz and Tork pursuing pet projects while his solo career atrophied.

Money was another issue. Forever frustrated by any perceived financial disparity, Jones read the riot act to anyone who cared to listen. Furious the group was still paying royalties to use the Monkees name on tour, he told the *San Francisco Chronicle*, "It's a criminal shame. I think we've earned the right to use that name."

On this latter issue Jones certainly had a point. Anybody who could afford licensing rights could, in essence, become the Monkees. In 1987, the name was licensed to producer Steve Blauner, the former partner third in Rafelson and

Nesmith joined forces for *Justus*. The highly improbable reunion ended acrimoniously.

Schneider's BBS Productions. Blauner had the woefully misbegotten idea of creating the "New Monkees." With the backing of Columbia Pictures, he held open auditions attracting 3,000 hopefuls, including Nesmith's son Jason.

So why did Dino Kovas, Jared Chandler, Marty Ross and Larry Saltis—the four young men who won the roles—fail to become the old Davy, Micky, Peter and Mike? The Monkee-faithful simply found the idea repugnant. Predictably and mercifully, the New Monkees died a quick death. But the very fact it had gotten beyond the initial stage of development made it clear how executives in charge of the Monkees' trademark viewed the original members as disposable non-entities.

The arrogance and avarice outraged Bert Schneider. "Movie companies are no longer movie companies," Schneider complained. "They are divisions of larger entities, managed by different kinds of people whose energies are focused elsewhere, not in show business. This is particularly true to the Monkees situation. Never has there been an act whose future is always in the hands of someone else. When you get up to the level of Coca-Cola, it [the Monkees] just falls through the cracks. It doesn't get watered like orchids need to be."

Never shy when it came to litigation, Schneider sued Columbia Pictures, claiming the Monkees' comeback had been botched. After a protracted dispute he and Rafelson won back the licensing rights. In their last act as Raybert, they turned around and sold those rights to Rhino Records for $4 million, setting the stage for one last chapter in the group's unlikely, but surprisingly durable, second life.

Chapter Sixty-Two

THE LEGACY OF THE MONKEES seemed complete, but the tours went on and on and on. As always, the three remaining Monkees were willing to mask private fissures with public fraternity, as long as the offers kept rolling in. In 1988, they toured Australia, in 1989, the United Kingdom. Dates in Japan and Europe kept the trio busy, even as ticket sales in the United Sates slumped.

"Fourth Monkee" Michael Nesmith maintained his typical distance from the fray. "It would be fun to play the songs, it would be fun to be onstage, it would be fun to see the fans, it would be fun to be one of the Monkees," he said with a chuckle in 1988. "But it's probably not going to happen."

For the first half of the 1990s it seemed unlikely that any full-scale reunion would ever occur. Minus Nesmith, the trio briefly reunited in 1995 to make cameo appearances in *The Brady Bunch Movie*, a satirical update of the '70s sitcom. A highlight of the movie found Jones reprising the song "Girl" at Marcia's prom, only this time it was middle-aged mothers who did the swooning.

By the mid-'90s, all four of the ex-Monkees were well into middle age. Except for Jones, who looked suspiciously young and tanned, the skinny guys riding shotgun in the Monkeemobile were nowhere to be seen. Somewhat disconcertingly, cute Monkee Micky—"old pancake face" as Jones endearingly dubbed him— began to look like former Vice-President Hubert Humphrey. To hide his balding pate, Dolenz donned a series of stylish hats.

The ex-Monkees still shared many of the same predicaments—all had been married, divorced, and later remarried and then divorced again—but they had grown apart as people. Still, money has a way of patching up differences and it remained a motivating factor. There was alimony, college tuitions and other expenses associated with being a pop star. Jones spoke of his expensive "horse habit," the one that came with his purchase of a farm in western Pennsylvania.

In the midst of the deadly-earnest grunge era, the Monkees were out of sync with the times. But in early 1995 the project received a much-needed shot of adrenaline with a presentation of platinum certification awards by Rhino Records president Harold Bronson. Intriguingly, Nesmith was on hand for the event, and hinted he might participate in 30th anniversary projects the following year.

Back on the circuit for the first time in seven years, the trio of Jones, Dolenz and Tork were on the upswing, pulling in the crowds and getting good notices. A reviewer in the *Hollywood Reporter* claimed the show was "a refreshing, nostalgic blast of good clean family fun for the angst-ridden '90s." Thanks to a solid promotional push from Rhino Records, the Monkees were proving they still had legs.

For Nesmith, they were trying times. His media company, Pacific Arts, had declared bankruptcy after PBS filed a $2.3 million lawsuit against the company for unpaid video distribution commissions. Nesmith was counter-suing PBS for $35 million in damages.

The traumatic series of events had an unexpected side effect: for the first time in a long time, Nesmith was ready to reunite with the act he had studiously avoided. News leaked that he had been on an all-original Monkees album with Dolenz, Jones and Tork. Not only that—a TV special was being planned and a reunion tour seemed likely.

Chapter Sixty-Three

HAVING NESMITH ONBOARD, certainly an exciting prospect for any longtime Monkee fan, did leave some scratching their heads. Under what circumstances had the reluctant warrior agreed to reunite? The logical assumption was money, given Nesmith's imperiled fortune and the PBS lawsuit.

It is also possible Nesmith wanted to come full circle and make peace with the project that had dominated his adult life. "It's always great to walk on stage and have the place go up in smoke," he confessed after the 1986 reunion at the Greek Theatre. "It's not the sort of thing that performers tend to avoid. And I enjoyed it. It made me really want to go out and play."

Nesmith pledged to make a full-time effort to the reunion. There would be records, videos, a TV special, touring, and the possibility of doing a movie. "It is current; it is of its time right now," Nesmith said of the Monkees. "The values that have been brought forward, the new fans and the old fans, are all connecting."

Always commitment-adverse, he was vague when it came to long-term plans. "So far what we've done is make a record," Nesmith informed *Variety*. "From there I don't have any idea where it will go. It's like having a great old car in the garage that you take out on the weekends and suddenly it dawns on you that 'Wow, I can drive this thing from New York to Los Angeles!'"

Tork was more direct. "We're all still alive, still getting along, and why not try it out?" he told an interviewer.

The quartet's first creative collaboration in over 25 years was the album *Justus*. The punning title, and the fact the group played every note and used only original songs, was a statement of intent. Track one was a gritty reprise of "Circle Sky." Were they reasserting their garage band credentials or was Nesmith making amends for leaving the electrifying live version off the soundtrack of *Head*? Either way it was a curious choice.

The highlight of the set was a heartfelt Dolenz and Jones duet called

"You and I," a rare collaboration between the two "Sunshine Boys." The lightweight middle-of-the-road pop song sat uneasily alongside "Admiral Mike," Nesmith's vitriolic diatribe against the media. Featuring a blunt edge rarely heard on a Monkees record (sample lines: "you're selling ads you slimy toads," "go back to hell you giddy fools,") the song was a peculiarity. Unwisely, vocal duties had been handled by Dolenz, whose genial personality undermined the song's urgency.

The same could be said of the rest of *Justus*. It was pleasant, mid-tempo rock that possessed moments of charm but lacked the urgency and passion of its predecessor, *Headquarters*. Reviews were middling. The *Los Angeles Times* found the album a "fitting coda" and felt the band sounded "remarkably spry." *Entertainment Weekly* wasn't as enthusiastic. "Harmonizing woozily like weathered sailors" was reviewer David Browne's description, who knocked Nesmith's "Admiral Mike" as "bad psychedelic rock."

The review hit a raw nerve with Nesmith. Firing back on the Internet, Nesmith wrote, "bad reviews are part of the territory and don't bother me (but) mindless digs and blanket indictments are usually someone carrying on something they have heard or have been taught to think. It is correctable with a swift, strong, intelligent response."

To prove his point, Nesmith also posted a letter written to *Entertainment Weekly* in which he assailed Browne's "shallow review" as "half-witted journalism, combined with poor writing skills and even less insight." Unsurprisingly, the letter was never printed.

Nesmith's reaction revealed a certain prickly pride and a sense of resignation. "I realize that if I were ever fortunate to win the Nobel Peace Prize," he told interviewers, "it will be reported that, 'Monkee Mike Nesmith Won the Nobel Peace Price.'"

To boost their public profile and provide *Justus* with a promotional push, the self-contained quartet reunited to perform a brief set on November 22, 1996. News crews from CNN, CBS, ABC and Fox gathered at Billboard Live in Hollywood to witness the event. The group was in fine form. Dolenz's forceful drumming was better than ever, Nesmith's guitar stomped and he even took a rare solo on "Regional Girl," Tork's rumbling bass provided a fat bottom and the tambourine-banging Jones looked content to shake and shimmy.

In a behind-the-scenes interview, a surprisingly-relaxed Nesmith expressed nothing but good feelings towards his former cast members. "The miracle is that when the four of us get together the Monkees come alive. Well, that's a lot of fun."

This rosy image is the one that Nesmith retained. "It was a very important and happy time of my life," he said of his Monkees tenure, "so I'm comfortable with it in whatever incarnation."

Chapter Sixty-Four

MORE FUN WAS BEING PROMISED. The group reconvened in January 1997 to spend a week filming a one-hour TV special entitled *Hey, Hey, It's the Monkees*. The show featured a potentially-clever comic twist: the Monkees were living in a time warp, still making the old TV show and living in the same beach house.

Nesmith had written and directed the special. On Internet message boards, he bragged about "wonderful Monkee moments" but when the show aired on ABC on February 17, 1997, the sight of middle-aged men dressed in shorts making sophomoric jokes about bodily fluids betrayed a total lack of group chemistry. The only such moment occurred in an updated medley of greatest hits, a delightful, well-edited segment that deftly combined old and new footage. But when the music ended, it was back to cringe time.

Despite fans' efforts to put a positive spin on it, the TV special was a dispiriting let-down. The low ratings reflected the public's lack of interest in the aging franchise. ABC came in dead last for the timeslot, which was bad news for a motion picture in the works. From there, things went rapidly downhill. Dolenz's assertion—that there "never was a brand consensus about anything"—was becoming painfully clear to everyone involved.

The breaking point would occur on the *Justus* tour. Trouble was already brewing in the ranks before the 10-stop jaunt in England, Scotland and Ireland got underway. Nesmith had flown in on a private jet and had booked himself in separate hotels.

A scoop-hungry press corps grilled the group at a press conference in London. "We're ferociously good," Tork announced, but his enthusiasm was undermined by Dolenz's admission that, creatively, it had all been done before. "There are a lot of people who have tried to catch lightning in the bottle again—it's a very tough job to do and nobody has been successful," he confessed.

Jones had money on his mind. Pointing out his homes in England and the USA,

The "Sunshine Boys" were initially buddies but their intense rivalry lead to deep divisions.

plus alimony and horses to feed, he gleefully announced "it's just wonderful to be making money, and have fun. Ah…money, pleasure, the orgasmic rush of being a heartthrob again!"

A sullen-looking Nesmith would not elaborate his motivations. "I just wanted to get back to playing," he told reporters. Asked whether the tour was a comeback, an irritated Nesmith lashed out. "Comeback? I have absolutely no intention of making a comeback," he barked. "We've had the '60s. Been there, done that." He then tersely added, "We have nothing to vindicate. You either get it or you don't."

When the tour opened in Newcastle, England on March 7, 1997, critics unleashed their poisoned pens. A review in the *Telegraph* typified the reaction. Noting the half-empty hall, the reviewer felt the show had a "ramshackle, disjointed air," adding "I found the sight of four middle-aged men playing songs that once encapsulated youth and freshness strange and distressing."

From all outward appearances Nesmith agreed with the critics. He objected to Jones' corny solo turn which found him donning a wig to impersonate Elvis Presley. It was an embarrassment. "There was little left of the public mandate so it was difficult for me," Nesmith said in 2009. When asked if it was the bookend of his Monkees' career, Nesmith was more specific: "it was the final chapter."

It was a sad chapter indeed. As the tour trudged on, reviews grew more and more vituperative. "Many moments of toe-curling embarrassment," read a review of one of the group's two shows at London's Wembley Arena. The *London Times* reported a "mood of desperately forced frivolity" by "participants clearly of an age to know better," concluding "the real sadness was that, whatever the aesthetic considerations, the show as a whole had failed to entertain."

Despite the critical lashing, an American tour by all four Monkees had been booked. Back in the States, however, Nesmith disappeared from view. Inquiries from the other Monkees went unanswered. Nesmith's silence spoke volumes.

Chapter Sixty-Five

DESPITE THE ANIMOSITY BEHIND THE SCENES, there was a full-length motion picture in the planning stages with a targeted 1998 production date and Papa Nez was still on board. It was based on Nesmith's screenplay, a surrealistic comedy with a sci-fi twist. "We have begun work on the movie which should be out next year," Nesmith told an Internet message board.

No movie materialized. Jones made sure of that. Asking for an outlandish fee during contract negotiations, his demands were the deal breaker—a second Monkee movie would not be produced.

Jones pointed to Nesmith's mercurial behavior as the root cause of the problems. "He made a new album with us. He toured Great Britain with us. Then all of a sudden, he's not here. Later, I hear rumors he's writing a script for our next movie. Oh, really? That's bloody news to me," Jones told the *Los Angeles Times* with characteristic peevishness. "He's always been this aloof, inaccessible person...the fourth part of the jigsaw puzzle that never quite fit in."

But whether or not the Monkees were bosom buddies had always been commercially immaterial. In the world of pop music, timing was everything. Such was the case of the Dolenz, Jones and Tork reunion tour of 2001, which received an unexpected boost when the group's signature song, "I'm a Believer," made a high-profile appearance in the blockbuster animated movie *Shrek* (the version heard in the film was a cover by the lounge-pop group Smash Mouth).

Thanks to the popularity of *Shrek*, interest in Monkees music had once again awakened. But once again the group was in the process of breaking up. Fed up with the pettiness and squabbling, Tork gave notice to Dolenz and Jones—he was quitting the Monkees and this time it was for good.

"I'm a recovering alcoholic," Tork told the press, "and haven't had a drink in several years. I'm not against people drinking—just when they get mean and abusive. I went on the anniversary tour with the agreement that I didn't have to put

up with drinking and difficult behavior offstage."

Like the end of most relationships, the final stages of disentanglement were messy. Before Tork could play his final commitments he was summarily fired for "irreconcilable differences." The trio's final performance occurred at the Sun Theater in Anaheim, California on August 31, 2001. The show was professionally recorded and would later be made available for release.

For the second time, Tork was walking away from the Monkees. This time, however, no gold watch awaited him, only a nasty parting shot from Dolenz, "Once a quitter, always a quitter."

Unlike the old days, when handlers made sure bad press never reached the fans, the dirty laundry between the band's members was now being aired. To those who had worked with them this development was no surprise. "The Monkees never got along," noted David Fishof, who was promoting the 2001 tour. "They didn't get along in the 1960s and they didn't keep in touch. From the beginning of the reunion in 1985, they bickered and fought and sabotaged each other."

Despite the bitterness, there was no question in the mind of Bert Schneider that the three Monkees, for better or worse, needed each other. "They are symbiotically good as performers," Schneider contended. "They feed off each other. The fact of the matter is they were never as good alone as they are together; otherwise they would have had successful performing careers on their own."

This was a rueful fact that the four ex-Monkees had a hard time escaping. As Jones succinctly put it, "The Monkees are like the mafia. You're in for life. Nobody gets out."

Chapter Sixty-Six

LAST MONKEE STANDING. That was the name of the game now that Tork was gone. Dolenz and Jones found themselves playing to sparse crowds. The demographics of a Monkees concert were now heavily skewed towards middle-aged female fans. When Dolenz joked, "they don't throw underwear anymore, they throw Depends," it revealed a hidden truth. Singing "we're the young generation" was getting harder to do with a straight face.

Perhaps as a sign of desperation, the stage patter and choreography grew looser as the final Monkee tour ground to a halt. Dolenz adlibbed lines about "gin and Viagra," but if his blood-alcohol level was elevated it did not show onstage—he sang with gusto and proved, night after night, he could still deliver the goods.

The duo weren't done yet. In March 2002, they returned to the UK and Ireland for a short tour. At a homecoming show in Manchester, Jones belted out his song "Manchester Boy" to the delight of local fans. This time the British press took it easy on them.

Back in the States, however, it was clear the well had run dry and by September it was over. Phony Monkeemania had bitten the dust. After four decades of partnership, the "Sunshine Boys"—Jones and Dolenz—were no more. Once the closest of the Monkees, the friendship was over and so was their professional affiliation.

At the tour's conclusion, Dolenz entered into another marriage, the real kind, to longtime partner, Donna Quinter. Matrimonial bliss seemed to suit him and a variety of opportunities came Dolenz's way. He won the job of morning disc jockey on New York oldies station WCBS—a position that ended abruptly when the station changed formats in the middle of Dolenz's live musical performance. He also directed cable television movies, joined the national touring companies of musicals, such as *Grease* and *Pippin*, competed on the reality TV show *Gone Country*, and even patented and marketed a home improvement gizmo called Hang-it-All.

While he never ran away from his past, Dolenz was careful to disassociate himself from his role on *The Monkees* TV show. When asked to describe the evolution of the project, he always trotted out the same analogy, "The Monkees were no more a rock group than Leonard Nimoy was a Vulcan on *Star Trek*."

In case anybody misunderstood, Dolenz was making it perfectly clear that after years of typecasting, he was free, and, from all appearances, thrilled to show off the full range of his talents in whatever medium was available—from writing a book about rock trivia to providing the voice of Snuggle Bear in TV commercials for fabric softeners.

Fulfilling one of his life-long dreams, Dolenz joined the Broadway cast of the Elton John/Tim Rice musical *Aida* on January 6, 2004. Playing the evil Zoser went against type but his debut on the Great White Way was greeted with acclaim.

"When he's willing to let his brain loose and flash out and act in unknown territory he's brilliant," explained Tork, hastening to add that Dolenz's reluctance to repeat his achievements made many underestimate his talents. "I think he could be one of the world class artists of the day. He's got that much going for him, but the unwillingness to go back keeps him on a more muted artistic level."

The always-quotable Tork moved to rural Connecticut and seemed grateful to be demon-free. He found his musical sweet spot in an exalted bar band called Shoe Suede Blues, happily touring small clubs playing tasteful R&B, mixed in with chestnuts like "Take a Giant Step."

Tork's parting words in 2001, "Thank God I don't need the Monkees anymore," seemed to define his outlook on life. Wiser and slightly wizened, he enjoyed his perch in life. He started an online advice column offering words of wisdom to troubled souls. Asked by one fan whether he still embraced the hippie ideals of his early Monkees days, Tork answered, "I believe very much in all that I believed in back in the '60s. I hope I'm more aware of the practicalities than I was then, but I am positive that the values and principles I held then are critical to the well-being of the planet."

One subject did seem to roil Tork—the Rock and Roll Hall of Fame. Even though he and his fellow Monkees had entered the cultural firmament in every other way, Tork was irked that, despite the effort of fans, the high-profile institution had continued to deny them credit for their accomplishments. This outcome was hardly a surprise. *Rolling Stone* publisher Jann Wenner, a founding member of the museum, was never a fan and, by all accounts, the feeling was mutual (Dolenz always took pains to describe Wenner's rock magazine as "Rolling Stain").

Tork took his case public, alleging Wenner harbored a personal vendetta. "It is an abuse of power," Tork told the *New York Post* in 2007. "I don't know whether the Monkees belong in the Hall of Fame, but it's pretty clear that we're not in there because of a personal whim."

Tork was attempting to slay the last of the dragons—the still-persistent notion among his Aquarian-Age peers that the Monkees had invalidated their right to be praised because they had not played their own instruments on their early hits. Tork argued, "40 years later, everybody says, 'What's the big deal? Everybody else does it.' Nobody cares now except (Wenner). He feels his moral judgment in 1967 and 1968 is supposed to serve in 2007."

There was plenty of support for Tork in the court of public opinion. A petition began circulating to induct the Monkees into the music shrine. Over 20,000 signatures, including legends such as Brian Wilson, were collected as the campaign went viral.

Were the Monkees worthy of entering the Rock and Roll Hall of Fame? It was the kind of argument that was perfect fodder for a lively bar conversation. The dubious nature of the Rock and Roll Hall of Fame was one factor—many other popular acts had also been overlooked—while some inductees, like the Sex Pistols, refused to show up at the ceremony altogether. In an ironically-worded statement about their absence, the Pistols sent a note that read, "We're not coming. We're not your monkeys."

Chapter Sixty-Seven

EVEN WITHOUT THE CANONIZATION OF the Rock and Roll Hall of Fame, the Monkees had been elevated to the status of an entertainment institution. Their legacy was unique—a time capsule of TV episodes, movies, and a pop-rock catalog unrivalled by any group of its kind.

Was the glamour cheapened when ex-Monkees started peddling their wares on eBay? Dolenz auctioned off a celebrity lunch and Jones listed his x-rays. Nesmith was selling autographed horseshoes and mugs on his website Videoranch. Tork played small clubs for chump change.

Aging gracefully is difficult for any rock star. Eternal youth was one of the promises of *The Monkees* and in a strange twist of fate, even as they grew older, the ex-Monkees shared a collective identity that never aged.

They shared something else—bitterness. For all intents and purposes, they had signed a lifetime contract. Their public identity was inescapable. No matter what they did, they would always be one of those happy-go-lucky guys locking arms doing the Monkee walk. It was a Faustian bargain times four and, despite the distance in their lives, a private dilemma each shared.

As a group of four sharply-different personalities who rarely agreed on anything, all four of the Monkees seem to draw the same conclusion about their creators, Rafelson and Schneider: they could have been treated better. Rafelson and Schneider did not have to deal with the legacy of being one of the Monkees in their day-to-day lives; all they had to do was cash the checks and be hailed as creative geniuses.

When it came to the subject of Rafelson, Tork did not mince words. "My personal belief is that Bob is an evil-minded man. He likes to bring people down," Tork told *Mojo* magazine in 2002. "Bob was often unsupportive as a human being and distinctly negative—and I was on the short end of that."

When Rafelson and Schneider lost interest in the project after *Head* they coldly abandoned their highly-pampered stars, leaving them to fend for themselves in an entertainment industry that had never fully embraced them in the first place. Viewed as puppets on a string, the individual Monkees were essentially typecast for life.

The perception that the Monkees were merely replaceable parts of a highly-sophisticated marketing machine was particularly disturbing to Nesmith, who felt the group was "tolerated" but the "talent of the four principals was really very low in the pecking order."

"The creative team behind the Monkees television series was the heart and soul," he contended. "If Bob Rafelson was the soul of it, Bert Schneider was the heart of it. Well, what does that make us? Are we just hired guns? Well, no, it doesn't because we had a heart and soul, too. And we brought to it the force of our individualities. And I don't think these guys—meaning Bob and Bert—ever really understood that."

Thanks, in part, to Raybert's "you can fool some of the kids some of the time" arrogance, each of the members continued to grapple with the implications of the group's manufactured image. "Looking back, I realize that the producers of the show—and I won't name names—I think there might have been an element of trying to trick somebody, trying to fool the public a little bit," claimed Dolenz.

But, of course, defining what made the Monkees tick—and what accounted for their immense popularity—had always been a tricky proposition. Even the four members struggled to come up an adequate theory. "Was it a TV show? Was it a rock and roll group? I don't have any idea," Nesmith told an interviewer in 1996. "It was neither and it was a little of both."

Nesmith harbored little doubt, however, that any four good-looking guys with a modicum of talent could have become the Monkees. "There was a willingness on the part of the press to believe that a phenomenon on the scale of the Monkees could be manufactured," he argued. "But it can't be. Let me tell you, if they could do it, they would. But it's not manufacturable. When it gets up into a certain level it has to have within it its own breathing life."

Not all the memories were bitter ones. Shared experiences, both good and bad, remained a common bond between them. "We were comrades in arms," Nesmith said. "That's exactly what we were. We were never really close, good buddies. But I have to tell you…there was an abiding kind of love that we all had for each other; a real bond on some odd level."

"Once you've bonded," Jones explained, "and you've had this thing such as the Monkees, to me, a friend is a friend for life. But this was more, this was finding three brothers I never had."

Tork also expressed "an abiding love" for everyone in the inner circle. "I have an awful lot of respect for those guys," he fondly recalled. "Each one of them in his own right is an enormous and amazing talent." And he displayed a defiant pride about the group's accomplishments: "We did play, we did perform, we did make music. It's not like we weren't anything. We were something."

Where does the credit lie? Ultimately, Nesmith claimed, it did not matter. "It's not really until we're all dead, it's all over and it's just a part of history (and) becomes nothing but artifacts, that anybody will get any kind of perspective on it."

Chapter Sixty-Eight

IN 2009, TORK ANNOUNCED he was suffering from adenoid cystic carcinoma, a rare form of cancer. Reacting to an outpouring of concern from friends and fans, the ailing Monkee decided to utilize social networking tools such as Facebook to update his condition. Going public, Tork explained in the *Washington Post*, would help him "keep a right-sized attitude about life and myself. Otherwise, you know, it'd be like: I'm a celebrity, get me offa this planet! Can't have that."

In-between radiation treatments, a vibrant-looking Tork played sets with his band Shoe Suede Blues. He also found time to pen an editorial for the *Hartford Courant* after the death of Michael Jackson. He found a parallel to his own experience: "As I was going through all the attention the Monkees generated, I wondered why there was no way to prepare for being famous. Now, I'm pretty sure there is no preparation possible. How are you going to listen to people if you have ample reason not to trust anybody?"

That rhetorical question could well have been asked of Davy Jones whose sunny onstage persona seemed to contrast a darker character offstage. "Jonesy got my heart," noted Tork with great affection. "I don't know why, because I don't like him very much—very interesting. Sometimes he's great to hang with and sometimes he's very difficult."

The pint-sized dynamo with the pearly white teeth and impeccable grooming had long-ago secured a special place in the heart of loyal fans. They were no longer teenyboppers but many secretly harbored an incurable crush on the aging heartthrob.

"Davy being Davy" became an evergreen act on the nostalgia circuit. Whether it was a cruise liner looking for on-board entertainer, a "teen" idol tour or some self-consciously hip comedy requiring a Monkee cameo, there was a role for Jones. From the stages of Walt Disney World to Time/Life infomercials selling '60s pop music collections, the promise of good clean fun was an integral part of Jones' brand equity.

On occasion, the hard-partying side of Jones' private life slipped out. While being interviewed by conservative talk show host Bill O'Reilly on Fox-TV about the Rock and Roll Hall of Fame controversy, Jones digressed from the conversation. "I can give you lots of stories," he told the perplexed host. "Talk about the times we sat around, passing the joint in the room, watching life go by."

These streams of consciousness rambles were not out of character. At a screening of *Head* in Los Angeles, Jones said to laughter, "I play a character based on myself." It wasn't clear he was joking.

By default, the seemingly-ageless mop-top was the public face of the Monkees. Whether it was showing up as himself on the popular kids cartoon *SpongeBob SquarePants*, or making a surprise guest appearance at a U2 concert in Los Angeles (where Jones joined guitarist Edge for sing-along performance of "Daydream Believer" to a rapturous crowd), audiences loved every showboating minute.

Splitting time between southern Florida and the Amish community of Beavertown, Pennsylvania, Jones devoted himself to his first love—riding and raising horses—and even managed to ride a winner in an amateur race. Talk of building a Davy Jones shrine at the 19th Century Lutheran Church he purchased was also bandied about.

In 2006, Jones spotted striking-looking actress Jessica Pacheco on the set of a musical production of *Cinderella*. "I called up the producers to find out more about her," Jones told *Celebrity Parents* Magazine. "They told me she was 28 years old and I thought, 'Hmmm, that's OK then! I'm not as much a pervert as I thought I was!'"

The unlikely romance between the star of the Telemundo telenovela *Dame Chocolate* (*Give Me Chocolate*) and the former Monkee was easy fodder for the tabloids. Reportedly, none of Jones' four daughters attended their wedding in 2009. Soon after, hints of marital discord began circulating. These included allegations of physical abuse on Pacheco's part. The May/December couple denied all claims. "Jessica IS the love of my life," Jones told the *National Enquirer*. "I've never been so happy."

Nonetheless, details hinting at unhappiness kept emerging. Jones grew testy at the public reaction Pacheco received when he invited her to perform a flamenco dance at one of his solo performances. His increasingly erratic onstage behavior finally erupted into a full-scale public meltdown in Sunbury, Pennsylvania in late 2009 when an apparently inebriated Jones first challenged audience members to a fight and then threw his microphone across the room. Newswires picked up embarrassing reports about the incident.

Word also circulated that Jones had scuttled plans to reform with Dolenz and Tork. All three had been approached by Azoff Music Management with an offer

"I've never been so happy," Jones told the press after marrying Jessica Pacheco.

for an extensive tour throughout 2010 which included stops at the Hollywood Bowl and England's Glastonbury Festival. Despite a lucrative payday, high-profile management, and the backing of his former bandmates, Jones refused to sign on. No public explanation was offered.

"Remember me, as you hoped I'd be," he cryptically told the *Tecumseh Herald* in early 2010. Whether he was in a state of personal turmoil or not, Jones held it all at distance in interviews, preferring to put on a self-deprecating face. Other times, he was proudly defiant. He defended himself, in a message to fans in early 2010, with the old axiom "don't let the truth spoil the news." In it, Jones addressed his decision to marry Pacheco: "She made me realize that time is precious...life alone is not where anyone with dreams should find comfort."

In a BBC radio interview conducted in the same period, Jones admitted to some lingering bitterness about his stunted afterlife as a performer. "The Monkees ruined my acting career," he said. "What I should have done after the Monkees finished in 1970 is I should have either gone back to the stables or I should have gone to England and joined the Young Vic just to establish myself." Off-mic, in an unguarded moment, he told the interviewer, "sometimes I'm just a lonely frightened old man."

Chapter Sixty-Nine

IN A REMOTE OFFICE in Sand City, California, Nesmith was immersed in creating a virtual world via his website, Videoranch. It was about as far from the Jones' tabloid life as you could get. Having weathered the PBS lawsuit, Nesmith was once again financially stable. When a jury awarded him $46.8 million in compensatory and punitive damages in 1999, Nesmith did not celebrate the victory in public. "It's like finding your grandmother stealing your stereo," he said with characteristic offbeat wit. "You're happy to get your stereo back, but it's sad to find out your grandmother is a thief."

After PBS appealed the ruling, an out-of-court settlement was reached for an unspecified amount of money. Nesmith began keeping a lower profile. Having produced films such as *Repo Man, Tapeheads*, and *Timerider*, he turned his attention to writing. In 1998, St. Martin's Press published his first novel, *The Long Sandy Hair of Neftoon Zamora*.

An enthusiastic early adopter of online entrepreneurship, Nesmith became one of the first artists to offer his music as digital downloads in the 1990s. When he was honored with a Lifetime Achievement Award by the Texas Film Hall of Fame in 2010, Nesmith's long list of visionary exploits in media and communications technology barely mentioned a certain prefabricated group from his past.

While never denying his fame had roots in the Monkees, Nesmith was still reluctant to fully embrace its legacy. "It made some kind of peculiar mark, a kind of odd graffiti on the fence posts of society, but it never really had the ballast of a great work of art. It was a cultural and media phenomenon. And those things tatter and fray very quickly in the whims of the times and that's what began to happen to us," he told an interviewer.

The appeal of the Monkees remained elusive to Nesmith. "I just never got it; I just don't get it. I just don't quite understand it and I don't think I ever will."

In 2009, Nesmith's long-awaited second novel, *The American Gene*, became available for download. In weekly performances, he read the book aloud to an audience in his virtual world, Videoranch 3D, or VR3D for short.

VR3D had become Nesmith's new obsession. The member-only virtual community allowed users to pick an avatar and wander through the digital landscape, enjoying live concerts and movies, and the ability to conduct real-time chats. Nesmith extolled the virtues of his virtual world. "It is a real watershed," he wrote in a Web chat interview conducted on VR3D. "The scale of this is unprecedented."

But he bristled at the notion of any connection of the Monkees to the new medium. "The Monkees are a treasured part of things for many of the fans here. They talk about them and enjoy the memories, but I have to say I have watched them all mature and come to this new medium without too much push, and the Monkees don't help them here any more than the model of car they drive."

The virtual world of VR3D provided Nesmith with a platform to promote books and music, as well dabble in a futuristic communication technology. With characteristic enthusiasm, he filed patents, predicted great things and then patiently waited for the world to catch up with him.

On Christmas Day 2012 his patience paid off when the US Patent Office awarded VR3D patent number 8,339,418 for the invention of "embedding a real time video into a virtual environment." Nesmith was thrilled. "I didn't know the Fed was even open on Christmas Day," he wrote in a celebratory Facebook post, adding "the notion of handing me a patent on Christmas in the middle of the gift giving holidays was delightful."

Fleshing out his invention in greater detail, he explained "this allows the video images including people to appear seamlessly in the virtual world—as if they are a part of it—and for the virtual audience to see and talk to the video image live and in real time."

Much like his role in the development of MTV ("I made a little money from it, but not much") Nesmith claimed to have little interest in the commercial development of VR3D. "I have no idea what I will do with the patent—if anything. That may not be my chapter to write, but if it is then I don't see it yet."

Chapter Seventy

THERE HAD ALWAYS BEEN A DUALITY between the public and private life of the most popular Monkee: it was Disney Davy in public and Drama Davy in private. Increasingly, the less-glamorous side was being exposed. In one particularly cringe-worthy moment, he appeared on *Dr. Phil* with his wife Jessica Pacheco to deny allegations of an abusive relationship. What seemed obvious to everyone else seemed to elude Jones: his volatile union with Pacheco was doomed.

The boiling point between the two occurred on the Monkees' 45th anniversary tour in 2011. In almost every respect the tour was considered a resounding success. A briskly-paced bit of stagecraft which deftly utilized the group's deep songbook to emphasize their by-now unimpeachable position as a classic pop band, the concert was embraced by fans and critics alike. Even *Rolling Stone*, the magazine that rarely, if ever, had given them credit ran the laudatory headline "Monkees Terrific As Ever."

For the first time in his career, Jones exercised full control over a Monkees tour. After scuttling plans for a reunion in 2010 and pledging he would never want to work with Dolenz and Tork again, Jones seemed to relish the opportunity to assert some authority. Artistically the new show was his baby. He chose the band, the set list, and oversaw every facet of the production. His single most controversial decision—and one that would ultimately backfire in spectacular fashion—was paying his volatile wife to dance in brief cameo appearances. Despite reservations, Dolenz and Tork consented.

On May 12, 2011, for the first time in over a decade, the trio performed. Against all odds, the enterprise hit its stride from the very get-go. A glowing review in the *Liverpool Echo* conveyed the happy news: "Micky can still hit the (very) high notes, Peter is still the loveable clown, like a psychedelic Stan Laurel, and Davy still has the ladies swooning despite the years."

The show was helped immensely by a colorful multimedia show featuring vintage photographs and video clips, an effective way of distracting the audience from the bald spots and, in Jones' case, a barely-concealed paunch. OK, they were no longer the young generation but, despite the years, they did have something to offer: a deep understanding of what the fans wanted.

Writing in *Rolling Stone*, Rob Sheffield raved about the timeless brand of entertainment they offered: "The Monkees have never been far from the heart of American culture. People are always glad when they show up. This was an excellent show from a legendary pop band giving out much, much, much more than they had to. Hardcore crowd, too – the kind of Monkeemaniacs who roar when they see the roadies wheel a kettledrum onstage, because they know that means it's time for Micky's psychedelic rant 'Randy Scouse Git.'"

"It's hard to imagine anybody disappointed by this show," Sheffield concluded, "unless they just plain hate life."

Tork was particularly grateful for another turn in the spotlight. Looking no worse for wear after recuperating from throat cancer, he displayed his musical chops on a variety of instruments including flugelhorn. For good measure he even added a few hoedown steps to his dance moves. His rehabilitation seemed complete. Once a full-fledged has-been and now a durable still-was, Tork was, above all, a survivor.

Dolenz, having come straight off a UK-tour of the musical *Hairspray*, was singing as strongly as ever. Micky the Monkee was just another role to play, albeit his most popular role. Despite his familiarity with the material, he never seemed to mail in a performance—in that sense he was a throwback, a trouper from the old-school that dated back to vaudeville.

In an otherwise pitch-perfect show, there was only one moment of cognitive dissonance. It was the sight of Jessica Pacheco prancing onstage in a come-hither style while her husband Davy Jones beamed a high-wattage smile. It was not going down well with audiences.

Chapter Seventy-One

AT FIRST, DOLENZ AND TORK REMAINED SILENT about Pacheco's participation but there were indications that something was amiss. A hit piece appeared in the UK tabloid the *Sun*. "Their tour looks doomed before it's even begun," claimed an unnamed party, citing "bad blood" and the group's overall lack of communication.

Evidently someone within the inner circle was bearing a grudge. Not a particularly shocking development; after all, bitching and backstabbing were mainstays of a Monkees tour. Internal conflicts? Completely predictable. But what wasn't predictable was a new presence in Jones' entourage. Seemingly cast from a third-rate gangster movie with his slicked-back hair, dark suits and brusque demeanor, Joseph Pacheco's last name was no mere coincidence. The brother of Jones' wife Jessica was now, rather ominously, functioning as his full-time personal manager.

It was his sister, however, who was drawing the wrath of fans. Their reaction wasn't difficult to understand—by pulling "a Yoko," Jessica Pacheco's performances were destroying the fantasy of three band mates united in song, together as one.

Promoting Pacheco's skills had been on the agenda for some time. Already her sexy Flamenco had wormed its way into Jones' solo shows but, from the start, these seductive displays alienated middle-aged women, his prime demographic. Was he willingly ignorant that the sight of a woman three decades younger—a woman, moreover, who had been accused of physically abusing him—might agitate and upset his fan base? Or was he so besotted with love that his judgment had been impaired?

Whatever the case, by the time the reunion tour touched down in the US, Jessica Pacheco was suddenly nowhere to be seen. Reportedly at the insistence of tour management as well as Dolenz and Tork, her onstage appearances had been excised from the stage show. Boiling mad, Pacheco bolted the tour in a high state of dudgeon. Incensed at what seemed like betrayal, she left her husband alone and bereft. On July 28, 2011, she filed for divorce in Miami-Dade County, Florida.

There was one remnant of their tattered marriage, however, that was still lurking. For the rest of the tour Joseph Pacheco continued to shadow Jones' every move.

Despite those private travails there was good reason for everyone to celebrate. Financially the concerts were doing very solid business, bucking the trend of slumping ticket sales that had been bedeviling the music industry. Almost every Monkees concert was sold out and lucrative offers were pouring in for more dates including overseas tours.

Then, without warning, the enterprise came to a screeching halt. On August 8, 2011, news broke: ten dates added to the tour had been canceled. "I'm not really at liberty to get into detail about what happened," Tork told *Rolling Stone*. "But there were some business affairs that couldn't be coordinated correctly. We hit a glitch...I can't say anything more without getting into the stuff that we have to keep down."

What was the "stuff we have to keep down?" Rumors circulated that Dolenz had been admitted to rehab. "Absolute horseshit," was Dolenz's response. "We got the best reviews I think we ever had. And I particularly am very pleased with some of the reviews I got for my vocal work."

As for Jones, his explanation seemed vague at best. "The tour was only supposed to go until July. And it was great, the best time we've had because we're all on the same page now. We gelled onstage and off. But then more dates were being added. And more. And then the next thing we knew, they were talking about Japan, Australia, Brazil, and we were like, 'Wait a second. This is turning into something more than a tour.'"

This was cagey logic (were more tour dates really a problem?) and it conspicuously avoided addressing the "business matter" that Tork and Dolenz had alluded to in interviews. And what exactly was that matter? A source privy to the ugly details spilled: Joseph Pacheco had been allegedly engaging in strong-arm tactics on Jones' behalf, extracting cash payments from concert promoters in advance of the group's appearance.

Had Jones privately encouraged this alleged behavior at the expense of his band mates? Although the source could not be corroborated, and therefore the answer remains speculative, even a shred of truth about the suspected hanky-panky (the scheming duo had reportedly benefited from the arrangement to the tune of several hundred thousand dollars, all without the knowledge of Dolenz, Tork or the tour managers) represented an unprecedented breech in trust and civility.

This news never reached the public. Once the chicanery was discovered, the tour was summarily canceled and Dolenz and Tork zipped their lips. Legal scrutiny hung in the balance, not to mention the reputations of everyone involved. But the damage was already done and no amount of reprisals would solve Jones' growing laundry list of personal problems. "We need to work on this stuff outside the public eye," Tork told *Rolling Stone*.

There were many reasons to be genuinely concerned about Jones' well-being. He was said to have given up drinking during the US tour but after he returned to Florida and reconciled with Pacheco all bets were off. She may have withdrawn her divorce papers but, by all accounts, the union remained stormy.

What transpired behind closed doors? Internet chat boards were rife with rumors, including allegations of screaming rows, smashed objects and nights Jones spent alone sleeping on park benches. In public Jones kept a brave face despite the inevitable stress he must have been experiencing. He mounted solo shows, conducted TV and radio interviews, made endorsement deals and comported himself like a professional.

Meanwhile, Dolenz and Tork could only lick their wounds. It must have been doubly galling to have a financial transgression mar their moment of glory, especially now that critics were in their corner. How could they capitalize on the good will? The answer arrived in the form of an idea proposed by Monkees archivist Andrew Sandoval—a one-off performance of the group's classic *Headquarters* album to be staged in Los Angeles in the spring of 2012.

Sandoval, whose meticulous effort to burnish the group's reputation through lavish reissues he lovingly produced for Rhino Records, received a quick endorsement from Dolenz and Tork. Astonishingly he also lassoed the "missing Monkee," the one who had previously claimed the group's 1997 UK tour was the "final chapter": Michael Nesmith.

Jones, however, would not be involved. This bit of intrigue—Nesmith in, Jones out—was never revealed to the fans. Before the show could go into rehearsals a stunning event changed everyone's plans.

Chapter Seventy-Two

DAVY JONES GALLOPED OFF for a routine ride. It was a picture perfect day—Leap Day, February 29, 2012. The sky was clear and the track was dry at the J-V Ranch in Indiantown, Florida.

For the "Manchester Cowboy," horses were a way of life, a lifelong passion that kept him out of "silly red-carpet clubs and the rest of that Hollywood baloney." They were also a convenient way to escape his increasingly chaotic private life. When things got hairy on the home front, Jones could always take refuge in the dozen prized steeds he maintained in Florida and Pennsylvania.

But on this day something was terribly wrong. Jones was experiencing chest pains. Dismounting his horse and struggling for breath, he retreated to his vintage Thunderbird, a car long coveted and recently purchased. A staff member discovered him and issued a frantic 911 call. An ambulance arrived but it was already too late. At a local hospital, Jones was pronounced dead.

For fans of the group, it was extremely difficult news to process. Davy Jones, the eternally youthful pop idol who occupied a happy and uncomplicated place in their lives, seemed invulnerable to the toll of time. Now he was gone at age 66, the victim of a massive heart attack.

The news went viral, condolences poured in and hastily the surviving Monkees issued heartfelt tributes. Perhaps the most touching came from the least likely of Monkees. "I will miss him, but I won't abandon him to mortality," Nesmith posted on Facebook. "David's spirit and soul live well in my heart, among all the lovely people, who remember with me the good times, and the healing times, that were created for so many, including us."

Although the two former band mates were polar opposites in almost every way, Nesmith emerged from a long media exile to reminisce fondly. "David had a wonderful laugh, infectious," he told *Rolling Stone*. Not hesitating to give credit where it was due, Nesmith insisted Jones had always been the primary force behind the Monkees' success: "For me, David was the Monkees. They were his band. We were his side men."

Monkees co-creator, Bob Rafelson, seconded that opinion, telling the *Los Angeles Times* that Jones "deserves a lot of credit, let me tell you. He may not have lived as long as we wanted him to, but he survived about seven lifetimes, including being perhaps the biggest rock star of his time."

Jones had lived several lifetimes—Rafelson was right about that—and judging from the evidence he expressed no interest in a rocking chair life. "Dad didn't want to get old," his youngest daughter Annabel later told an interviewer.

Up until the very end, Jones seemed the embodiment of inexhaustible energy. His "surprisingly nimble boogaloo moves" had been singled out for praise by *Rolling Stone* magazine. Self-referential jokes about his advancing age ("I'm Davy's dad," he told audiences. "Davy will be out in a minute") were entirely keeping in his character. According to his daughter Annabel, "Dad was so self-deprecating; he was the most humble guy ever."

In person, Jones did exude generosity, warmth and approachability. "I love making people laugh and making them happy and the most comforting place for me to be is on stage. It's what I wanted to do when I was a little boy and I still get to do it," he told the *Daily Mail* shortly before commencing on the Monkees' 2011 tour.

Thriving on the buzz he generated, from his Broadway debut in *Oliver* to his last solo show at a casino in Thackerville, Oklahoma just ten days before he died, Jones tirelessly engaged with his fans, signing untold thousands of autographs and posing for photos in meet-and-greets. In doing so he cemented a bond with those fans that proved unbreakable.

Away from the limelight Jones often lent a helping hand to friends. In his final years he provided financial support for Basil Foster, the horse trainer who, fifty years earlier, had set him on the path to stardom. At his own expense, Jones flew the ailing Foster to Florida and placed him in a health care facility. "He is just like a son to me," a glowing Foster told the *Daily Mail*. "He's looked after me for a long time and I'm very grateful to him."

The article in the *Daily Mail* was published weeks before Jones passed away. It was accompanied by photographs of the old friends posing together. These were some of the last images taken of Jones and they revealed the impish side of his personality. Jones and Foster were seen sporting giant sombreros and rascally grins.

Although he was a complicated person whose private struggles increasingly played out in public, Jones, in death, received the kind of royal treatment accorded to only the top rank of celebrities. The extraordinary outpouring was appreciated by Jones' bereaved family. "It was like falling from a great height and landing on a feather pillow," his daughter Annabel said, describing the reaction. "All these people were calling and fans were telling us all the things he'd done for them. It made me feel like I was getting a big hug."

No one could say Jones did not appreciate his audience and they certainly loved him back.

Chapter Seventy-Three

AS THE WORLD MOURNED the death of a much-beloved performer, the spotlight briefly turned to his widow, the controversial partner in his train-wreck marriage who fans had derisively nicknamed Jessica "Pay-checko." Reportedly, she had been on a cruise ship when she learned of her husband's demise.

Sadly, but predictably, the way Pacheco handled the funeral arrangements did nothing to tamp down suspicions she never had Jones' best interests in mind. One of her first acts after his passing was to inform the surviving Monkees in no uncertain terms they were not to attend the funeral. Although deeply wounded, Dolenz, Nesmith and Tork took the high road, claiming to the press they had avoided the services to prevent a media circus. They later held their own private tribute, without Pacheco, in Los Angeles.

On March 7, 2012, a private ceremony for Jones was held at the Holy Cross Catholic Church in Indiantown, Florida. The eulogy was delivered by Joseph Pacheco. In every way it was a non-Monkees event. "Daydream Believer" did not play over the PA system. Instead solo recordings by Jones—"I'll Love You Forever" and "Written in My Heart"—were heard.

The frustrated loyalists who sustained Jones in good times and bad were given no outlet for expressing grief for their fallen hero. There was no grave site— Jones had been cremated—and the funeral had been a closed affair. With no other choice his fans improvised. On March 10, 2012, hundreds flocked to the small Pennsylvania hamlet of Beavertown where Jones owned land and celebrated his life in speeches and song.

An officially-sanctioned tribute later staged by Jones' daughters Annabel and Talia was held at B.B. King's Blues Club, a New York City nightclub that had hosted one of his last performances. The event was held to raise money for the newly-established Davy Jones Equine Memorial Fund with profits earmarked to provide ongoing care for his horses. This time "Daydream Believer" took center place. At the end of an emotion-packed evening, Dolenz and Tork lead the audience in a poignant sing-along rendition of the ever-wistful tune.

Missing in action was Michael Nesmith (unsurprisingly neither Jessica nor Joseph Pacheco was there as well). Unbeknownst to fans, Nesmith's eyesight had deteriorated to an alarming degree where he was, in his own words, "practically blind." He discussed his ordeal on Facebook. "I had been slowly losing my sight since 2007, and then in 2010 it took a dramatic turn for the worse." Describing the situation in classic Nesmith fashion he wrote "my world was a Monet painting with pretty colors but no distinct identities."

It had been a rough couple of years for Nesmith. Videoranch, the hermetic online world he lovingly designed, had never broken through to the general public. His book *The American Gene* had barely registered a blip. His latest marriage had ended in divorce. But after cataract surgery successfully restored his eyesight, Nesmith seemed a changed man willing to engage the public. Were intimations of mortality influencing his willingness? Certainly the death of Davy Jones would have been hard to ignore.

Other members of the Monkees' inner circle were now gone as well. Just two months before Jones' demise, the group's co-creator Bert Schneider passed away at age 78. Like Jones, the final chapters of Schneider's life were a sad ending to an otherwise storybook life. It emerged that the once-vibrant producer had spiraled into heavy drug abuse and sadly even close friends and family had lost touch with him.

For such a charismatic figure, it was an inglorious end. Schneider, a product of privilege, had apparently become disillusioned by the political changes that had occurred since his heyday as a countercultural rebel. An exponent of what writer Tom Wolfe termed "radical chic," he funded underground movements, including the escape of fugitive Black Panther Huey Newton, but also lived opulently in a Beverly Hills mansion. It was a life of seeming contradiction into which he slowly receded before disappearing altogether.

One month after Schneider's death another member of the Monkees family, albeit one long exiled, Don Kirshner, was gone as well. The passing of the Man with the Golden Ear, whose command of the Brill Building hit factory had been essential to the group's success, elicited a fascinating, if slightly elliptical, comment from his former nemesis Michael Nesmith.

"Sad to learn of the passing of my old adversary Don Kirshner," Nesmith wrote on his Facebook page. "He was a formidable foe and I send my condolences and sympathy to his family and his many friends. Donny, where ever you are—I want you to know I put my fist thru the wall just for dramatic effect. Apparently it worked. It is all behind us now, and we wrote what we wrote. Rest in Peace."

In an interview conducted shortly before his death, Jones also made amends for comments about Kirshner's lack of talent. "I've come to appreciate the choices he made for us musically," Jones told a Kirshner biographer. "I guess he wasn't such a bad guy after all."

Kirshner was posthumously inducted into the Roll and Roll Hall of Fame, a bittersweet irony since it was an honor he had long sought. "They've got people in there that I *trained,* and I'm not in? It bothers me on principle," he told the *Washington Post* in 2004. Like Schneider, Kirshner had faded from view but, apparently, his ego was intact and undiminished. "My body of work is as big as anyone's," he insisted, "and nobody knows the half of it."

One very public fan, Paul Shaffer, seemed to understand. The band leader of *Late Night with David Letterman*, whose spot-on impression of Kirshner had been a staple of *Saturday Night Live*, had become a close friend. Kirshner was "a character, so colorful," recalled Shaffer, who reveled in the anecdotes Kirshner would share of his glory days. "If he loved a record, he'd call people from the studio and hold up the phone to the speaker," Shaffer recalled. "He'd describe how excited he was when Neil Diamond came in with 'I'm a Believer.' He really loved this music."

Schneider, Kirshner and then Jones—three key figures in the evolution of the Monkees—were gone but the marketing machine never seemed to slow down. If completists had enough money in their PayPal accounts they could purchase *America Lost and Found: The BBS Story*, a DVD box set featuring a stunning restoration of *Head* along with other Rafelson/Schneider productions including *Easy Rider*, *Five Easy Pieces*, and *The Last Picture Show*.

Reviewing the BBS box set for the *New York Times*, film critic Monohla Dargis singled out *Head* as "the most subversive of the seven titles." The critical re-evaluation of the movie—and the Monkees as a whole—now seemed complete. The stigma that defined the past had been replaced by a big communal hug. Even director Quentin Tarantino was name-checking *Head* as a seminal influence on his work. "Believe it or not," he gushed before an audience in 2011, "even though I was too young to understand it... in 1970 I saw *Head* at a movie theater, one of the greatest movies ever to use music."

More than ever, the Monkees were a hip signifier, a cool reference point for a pop-obsessed culture. When the producers of the acclaimed TV series *Breaking Bad* chose to use "Goin' Down" as the soundtrack for a key scene, it wasn't some outré move on their part—it was simply using an evocative song and therefore it just made perfect sense.

It took nearly fifty years but the world had caught up to the Monkees.

Chapter Seventy-Four

A POST ON FACEBOOK made it official: Dolenz, Tork and Nesmith had all signed on for a 12-date tour in late 2012. "This seems like a good time to do this—the right time," Nesmith said. "Who knows when we will get another chance?"

Nesmith's seize-the-day logic was difficult to argue with but a bit revisionist history was necessary to explain why, after so many opportunities in the past, he felt motivated to get back together with his buddies. Was it merely a coincidence that he was willing to reunite now that Jones was dead and gone? It was Jones, after all, who persistently needled Nesmith in interviews and vetoed his possible cameo on the 2011 tour.

So what was Nesmith's explanation? "I never really left," he told *Rolling Stone*, presumably with a straight face. "It is a part of my youth that is always active in my thought and part of my overall work as an artist. We did some good work together and I am always interested in the right time and the right place to reconnect and play."

Could the surviving trio have waited longer? Out of deference to Jones it might have been the right thing to do—after all, it had only been five months since the most popular Monkee had died. Yet for every naysayer there were plenty of eager fans willing to pay a premium to see the surviving Monkees reunite.

How would the group handle the absence of Davy Jones on stage and who would sing his signature song "Daydream Believer?" To hardcore fans these were sensitive issues, ones that Nesmith, rather embarrassingly, failed to grasp. In a series of Facebook posts he lampooned the speculation, making specious claims that fans were threatening to boycott the tour unless actor Kevin Spacey took Jones' place. This was Nesmith's idea of a joke. Later he suggested talk show host Jimmy Fallon could step in to do the job. "I am thinking seriously about inviting him to come and do it with us—just a couple of nights. I am giving it a lot of careful thought," he wrote in a facetious post.

Nesmith's satirical whimsy was remarkably tone deaf. Suggesting Davy Jones could be replaced, even in jest, seemed to merely validate suspicions that his participation in a reunion tour was for selfish, not sincere, reasons. The Davy Jones faction of the fan base was extremely riled up.

Even Jones' ex-wife Anita Pollinger mistook Nesmith's intentions. "There is no rhyme or reason for trying to replicate or replace this special man and his performances," Pollinger wrote in an emotional post on Facebook. "It is hard enough for his children right now—trying to handle the loss of their dad—I really hope that you will give them some thought in your decision making. It was hard for them when the tour was organized so fresh on the heels of their dad's death. It may be particularly hard for them to think that he is to be 'replaced.'

"The credibility of The Monkees was incredibly important to him," Pollinger concluded. "I have to wonder what on earth he would say to this 'idea.'"

Nesmith loved defying expectations and messing with people's heads but the consensus opinion was pretty clear on this issue: he should knock it off. Perhaps—and this was a charitable explanation—he had become giddy with the excitement of it all. The fact that he jumped the gun on the tour's official announcement by breaking the news a day early suggests this may have been the case (although that, too, was done in eccentric fashion in a Facebook post about making gazpacho).

He was one quirky dude, there was no doubt about that, and more bizarre behavior was on the way. During a run of solo shows conducted in the UK prior to reuniting with the Monkees, Nesmith baffled audiences with rambling monologues about his "children" (i.e., his songs), then treated them to re-mixed electronic versions he dubbed "movies of the mind" with instrumentation supplemented by iPads and MacBooks. "Some in the crowd looked anxious," a reviewer wrote after attending his concert at Queen Elizabeth Hall. "It seemed as if it might be interesting. The reality wasn't. Many songs sounded as if they were being played to an odd karaoke backing track."

It was fair to wonder whether Nesmith was really up for the rigors of a 12-date reunion tour. Would he flake out before the enterprise would get underway and even if he did show up would the unit truly gel? "The dynamic is seriously different," Tork said of Nesmith's involvement. "Mike is much more laid back. Davy was all buzzy and energetic, so there's a huge difference there.

Tork had the guts to address the elephant in the room. "I have to say that I don't regard this as anything of a wake," he said of the tour plans. "We note Davy's passing, because it's the right thing to do."

Chapter Seventy-Five

"THIS SONG BELONGS TO YOU NOW," Dolenz told the opening night audience in Escondido, California on November 8, 2012. The song in question was "Daydream Believer." Two audience members had been selected by Dolenz to come onstage and lead a mass sing-along.

The gesture was classy and it struck just the right emotional chord. It was impossible not to miss the presence of Davy Jones at a Monkees concert—there was no way to replace his pizzazz and panache—but any doubts about the legitimacy of this reunion were quickly laid to rest. It had been the right thing to do. The concert not only honored Jones' memory but made a life-affirming statement he undoubtedly would have endorsed: the show must go on.

Accompanied by an excellent backing band which included Nesmith's son Christian and Dolenz's sister Coco on vocals, "An Evening with the Monkees" was satisfying and compelling. "Nothing could have prepared the uninitiated for the powerful concert the Monkees delivered," wrote the *Chicago Tribune*. "It wasn't just a recap of the band's greatest hits. It was an emotionally disarming multimedia show that, for all its backward glance, felt fresh and electric."

Audience members were treated to several lesser-known songs from the Monkees' canon. These "deep cuts" may have baffled a few, particularly the inclusion of nearly every song from *Head*, but for those who harbored a not-so-secret love for that very strange movie, it was pure nirvana. Just hearing Micky's soaring tenor on "As We Go Along" was worth the price of admission.

Was that really Michael Nesmith onstage looking so relaxed and friendly? For skeptics questioning his motives his steady performance was sufficient proof to silence any doubts. Nesmith lent a sense of gravitas to the proceedings but he left the solemn posturing at home; instead, he displayed an acute and endearing sense of humor. One inspired bit of tomfoolery featured Nesmith's freewheeling imitation of a Moog synthesizer on the psychedelic oddity "Daily Nightly." For many it was the highlight of the evening.

Another of the evening's pleasant surprises was the durability of Nesmith's songs, ten of which were performed. From a moody slowed-down version of "Sweet Young Thing" to the underrated pop confection "The Girl I Knew Somewhere," these songs had stood the test of time. The latter number featured Tork's perfectly-rendered harpsichord parts (albeit played on a synthesizer).

Tork gracefully ceded the spotlight to his partners who sang the majority of the leads and didn't even seem to flinch when Nesmith playfully flipped him the bird at the closing concert at the Beacon Theater in New York on December 2, 2012.

The show at the Beacon caught the trio in rare form. The audience, on their feet for nearly the entire two-hours-plus performance, showered the group with adoration and deafening cheers. Sensing the momentousness of the occasion the trio seemed to rise to greater heights.

And, thus, the tour ended on a high sweet note with Nesmith seemingly reinvigorated. In spring 2013, he undertook an extensive solo tour and then joined forces with Dolenz and Tork on a series of dates dubbed "A Midsummer's Night With the Monkees."

Paying tribute to Davy Jones had become part of the act but it was clearly no longer a motivating force. An audience awaited, the Monkees were still selling tickets, and nobody was getting any younger. "I think we have to move on," Dolenz told Rolling Stone, "Everybody has to move on."

Epilogue

COMPARED TO 1966, we are infinitely more sophisticated about media, how it is created, how it is consumed, how we are deliberately manipulated by it. We are no longer shocked to discover Oz behind the curtain of the Next Big Thing, pulling the levers and intentionally blurring the lines between fantasy and reality.

Connecting with your audience, using multiple media platforms to get your message out, maximizing the tools of promotion—this is how business gets done. In the age of YouTube and iPhones, you must create an image that stands out in the crowd or you'll be lost in the shuffle.

Judging by the new rules of attention-seeking, Rafelson and Schneider played the high-stakes game of manufacturing idols perfectly. Like geneticists decoding a crucial sequence, they searched, and found, the magic combination of personalities to breathe life into their perfect pop beast. The success of the illusion was so total that the public had difficulty separating the characters the Monkees played on TV from their personas in real life.

The notion of "famous for being famous" did not start with the Monkees, but each of the four discovered how difficult it could be to disassociate yourself from the project that defined you. This was a new kind of notoriety, one you could never escape.

In the new-media age of the early 21st Century, participants face similar obstacles. Whether it's a tweet, a Facebook page, a blog entry or a gossip site, up-and-coming entertainers leave a permanent electronic trail and, like the Monkees in their heyday, they often face non-stop scrutiny.

For the always-connected generation, vexing questions have arisen: Must you surrender your private identity to become a public figure? Should you compromise your artistic vision to reach a wider audience? What is the line you won't cross to gain attention?

Long before any of these newcomers were born, the Monkees were wrestling the implications of their fame. What do you do with your metaphorical fifteen minutes? Use it to spread happiness and make money? Those were the obvious goals. But how do you embolden the power of the artist?

The four Monkees stepped into a brave new world, a future where the weapons for marketing were set to stun. Cutting-edge techniques were deployed to ensure they would attract unprecedented exposure in the marketplace.

The tools are even more powerful today. Aided by the pulsating, cross-promotion multimedia marketing of the Internet, anyone with a camera and a broadband connection can now create the trappings of the Monkees.

Ironically, in spite of the elegant artifice that had been constructed for the Monkees, the goal, in terms of audience identification, was always "keeping it real," to maintain the illusion that this was an organic creative unit.

Rafelson and Schneider, in this sense, faced the same perplexing conundrum that producers of reality TV face today. Once you turn on the cameras and consciously start filming people in unnatural circumstances, can you still call it reality?

Fusing reality and fantasy into the same narrative—there isn't a name for that kind of programming yet. The closest metaphor, as Nesmith pointed out, was a cinematic one. "The whole thing," he told author Andrew Sandoval, "was like being in a continuous movie. You keep watching all the things going on around you, but you aren't really part of it."

If reality was slippery, the group's desire to transcend their synthetic origins added even more layers of complexity. The more real the Monkees sought to be, the more vulnerable they became. The more vulnerable they became the more human and relatable they were. And on and on it went. But there was an invisible tripwire. When you had gone too far, reality vanished altogether and the identity you surrendered to the public domain could no longer be recovered.

The implications of over-exposing your persona to the insatiable demands of a celebrity-obsessed culture are more familiar today. Dolenz, Jones, Nesmith and Tork confronted these unforeseen dangers without a road map. Given the surrealistic twists and turns of their individual careers, it's quite amazing that all four of the Monkees survived with their sanity intact.

Of course, as with any Faustian bargain, the devil is in the details—the unforeseen consequences of exposing yourself to 24/7 media barrage, the possibility of stunted career ambitions and unwanted intrusions into your privacy. As the factory worker in Head said so wisely, "The tragedy of your times, my young friends, is that you might get exactly what you want."

Always ahead of their time, the Monkees have exerted different meanings in new eras—prefabricated band, video pioneers, reality TV stars. How will future generations relate to them? Their well-documented lives may hold the key. Having been captured in pristine sound and vision, each of the four Monkees can look back on their youthful vitality and experience the strange sensation, as they grow older, of seeing their personalities in full flower, never aging or diminishing in form.

This may well be the new illusion that is available to us all now, the ability to gaze back in wonder upon a vast archive of memories—a permanent electronic trail of photographs, videos, and blog posts—and ask ourselves the same ambiguous question: *was* that really me?

Photo Credits

Page 2/From the Collection of Marley Roberts; Page 6/From the Collection of Marley Roberts; Page 9/ Photograph by Henry Diltz; Page 14/From the Collection of Kevin Schmid and Marley Roberts; Page 19/ (Top) From the Collection of Kevin Schmid (Bottom) From the collection of Randi Waddell; Page 22/ From the Collection of Marley Roberts; Page 24/ From the Collection of Marley Roberts; Page 26/From the Collection of Marley Roberts; Page 27/From the Collection of Marley Roberts; Page 30/From the Collection of Randi Waddell; Page 32/From the Collection of Randi Waddell; Page 38/Photograph by David Gahr; Page 42/Photographs by Henry Diltz; Page 44/From the Collection of Marley Roberts; Page 48/From the Collection of Marley Roberts; Page 54/From the Collection of Randi Waddell; Page 57/From the Collection of Marley Roberts; Page 58/Photo by Henry Diltz; Page 60/Photographs by Henry Diltz; Page 62/From the Collection of Marley Roberts; Page 63/Photograph by Henry Diltz; Page 67/From the Collection of Kevin Schmid; Page 68/Photographs by Henry Diltz; Page 72/Photographs by Henry Diltz; Page 79/Photographs by Henry Diltz; Page 80/From the Collection of Randi Waddell; Page 89/From the Collection of Marley Roberts; Page 90/Photograph by Henry Diltz; Page 92/Photograph by Henry Diltz; Page 98/From the Collection of Randi Waddell; Page 102/From the Collection of Marley Roberts; Page 103/From the Collection of Marley Roberts; Page 105; Photographs by Henry Diltz; Page 109 (Top) From the Collection of Marley Roberts (Bottom) Photograph by Henry Diltz; Page 110/Photograph by Henry Diltz; Page 113/Photograph by Jim Marshall; Page 114/Photographs by Henry Diltz; Page 115/Photographs by Henry Diltz; Page 118/Photograph by Nona Hatay; Page 120/Photograph by Henry Diltz; Page 124/ From the Collection of Marley Roberts; Page 125/Photographs by Henry Diltz; Page 128/Photographs by Henry Diltz; Page 132/From the Collection of Kevin Schmid; Page 134/Photograph by Henry Diltz; Page 137/Photograph from the Collection of Randi Waddell; Page 138/Photographs by Henry Diltz; Page 142/Photograph by Henry Diltz; Page 145/Photographs by Henry Diltz; Page 146/Photograph by Henry Diltz; Page 149/From the Collection of Randi Waddell; Page 150/Photograph by Henry Diltz; Page 152/ Photograph by Henry Diltz; Page 157/Photograph by Henry Diltz; Page 158/From the Collection of Marley Roberts; Page 162/From the Collection of Marley Roberts; Page 165/From the Collection of Marley Roberts; Page 169/From the Collection of Marley Roberts; Page 171/Photograph by Henry Diltz; Page 172/ From the Collection of Kevin Schmid; Page 174/From the Collection of Randi Waddell; Page 177/From the Collection of Kevin Schmid; Page 184/(Left) Photography by Henry Diltz (Right) From the Collection of Kevin Schmid; Page 186/From the Collection of Marley Roberts; Page 191/From the Collection of Jodi Hammrich; Page 193/From the Collection of Marley Roberts; Page 201/Photograph by Chester Simpson; Page 202/(Tork) Photograph by Michael Ventura (Nesmith) From the Collection of Kevin Schmid (Jones) From the Collection of Kevin Schmid (Dolenz) From the Collection of Marley Roberts; Page 206/ Photograph by Henry Diltz; Page 208/Photograph by Henry Diltz; Page 214/Photograph by Henry Diltz; Page 221/Photograph by Henry Diltz; Page 226/Photograph by Henry Diltz; Page 229/Photograph by Henry Diltz; Page 232/(Tork) Photograph by Ivan Iannoli (Dolenz) Photograph by Robert Milazzo (Jones) Photograph by Kevin Scott Hess (Nesmith) Courtesy of Videoranch.com; Page 242/Photography Courtesy *Celebrity Parents* Magazine; Page 259/Photograph by Winifred Boyd; Page 260/Photograph by Winifred Boyd; Page 261/Photograph by Winifred Boyd; Page 262/Photograph by Winifred Boyd.

To purchase Winifred Boyd's photography, including photos of the 2012 Monkees tour, please go to her website: http://www.winifredboydphotography.com/

Song lyric credits:

CPSIA information can be obtained at www.ICGtesting.com
Printed in the USA
BVOW08s2336140616

452101BV00001B/6/P